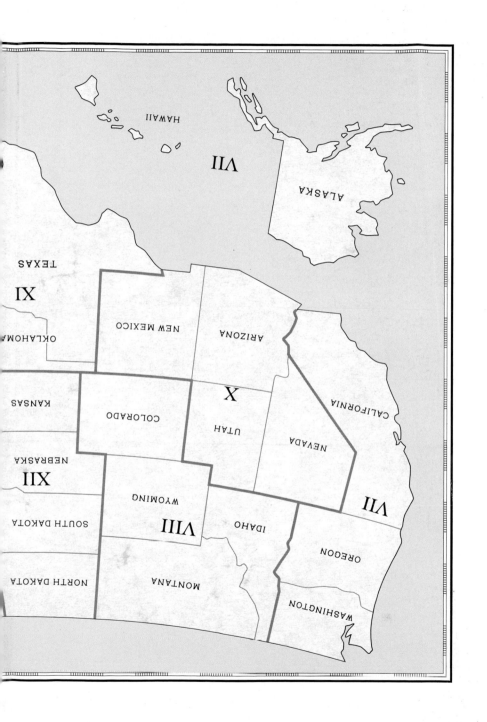

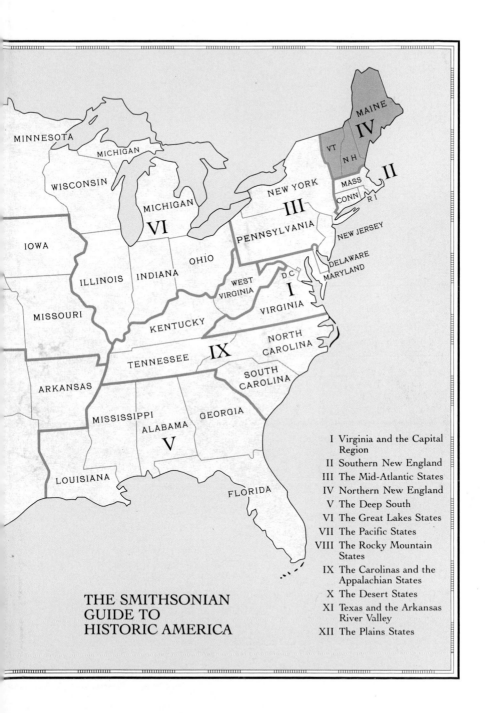

MINNESOTA

MICHIGAN

WISCONSIN

MICHIGAN

VI

IOWA

ILLINOIS   INDIANA   OHIO

MISSOURI

KENTUCKY

WEST
VIRGINIA

VIRGINIA

I

D C

NEW YORK

III

PENNSYLVANIA

NEW JERSEY

DELAWARE
MARYLAND

MAINE

IV

VT   N H

MASS

CONN

II

R I

TENNESSEE   **IX**   NORTH
CAROLINA

ARKANSAS   SOUTH
CAROLINA

MISSISSIPPI   GEORGIA

ALABAMA

V

LOUISIANA

FLORIDA

I Virginia and the Capital
  Region
II Southern New England
III The Mid-Atlantic States
IV Northern New England
V The Deep South
VI The Great Lakes States
VII The Pacific States
VIII The Rocky Mountain
  States
IX The Carolinas and the
  Appalachian States
X The Desert States
XI Texas and the Arkansas
  River Valley
XII The Plains States

THE SMITHSONIAN
GUIDE TO
HISTORIC AMERICA

THE
SMITHSONIAN
GUIDE TO
HISTORIC AMERICA

NORTHERN NEW ENGLAND

TEXT BY
VANCE MUSE

SPECIAL PHOTOGRAPHY BY
PAUL ROCHELEAU

EDITORIAL DIRECTOR
ROGER G. KENNEDY
DIRECTOR OF THE NATIONAL MUSEUM
OF AMERICAN HISTORY
OF THE SMITHSONIAN INSTITUTION

Stewart, Tabori & Chang
NEW YORK

Published in 1989 by Stewart, Tabori & Chang, Inc., 740 Broadway,
New York, NY 10003.

FRONT COVER: Waits River, VT.
HALF-TITLE PAGE: Scrimshaw, Shelburne Museum, VT.
FRONTISPIECE: Acadia National Park, ME.
BACK COVER: North Ferrisburg, VT.

SERIES EDITOR: HENRY WIENCEK
EDITOR: MARY LUDERS
PHOTO EDITORS: DAVID LARKIN, MARION PAONE
ART DIRECTOR: DIANA M. JONES
DESIGNER: PAUL P. ZAKRIS
ASSOCIATE EDITOR: BRIGID A. MAST
PHOTO ASSISTANT: BARBARA J. SEYDA
EDITORIAL ASSISTANT: MONINA MEDY
DESIGN ASSISTANT: KATHI R. PORTER
CARTOGRAPHIC DESIGN AND PRODUCTION: GUENTER VOLLATH
CARTOGRAPHIC COMPILATION: GEORGE COLBERT
DATA ENTRY: SUSAN KIRBY

LIBRARY OF CONGRESS CATALOGING-IN-PUBLICATION DATA

Muse, Vance
    Northern New England.

    (The Smithsonian guide to historic America)
    Includes index.
    1. New England—Description and travel—1981-   —Guide-books.
2. Historic sites—New England—Guide-books. 3. Maine—Description and travel—1981-
    —Guide-books. 4. Historic sites—Maine—Guide-books. 5. Vermont—Description and
travel—1981-   —Guide-books. 6. Historic sites—Vermont—Guide-books. 7. New
Hampshire—Description and travel—1981-   —Guide-books. 8. Historic sites—New
Hampshire—Guide-books.
    I. Rocheleau, Paul. II. Kennedy, Roger G. III. Title. IV. Series.
F2.3.M8 1989   917.4   88-33092
ISBN 1-55670-066-0 (pbk.)   ISBN 1-55670-049-0

Distributed by Workman Publishing, 708 Broadway, New York, NY 10003

Printed in Japan

10 9 8 7 6 5 4 3 2 1
First Edition

C O N T E N T S

INTRODUCTION   10

WESTERN VERMONT   16

EASTERN VERMONT   56

PORTSMOUTH AND SOUTHEASTERN
    NEW HAMPSHIRE   84

WESTERN AND NORTHERN
    NEW HAMPSHIRE   126

SOUTHERN MAINE   160

THE MAINE COAST   212

THE MAINE INTERIOR   252

NOTES ON ARCHITECTURE   282

INDEX   284

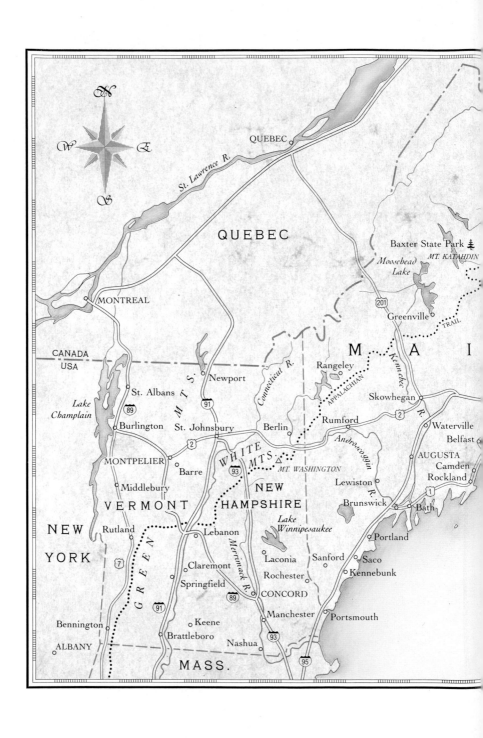

such as Katahdin, so uncompromising that their slopes will have nothing to do with trees or even bushes.

The Saco River has always divided this difficult terrain from the more fertile portions of New England and has divided occupations for so long that the woodland Eastern Abenaki spoke one set of dialects and the agricultural Western Abenaki, who commanded much of New Hampshire and Vermont, spoke another. The eastern cousins knew as much about fishing as the western knew about corn and squash, beans and tobacco; accents and occupations still are divided roughly along those ancient lines.

The Abenaki were fierce fighters; they first held the English to a few starveling settlements along the coast and then drove them out of Maine entirely. Until European diseases and intertribal warfare weakened them, they also held their villages and fields along the Connecticut River. When the remaining Abenaki ultimately retreated northward to take shelter with their French allies, they left those terraces to be assumed by the English, who simply continued to plant as the Indians had done.

Along the Connecticut River Valley there are architectural vestiges of the great merchants, called "the River Gods" by their contemporaries, who occupied the valley once the Indians had receded. These vestiges are the famous "Connecticut River door-ways," bold statements, curving into mannerist, with overscaled celebrations at the top. In their most magnificent versions, they are supported by piles of simulated blocks up the side that frame the door opening. Headstones in valley cemeteries took similar forms at the end of the eighteenth century. Deerfield, in Massachusetts, has the most famous of these artifacts, but there are examples to be found all the way up the river to the point where the moose and the wild-rice meadows take over.

Architectural form is an eloquent evoker of character: The Connecticut River doorways and headstones display a strutting bellicosity. This is the noisy, passionate side of the English character, the Shakespearean side. The River Gods had only a brief reign; toward the end, in the 1780s, their doorways shut out an increasingly disrespectful outside world. Their headstones, full of pride, were entryways from a revolutionary world into the silent order of the grave.

INTRODUCTION

ROGER G. KENNEDY

T he Northland is irreconcilable, an Old Testament place of absolutes: sky and sea, rock and marsh. Ambiguities and meadows are luxuries for summer people. This is an unfor-giving land; the scars men make last almost as long as they do in the desert. The "duff" holds together grass and moss and pine needles in a poultice, but when it is ripped by a hiker's boot a tear opens that the wind will worry until all that is left is the gray-rock plat-form upon which northern New England is built. The miracle is that between the dark spruce forest of the far north and the hardwoods of Massachusetts so many tall pines managed to grow, finding nutriment and anchorage in crevices, to rise above 160 feet on trunks six feet across at the base. When loggers climbed a pine they would drop a spruce diagonally against the trunk to use as a ladder to the first pine branches, sixty feet up. The first Europeans to search for the big pines wanted a few of those branchless trunks, entire, for the making of masts; it was only much later, in the 1820s, that the great lumber booms began, and sliced pine became a great commercial crop.

Whatever their ultimate destination, whether for fleets, floors, or furniture, the pines have mostly gone. Paul Bunyan, the myth-ical logger, left large footsteps. Some say they are the chains of elliptical lakelets of the north, but more likely, the record of his passage is in patches of desolate stumpage, slowly, slowly healing.

Inland Maine and New Hampshire were depicted as a vale of ease only by those who had an interest in selling pieces of them: Sir Ferdinando Gorges and Sir John Popham, who thought of Maine as a fine place to colonize with English Catholics, and French entrepreneurs who, in 1604, established the first European agricul-tural colony in North America and thought it ideally situated to receive French Protestants. In southern New England there was Indian agriculture to poach upon, and in its hardwood forests a profusion of deer and small animals browsed upon the berries, nuts, acorns, edible bark, and tender understory. Massachusetts was a hospitable wilderness. But Maine, though bracing, is only intermittently salubrious. The growing season is short, and in the gloom beneath the giant pines one might walk for days without seeing a deer or turkey. The northern spruceland is treacherous with unexpected bogs and disrupted by sudden granite mountains,

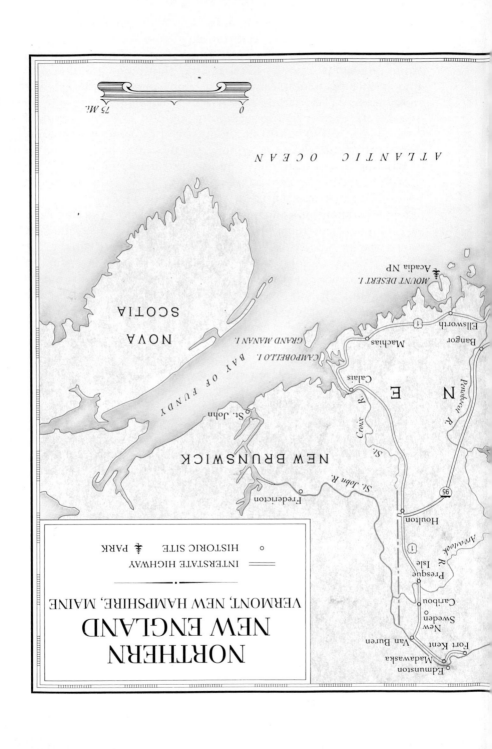

Northern New England was a landscape dominated by huge landholdings. Maine was a proprietary colony: Its people owed fealty to courtiers of the king who held the land grants to their settlements. Between 1690 and 1750, western Vermont and much of New Hampshire had been organized into "seigneuries" by French colonial officials and two English governors, George Clarke of New York and Benning Wentworth of New Hampshire. These two shrewd politicians made use of their posts as the chief representatives of the Crown to swell their own fortunes, distributing the best land to themselves and their supporters. The Wentworths ultimately owned nearly 100,000 acres—the reach of Benning Wentworth's aspirations is disclosed by the very name of Bennington, Vermont—and the Clarkes came to own 120,000 acres, some of it in the Green Mountain State.

The Clarkes and their "Yorkers" were opposed by the redoubtable brothers Ira and Ethan Allen. Ethan had already given Vermont its patriotic text in an altercation with the Clarkes' lawyers: "the gods of the hills are not the gods of the valley"—a deliberately ambiguous utterance that might be loosely translated as "come and get me." Ethan Allen's Green Mountain Boys were first organized in 1770, not to gain independence from Britain but to rid themselves of the Clarkes and their rent-collectors. From 1770 onward there was a small-scale civil war in Vermont between the Green Mountain Boys and the settlers from New York, marked by beatings, burned-out farms, and the rough expulsion of New York sheriffs. Later, Ethan Allen moved to wrap himself in larger causes and to unhorse the Portsmouth landlords, the Wentworths, by leading the Green Mountain Boys against the source of all royal titles, the British Crown. They captured Fort Ticonderoga from the British in 1775; Allen was captured by the British later in that year.

His followers, however, proclaimed Vermont to be independent of everybody in 1777; some New Hampshire towns on the eastern side of the Connecticut enthusiastically applied to join, which enraged the patriots of New Hampshire and encouraged Massachusetts to claim a portion of the new republic for itself.

Between 1779 and 1783 Ethan Allen, released with suspicious ease from his Canadian jail, negotiated on the part of the republic of Vermont with the governor-general of Canada—perhaps the

OPPOSITE: *Shelburne, Vermont, after an autumn rain.*

Green Mountain State might become re-attached to the British Empire, under the right conditions. But Lord Cornwallis surrendered at Yorktown, and the British conceded Vermont to the United States in 1783. Though its neighbors punished its ambiguities by denying it membership in the original thirteen states, Vermont was not quite done with its Balkan politics: As late as 1796, Ira Allen had 20,000 muskets and 24 cannon on board a ship from France to provide for a new revolutionary army, this time to create "New Columbia." Northern Vermont supplied most of the provisions that fed the British armies of the north during the War of 1812. Southern Vermont settled into the United States with greater equanimity as the seigneuries and the great Clarke and Wentworth landholdings came apart.

After independence, the distant aristocrats and oligarchs were replaced by merchant speculators. Maine, especially, was hustled by land-merchants of genius: William Duer, who coupled Old Etonian charm with a total absence of scruple; William Bingham, the "Golden Voyager" with three million acres to dispose; and Alexander Baring, who, as Lord Ashburton, held a million acres of timberland and negotiated its borders with the government of the United States, under whose jurisdiction it came. Bingham's landholdings came as a purchase from Duer, who had bankrupted himself in a frenzy of avarice, devouring confiscated Tory holdings. They constituted the largest holdings east of the Appalachians still remaining under one man's dominance after American independence, and his heirs held on to some bits and pieces until the 1960s.

Traces of these patterns of landholding persist. Six and a half million acres of northern Maine are, to this day, served by 5,000 miles of roads, all of them private. The Brown Company, a logging concern, is more important to the daily life of several townships than is any agent of the state government. Robert Hallowell Gardiner still occupies one of the few continuous squirearchies in the United States, in the town of Gardiner, on Gardiner lands that have been in the family since the mid-eighteenth century and were parts of the Kennebec purchase, thirty miles square. (These Gardiners are not to be confused with the Gardiners of Gardiners Island, New York, though the latter have held their isolated manor even longer.)

Despite our democratic preference to think of this region as owing its charm to the reign of independent yeomen, there is no denying the fact that some of its large landowners have bestowed upon it a benign tradition of conservation practices and public service. The remarkable legacy of the Gardiners is just one example. It is the strange outcome of Maine's reliance upon lumber as a cash crop that some of its proprietors have taken a very long view of their interests and responsibilities. Three-quarters of the "old-growth" timber in all northern New England was recently transferred to a conservancy in the block around Seven Ponds, north of Mount Katahdin, by the heirs of David Pingree, who acquired this domain in 1820. The Seven Ponds reserve is one of the two largest surviving tracts of unspoiled America north of the Smokies (the other is Ramsey's Draft, in Virginia); both are considerably larger than any similar tract in the Adirondacks.

Much of what now looks "wild" in northern New England is merely abandoned, indelibly affected by the farming and grazing that were done in the eighteenth and nineteenth centuries. Even before the arrival of Europeans, the Native Americans had already altered the landscape by purposeful burning and by agriculture. But in Vermont there are thirteen acres of large, old-growth pines in the Fisher-Scott Memorial, north of the village of Arlington, and sixteen acres of climax sugar maples and beech in the Gifford Woods State Park, east of Rutland. Not far away, in the Tinker Brook Natural Area south of West Bridgewater, there are forty-five acres of hemlock and red spruce. Even with the addition of the Battell Stand in Middlebury and more remote stands of timber, such as the Lord's Hill Tract in Marshfield, the diminutive size of these remnants makes the point: We have left very little of the terrain unaffected by our ambitions.

In the countryside, life goes on much as it did in the past. Along the coast, the fishermen and subsistence farmers remain as suspicious of strangers as the Abenaki had been. It is to continuities like this that I wish to draw attention: The extent of northern New England's ancient landholdings, its perpetual clearing of land for planting and grazing, and, despite the felling of white pines so tall that their first branches were higher than the rooftops of a Manchester textile mill, the intractability of the fundamental North Country to any human intervention.

The moose go on searching for succulent stems of arrowroot, the mosquitoes seek the nourishment of blood, the eagles ride the currents sent upward by the sun's earnest effort to thaw Katahdin, and the wolves, it is said, are coming back.

WESTERN VERMONT

OPPOSITE: *Vermont, the most rural state, contains many farms such as this one near Middlebury.*

In its pre-colonial days, Vermont was the hunting ground of Iroquois and Algonquin Indians who traveled the small water-ways—the Winooski, Lamoille, and Missisquoi rivers and Otter Creek—to and from the territory's long western lake. Samuel de Champlain gave his name to that lake in 1609, when he sailed down from Canada, trading with the Algonquin along the way. The explorer's countrymen would attempt Vermont's first settlement on Lake Champlain in 1666 at Isle la Motte.

Shared by New York and Canada, Lake Champlain stretches for over a hundred miles within Vermont (its total length is 120 miles). The lake developed as an important artery for France's colonial commerce in furs and was a vital waterway during the Revolution. Britain's plan to send an invasion force down the lake to the Hudson Valley and split the rebellion was delayed for a year by Benedict Arnold's little fleet at Valcour Bay. During the War of 1812 another small American force, under Thomas Macdonough, won an important American victory on the lake. Later in the century Burlington grew into a rich port city as timber harvests were shipped south on flatboats and steam-powered sidewheelers.

The early French settlement at Isle la Motte failed to survive; it was the English, in 1724, who succeeded in establishing the state's first permanent European settlement at Fort Dummer, near the site of present-day Brattleboro. In 1764 Governor Benning Wentworth of New Hampshire, liberally interpreting his colony's royal charter, began granting towns west of the Connecticut River. The region between the Connecticut and Lake Champlain became known as the New Hampshire Grants. New York also had a claim to this area and began granting towns as well.

When the king decreed in 1770 that New York's claim was the valid one, settlers who had acquired land from New Hampshire found themselves thrown off their land or forced to buy it again from New York proprietors. Anger boiled into action, as Ethan and Ira Allen, Seth Warner, and other leaders organized the Green Mountain Boys, a vigilante group that resisted by force any effort of a New Yorker to evict a Vermonter. Settlers from New York were beaten and their houses burned; New York sheriffs were prevented from serving eviction papers and driven off.

The Green Mountain Boys launched the first offensive of the Revolution, taking Fort Ticonderoga from the British in May 1775. The only Revolutionary battle in Vermont was a rear guard action at Hubbardton in which the Americans stopped the British from

A view of Middlebury Falls, ca. 1865, attributed to James Hope (detail).

pursuing an American column retreating from Fort Ticonderoga. Although the 1777 Battle of Bennington is named for a Vermont town, the actual fighting in that engagement took place in New York. A Hessian raiding party, detached from General John Burgoyne's Hudson Valley invasion force, was on its way to seize supplies at Bennington when it was stopped by John Stark at Walloomsac in New York.

After the war, Vermont announced itself an independent republic. Still concerned about the possibility that New York's land claims would be held valid, Vermont held out the threat that it would join Canada instead of the United States. In 1781 Ethan Allen wrote a firm letter to Congress: "I am as resolutely determined to defend the independence of Vermont as Congress [is] that of the United States, and rather than fail will retire with the hardy Green Mountain Boys into the desolate caverns of the mountains and wage war with human nature at large." The dispute was settled in 1791, when Vermont was admitted as the fourteenth state. Its constitution prohibited slavery and guaranteed suffrage to males whether they owned property or not. The authors of Vermont's constitution also mandated free public education.

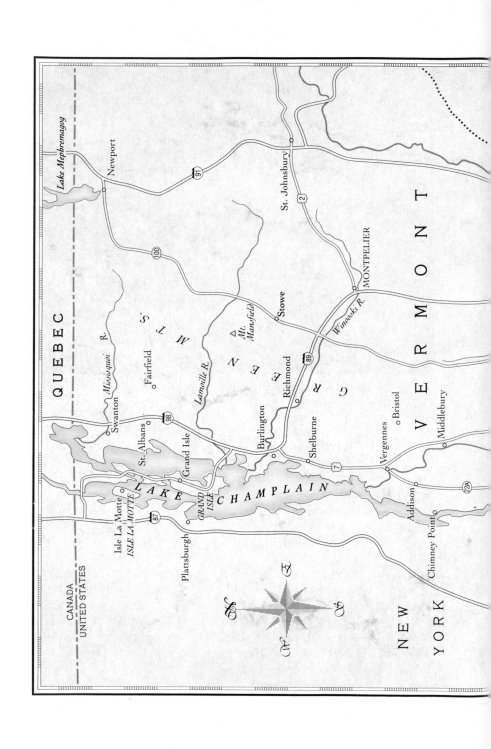

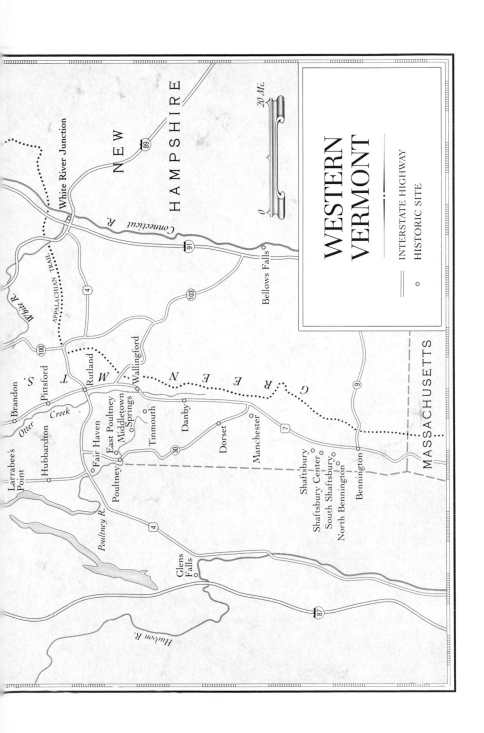

WESTERN VERMONT

—·— INTERSTATE HIGHWAY
  ○   HISTORIC SITE

20 Mi.

0

NEW HAMPSHIRE

White River Junction

APPALACHIAN TRAIL

Connecticut R.

White R.

89

4

100

91

103

Bellows Falls

MASSACHUSETTS

Brandon

Pittsford

Otter Creek

Hubbardton

Larrabees' Point

Rutland

Fair Haven

East Poultney

Poultney

Middletown Springs

Wallingford

Tinmouth

Danby

Dorset

Manchester

Shaftsbury

Shaftsbury Center

South Shaftsbury

North Bennington

Bennington

30

7

9

GREEN MTS.

Poultney R.

4

Glens Falls

87

Hudson R.

After 1791 the state's population surged. French Canadians settled on Lake Champlain and along the northern border. Scottish immigrants came to work the new state's rock quarries, as did Welsh, Italian, and Spanish settlers. Though Vermont lacked the natural water resources of its neighboring states, there were a sufficient number of rivers and streams to power some mills, and young manufacturing towns attracted other New Englanders as well as Polish and Scandinavian immigrants. The Irish came to build canals in the 1820s and railroads in the 1840s and 1850s.

Sheep and cattle raising dominated Vermont agriculture and led to the establishment of woolen mills and creameries throughout the state. Abundant maple trees made Vermont the sugar and syrup capital of the country. Native manufacturing often was small-scale and specialized—ranging from farm tools and fishing rods to papermaking and book publishing. Noah Webster's 1828 dictionary was among the state's early publishing enterprises.

The quiet countryside of Vermont has long attracted artists and writers—Rudyard Kipling, Emily Dickinson, Daniel Chester French, Sinclair Lewis, Pearl Buck, and Norman Rockwell among them. Anna Mary Robertson, the painter known as Grandma Moses, kept a summer studio outside Bennington. Vermont has also attracted sportsmen and vacationers—the state's year-round resort industry has thrived since the mid-nineteenth century. City people still come for the cool lakes and mountain air, foliage, and snowy slopes.

Vermont's towns, farms, and small cities reflect the modesty and thrift of their builders. Executed in clapboard and native stone, the buildings seem as sturdy and pure as the state character. Exuberant, highly decorated architecture is rare in this state—even the Greek Revival, often a showy style, is subdued here. More than any individual structures, entire villages make the strongest architectural impression in Vermont (and indeed, many are designated historic districts), the white steeple of a white church within a white picket fence identifying the scene as quintessential pre-industrial New England. The term "continuous architecture" describes the rural compound of farmhouse, barn, sheds, and other buildings, all connected to one another. The design made life easier in a cold climate, allowing the farm family to rise each morning, milk cows, gather eggs, and perform other chores without having to step into the sub-freezing outdoors. It also kept the family unto itself, out of view. Such compounds are no longer built (chiefly because of

sanitation), but many from the last century may be seen along
Vermont's country roads. Also identified with the state are covered
bridges, which still charm and confound visitors. Why build a roof
over a bridge? The best explanation seems to be the simplest one—
to protect the bridge structure itself from the weight and damp of
the snow.

Rocky and mountainous, with thin soil and lacking a network
of powerful rivers, Vermont never spawned major farming or
industrial centers, and over the years it has lost people to the more
populous, industrialized states to the west and south. Vermont
remains the most rural of the United States, with the fewest number of people residing in cities, and its population is the smallest
east of the Mississippi River. But it still exemplifies Yankee independence. For the most part, Vermonters are of Anglo-Saxon
descent, grassroots conservatives who continue to hold town meetings the first Tuesday of every March.

This chapter begins in the southwestern corner of the state at
Bennington (the first New Hampshire Grant town chartered by
Governor Benning Wentworth), then proceeds north to the Lake
Champlain area.

BENNINGTON

Built on the banks of the Walloomsac River, Bennington encompasses both the Old Town—established in the 1760s—and the
nineteenth-century industrial district of textile and paper mills.
The town is set off by hills to the north and east. It was on these
slopes that Ethan Allen organized his Green Mountain Boys in
1770. Seth Warner, who was elected commander of that group,
had his home in Bennington.

Bennington's earliest citizens, a group of families from Massachusetts, settled along a rise of land that now defines the **Old
Bennington Historic District,** site of a concentration of Federal
and Greek Revival houses along Monument Avenue, all private.
This district went into a decline beginning in the 1820s, when the
area that is now downtown Bennington started its industrial boom,
but revived later in the century as a fashionable residential enclave.
Some of the houses were remodeled in the late 1800s and early
1900s, and new houses, in the Colonial Revival style, were built into
the 1930s. A plaque on the avenue marks the site of the **Catamount
Tavern,** a gathering place for the Green Mountain Boys.

Bennington's Old First Church, built in 1805, has been officially designated "Vermont's Colonial Shrine." The poet Robert Frost is buried here, in the state's oldest graveyard.

Also on Monument Avenue is the handsome, white clapboard **Old First Church,** officially designated as "Vermont's Colonial Shrine." Built in 1805, it was designed by Lavius Fillmore, who followed a popular building handbook, Asher Benjamin's *The Country Builder's Assistant.* Fillmore made his own adaptations to the basic Federal scheme, adding a belfry to the steeple, and enormous Palladian windows above the front entrance and behind the high pulpit. In 1937 the church underwent restoration and Robert Frost was among the project's patrons; the poet and his family are buried behind the church, in the oldest graveyard in the state.

Located across the street from the church, the **Walloomsac Inn** (Monument Avenue and West Road, private) was built in 1766 by Elijah Dewey, the son of Bennington's first minister and later a veteran of the Battle of Bennington. British and Hessian prisoners taken at the battle were brought here for their meals.

Bennington Battle Monument

At the northern end of the historic district a 306-foot-high dolomite obelisk commemorates a 1777 Revolutionary War battle that occurred two miles away in New York. It was there that General

John Stark, reinforced by Seth Warner and the Green Mountain Boys, defeated two British columns advancing toward an American storehouse which was then located on the monument grounds. The New Hampshire and Vermont militia defended the supply depot in one of the significant battles of the Revolution. The battle denied General John Burgoyne crucial supplies, and contributed to the subsequent American victory at Saratoga. In 1891, the state of Vermont erected the monument near the old arsenal. An elevator takes visitors to an observation gallery 200 feet up the shaft.

LOCATION: Monument Circle. HOURS: April through October: 9–5 Daily. FEE: Yes. TELEPHONE: 802–447–0550.

The Bennington Battle Monument, erected in 1891, commemorates the historic defeat of the British by Vermont's Green Mountain Boys on August 16, 1777.

East of Monument Avenue, along the Walloomsac River, is Bennington's **nineteenth-century milling and manufacturing district.** Set up along both sides of the river were paper mills, gristmills, and brick and pottery factories. Two notable buildings are the 1865 **Big Mill** (Benmont Avenue, along the river), a brick structure in the Italianate style with a lofty bell tower, and the Romanesque Revival **Bennington and Rutland Railroad Station** (River Street), built of marble in 1898. The downtown historic district along Main, North, and South streets is a busy mingling of Victorian commercial architecture, including the **Putnam Block** at South and Main and the 1870 **Pennysaver Building** (107–111 South Street).

Bennington Museum

This museum, specializing in the region's art and history, displays the most complete collection of Bennington pottery in existence, as well as a collection of pressed glass, blown glass, and some items by the Tiffany studio. Its exhibits of local military items include the flag flown at the 1777 Battle of Bennington, believed to be the oldest surviving Stars and Stripes. The painting collections encompass works by Erastus Salisbury Field, a 1798 *View of Bennington* by Ralph Earl (one of the oldest landscape paintings in the country), and many works by Anna Mary Robertson ("Grandma") Moses. A collection of Moses memorabilia is displayed in the schoolhouse she attended, which was moved here from its original site in Eagle Bridge, New York, in 1972.

> LOCATION: West Main Street. HOURS: March through December: 9–5 Daily; January through February: 9–5 Saturday–Sunday. FEE: Yes. TELEPHONE: 802–447–1571.

A few miles northeast is **North Bennington,** where woodworking and furniture making were local specialties. Paran Creek powered the community's mills, few of which survive. Early mill-workers' housing, however, stands along Sage Street. Rail lines to Massachusetts and New York converged at the **North Bennington Depot,** a small brick train station and former headquarters of the Bennington and Rutland Railroad.

Park-McCullough House

This Second Empire–style, thirty-five-room mansion was begun in 1863 and completed in 1865 by Trenor Park, who made his initial fortune managing California gold mines. The house has important

Two of Vermont's governors, Hiland Hall and John G. McCullough, lived in North Bennington's Park-McCullough House, one of the country's earliest Second Empire style residences.

collections of nineteenth-century furnishings, decorative arts, and fine arts. It was home to two Vermont governors, Hiland Hall (Trenor Park's father-in-law) and John G. McCullough (his son-in-law). The house's archival collection includes the papers of Park and McCullough, as well as rare photographs by the renowned photographer of the American West, Carlton Watkins.

LOCATION: Park and West streets. HOURS: June through October: 10–4 Daily. FEE: Yes. TELEPHONE: 802–442–5441.

THE SHAFTSBURYS

Strung together by Route 7A, "the Shaftsburys"—**South Shaftsbury, Shaftsbury Center, Shaftsbury**—were settled by newcomers from Connecticut and Rhode Island in the 1760s.

Some of the Shaftsburys' earliest settlers (founders of Vermont's first Baptist congregation, in 1768) are buried in the eighteenth-century graveyard next to the **Center Shaftsbury Baptist Church** (Route 7A). The church, a Greek Revival structure built in 1846, houses the **Shaftsbury Historical Society Museum** (802–442–4580). Exhibits include church artifacts, hand tools, wedding dresses, locally made spinning wheels, historic flags, and tools used by the Eagle Square Manufacturing Company, which forged the first steel carpenter's tools. The **Peter Matteson Tavern,** a restored farmhouse and tavern operated by the Bennington Museum (East Road in Shaftsbury, 802–447–1571), is furnished with many pieces from the late 1780s period of its construction. The **Munro-Hawkins House** (Route 7A, 802–447–2286) is a fine two-story Georgian structure, built in 1808 by a successful wheat farmer, Joshua Munro, who exported wheat to France during the Napoleonic Wars. The house has been converted to an inn.

In 1920, the poet Robert Frost bought the oldest house in South Shaftsbury, the 1769 **Homer Noble Farm** (Route 7A, private), with twenty-two-inch thick stone walls. Just off the highway, the house did not afford sufficient privacy and Frost moved.

MANCHESTER

Manchester has been one of New England's prime resort towns since the middle of the nineteenth century. Along **Main Street,** which preserves its old marble sidewalks, are private houses and resort buildings once visited by Mrs. Ulysses S. Grant, Theodore Roosevelt, and William Howard Taft. Mrs. Abraham Lincoln stayed at the **Equinox Hotel** (Route 7A, Manchester Village, 802–362–4700), one of the great resorts of the day; it is still operating.

Hildene

Hildene was the summer home of Robert Todd Lincoln, the only one of Abraham Lincoln's four children to survive to adulthood. The twenty-four-room house was completed in 1904, when Robert was president of the Pullman Company; he died there in 1926. Today it is maintained as a house museum, with many original furnishings, including a 1908 Aeolian pipe organ, with 1,000 pipes and a player attachment. A narrow cabinet in the office contains a few of Abraham Lincoln's personal items, including a stovepipe hat.

The 400-acre estate includes a carriage barn (now the visitor center) and a magnificent formal garden in the shape of a Gothic window, designed by Robert's daughter, Jesse.

LOCATION: Route 7A South. HOURS: Mid-May through October: 9–4:30 Daily. FEE: Yes. TELEPHONE: 802–362–1788.

OPPOSITE: *Hildene, now a house museum, was built in 1904 by Robert Todd Lincoln, the son of Abraham Lincoln.* OVERLEAF: *Dorset is the site of America's first marble quarry.*

DORSET

Dorset is the site of the first (1785) marble quarry in the United States. In 1776 Vermont's leaders, including Thomas Chittenden, Seth Warner, and Ira Allen, convened at a tavern here and proclaimed the "Free and Independent State of Vermont." The town's eighteenth-century landmarks include the **Memorial Library** (Route 30, 802–867–5774), housed in a 1790 tavern, and the **United Church of Dorset and East Rupert** (Church Street, 802–867–2260), constructed of local marble. The **Kent Neighborhood Historic District** (surrounding the intersections of Dorset West Road, Lane Road, and Nichols Hill Road) contains clapboard homes from the eighteenth and early-nineteenth centuries.

DANBY

This village was settled largely by Quakers in the 1760s, and grew into a prosperous town in the nineteenth century as men opened quarries and harvested forests, and sent the stone and lumber south on the Rutland Railroad. Silas Griffith, one of Vermont's first millionaires, made his fortune cutting the Danby forests. The writer Pearl S. Buck moved to Danby toward the end of her life; by the time she died in 1973 she had restored several houses on the village's historic Main Street.

A manufacturing specialty developed north of Danby in the town of **Wallingford.** Hand garden tools (rakes, forks, spades) were produced at the **Old Stone Shop** (South Main Street), built in 1848, and other small factories. West of Wallingford, across Otter Creek, is **Tinmouth.** One of Vermont's first iron forges was started here in 1781. Later enterprises included sawmills, gristmills, tanneries, and creameries. Chartered in 1761, the town has a number of imposing Federal houses within its compact **historic district.**

MIDDLETOWN SPRINGS

This isolated mountain community came to life a century after it was founded in 1784 with the discovery of a spring. In the late-nineteenth century, people came to take the waters and relax in the Victorian "Springhouse," a replica of which has been built off Burdock Avenue by the **Middletown Springs Historical Society.**

Middletown Springs was founded in 1784 and became a fashionable spa and resort in the 1860s. One elegant place to stop was the Middletown Springs Inn, at right.

The society maintains a small **museum** (802–235–2322) on the town green that displays artifacts of local history. Fine Federal and Greek Revival houses surround the green on three sides.

POULTNEY AND EAST POULTNEY

Until the 1860s the village of East Poultney was the commercial center of the immediate area. The region's chief town is now Poultney, farther to the west. East Poultney was settled in the early 1770s by people from Connecticut, led by Heber Allen of the famed Allen family. They were driven from their new homes in 1777 by Burgoyne's troops during the British march from Canada to the Hudson Valley. The settlers later returned, establishing a string of busy mills and shops along the Poultney River up to Middletown Springs. These businesses, and the bridges that crossed the river, were wiped out by a flood in 1811, an event from which East Poultney never quite recovered.

The Poultney River plain is rich in slate. Federal and Greek Revival houses on East Poultney's **green** are roofed with the native slate—green, purple, or mottled. The handsome **United Baptist Church** (802–287–5577), with a Palladian window and clock tower, dominates the green. Built in 1805 from designs in Asher Benjamin's guide, *The Country Builder's Assistant,* it has been recently restored. The **Eagle Tavern** (on the green, 802–287–9498), a 1785 stagecoach inn, has put up many boarders, including the famous newspaperman Horace Greeley, founder of the *New York Tribune.* Greeley apprenticed at a local newspaper, the *Northern Spectator,* from 1826 to 1830. George Jones, one of the founders of the *New York Times,* was born in this town. Local history collections are at the **Poultney Historical Society Museum** (off Route 30, 802–287–4042). In the 1840s and 1850s Welsh quarry workers settled in the area to mine the slate deposits. The rise of the slate industry and the coming of the railroad led to the development of the town.

FAIR HAVEN

This town was another center of the slate industry in the nineteenth century, and like Poultney, attracted Welsh quarrymen. The town's early history was dominated by an Irish immigrant, Matthew Lyon, who arrived in 1783 and started sawmills, paper mills, an ironworks, and a printing press. Lyon also published the town's newspaper, and built its meetinghouse and school. He went on to become one of Vermont's best-known politicians, a controversial foe of President John Quincy Adams and the Federalists. In 1801 Congressman Lyon cast the tie-breaking presidential vote for Thomas Jefferson against Aaron Burr. Before the Civil War Fair Haven's houses were stops on the Underground Railroad, by which runaway slaves escaped to Canada.

RUTLAND

Vermont's "Marble City," Rutland is spread out in the Otter Creek valley, with the Green Mountains to the east and the Taconic range to the west. By the 1770s settlers, mostly from Connecticut, were farming in the town, which had been chartered by Governor Benning Wentworth in 1761. During the Revolution they built Fort Rutland, which burned in 1777. It was replaced the following year by Fort Ranger in Center Rutland.

The town boomed as a center of commerce and manufacturing after 1849 when the Rutland Railroad connected it to Boston. After the Civil War a returning veteran, Redfield Proctor, turned the town's sleepy marble business into one of the nation's biggest. Proctor's Vermont Marble Company employed thousands, many of them new immigrants from Ireland, Italy, Poland, and Sweden.

With its other attractions—milling and lumber industries, a lively retail trade, mountain resorts—Rutland tripled its population by 1880. The people built a handsome city, with some of the finest structures of that era in the **Rutland Courthouse District,** along Main, Center, and Washington streets. Two of the most notable and monumental are the **Rutland Free Library** (Court Street), designed by Ammi B. Young to house the post office and federal court, and the 1871 **county courthouse** (83 Center Street). The **Gryphon Building, opera house,** and other brick business blocks line **Merchants Row.** The former Rutland Bank at 101 Center Street was built in 1825. In 1989 the **Rutland Historical Society** opens its new museum in an 1850, Italianate-style building (formerly a firehouse) on Center Street. The 1892 Queen Anne–style house of marble magnate George Chaffee is now the **Chaffee Art Center** (16 South Main Street, 802–775–0356).

PROCTOR

The **Vermont Marble Exhibit** (61 Main Street, 802–459–3311), housed in the still-operating Vermont Marble Company, displays locally quarried marble and shows the process by which the raw material is turned into the carved and polished finished product.

The Vermont Marble Exhibit, with displays of locally quarried marble.

Wilson Castle, Proctor. OPPOSITE: *The grand stairwell of Wilson Castle.*

Wilson Castle

Wilson Castle, an eclectic blend of European styles surrounded by a 115-acre estate, has a facade of brick and marble, and, as befits its name, boasts a turret, parapet, and balcony, as well as nineteen proscenium arches. The thirty-two rooms, spread over three floors, feature French, German, Italian, and English antiques, as well as rugs, scrolls, and statues from the Far East. Particularly notable are the grand stairwell, with its mahogany panelling and frescoed ceilings, and the frescoed and gold stencilled walls and ceilings of the art gallery. Tiffany chandeliers hang in both the library and dining salon, and there are 84 stained-glass windows scattered throughout the Wilson home. Though it lacks a moat, the estate is suitably grand, with barns and stables, a carriage house, and an aviary stocked with peacocks, the bird traditionally owned by royalty.

LOCATION: West Proctor Road. HOURS: Mid-May through October: 8–6 Daily. FEE: Yes. TELEPHONE: 802–773–3284.

PITTSFORD

Saw and grist mills operated along two brooks that run through Pittsford, and the town was noted for its iron foundries. Nineteenth-century churches, commercial buildings, and houses surround the town's triangular green. Pittsford has three covered bridges, all built in the 1840s: the **Cooley,** the **Gorham,** and the **Hammond.** The **New England Maple Museum** (Route 7, 802–483–9414) has exhibits on the history of Vermont sugaring, beginning from the time of the Indians.

HUBBARDTON BATTLEFIELD

The only battle of the Revolutionary War fought on Vermont soil took place here on July 7, 1777. British and Hessian troops, commanded respectively by General Simon Fraser and General Baron Friedrich von Riedesel, were pursuing the American forces that were evacuating Fort Ticonderoga. The American rear guard, about 1,200 men commanded by Seth Warner of the Green Mountain Boys and two other officers from Massachusetts and New Hampshire, was waiting at Hubbardton with orders to delay the British advance as long as possible and then scatter. The British reached the American position just before dawn. In the sharp two-hour fight that ensued, the New Englanders were holding their own against highly trained, select British units, until the Hessians arrived. The Americans then scattered into the woods. Both sides suffered heavy losses; but the Americans achieved their purpose of stopping the British pursuit of the main American column.

The battle has been a controversial one: Warner was accused of tarrying at Hubbardton in defiance of his orders and of failing to post guards, thus allowing the British to surprise the camp. Recent scholarship, however, tends to vindicate Warner. There is evidence that he was in fact following orders when he made his stand here, that he did post guards, and was prepared for the British attack. The **Hubbardton Battlefield Monument,** a spire of solid Vermont marble, commemorates the battle and marks the burial spot of Colonel Ebenezer Francis, who led the Massachusetts detail and lost his life in the battle.

LOCATION: Seven miles north of Route 4, Hubbardton. HOURS: Late May through mid-October: 9:30–5:30 Wednesday–Sunday. FEE: None. TELEPHONE: 802–828–3226.

BRANDON

Northeast over the mountains is Brandon, birthplace of Stephen A. Douglas (1813), who later became the Democratic senator from Illinois and foe of Abraham Lincoln. In the senatorial campaign of 1858, the occasion for the famed Lincoln–Douglas debates, Douglas was the victor. In 1860, as the first Vermont native to be nominated for president, he lost to Lincoln. The village is sited on the Neshobe River, which powered its marble-cutting mills. Ironworks also were active in the area—ruins of the 1810 **Forestdale Iron Furnace** are preserved nearby (Route 73 and Furnace Road, 802–828–3226). Adding to the local industry were factories producing stoves and scales.

MOUNT INDEPENDENCE

After the Americans captured Fort Ticonderoga in 1775 they fortified this point on Lake Champlain, opposite Ticonderoga, and connected the two with a floating bridge. When Burgoyne recaptured Ticonderoga in 1777 the bridge served as the American garrison's escape route. Today the site contains the ruins of fortifications and gun batteries.

LOCATION: West of Route 22A, in Orwell. HOURS: June through mid-October: 9:30–5:30 Wednesday–Sunday. FEE: None. TELEPHONE: 802–828–3226.

Bunkers and foundations at Mount Independence.

The stately Old Chapel at Middlebury College is one of several early campus buildings constructed of local limestone.

LARRABEE'S POINT

Once a busy landing place for commercial traffic on Lake Champlain, this town became a trading center for quarried stone, lumber products, furniture, and textiles. Local black marble was a profitable export. The place was named for John Larrabee, who in 1823 built a **warehouse,** still standing on the lake's edge. Within the town's historic district are the **ferry dock** (for Ticonderoga traffic) and a few lakeside **cottages** dating from Larrabee's late-nineteenth-century resort days. Larrabee's Point lost its commercial thrust in the mid-nineteenth century when the northeastern network of railroads began to move merchandise more efficiently than had the waterways. The 108-foot **Shoreham Covered Railroad Bridge** was built by the Rutland Railroad in 1897.

Further up the Lake Champlain shoreline is the green promontory of **Chimney Point,** named for the ruins of an early French settlement on this strategic site. Indians had settled here before the French; in fact, this area has been settled for over 12,000 years. According to popular belief, Samuel de Champlain stood at this point in 1609 when he gave his name to the lake. The French raised their stone fortress in 1690. Nearly a century later, local ferry operator Benjamin Paine refashioned it as the **Chimney Point Tavern** (Route 17, 802–828–3226). Its taproom, visited by soldiers on both sides of the Revolution, is open to the public; a museum is scheduled to open in the summer of 1989.

MIDDLEBURY

Northeast toward Vermont's interior is Middlebury, lying on Otter Creek. Middlebury was chartered in 1761, though its early European settlers were unable to sustain their incursion into Indian lands; another settlement was begun twenty years later. The town sits on a deep bedrock of marble, quarried since 1803. Two important industrial innovations have come from Middlebury: the sand-and-water process of sawing marble, and the welding of cast steel. Falls on Otter Creek powered textile mills, and wool processing grew into Middlebury's major industry. Another important local enterprise was the manufacture of doors and window sashes.

In 1800 **Middlebury College** (College Street, 802–388–3711) was chartered. Among the campus's historic buildings (many made of local limestone) are **Mead Memorial Chapel, Hepburn Hall, Starr Hall, Starr Library,** and the college's oldest structure, the 1815 **Painter Hall.** The **Emma Willard House National Historic Landmark,** site of the Middlebury Female Seminary established in 1814, is now the admissions office for Middlebury College.

The village historic district, along Otter Creek, contains many eighteenth- and nineteenth-century structures. Among them are the **Battell Block** (Merchants Row and Main Street), the **Beckwith Block** (Main Street), and the **Congregational Church** (Main and

North Pleasant streets, 802–388–7634), completed in 1809 to designs by Lavius Fillmore. The Ionic columns inside are of solid wood, each made from a single tree.

Sheldon Museum

Located in an 1829 Federal-style house, the Sheldon Museum features everyday objects from the nineteenth century displayed in period settings. Permanent exhibits include furniture by Vermont artisans, fine and decorative arts, farming and carpentry tools, household utensils, and toys; these are supplemented by special exhibits. The house, built by local marble merchant Elias Judd, is a three-story brick mansion. Its Ionic columns, sills and lintels, and six fireplaces are made of black marble quarried in Shoreham.

LOCATION: 1 Park Street. HOURS: June through October: 10–5 Monday–Saturday; November through May: 1–4 Wednesday and Friday. FEE: Yes. TELEPHONE: 802–388–2117.

John Strong Mansion

This elegant brick mansion, built in the 1790s, stands near the site of Strong's first home, a frame house burned by the British in 1777. Shutters, door hinges, and iron-walled fireplaces all reflect fine craftsmanship. One of the bricks, on display in the mansion, bears the engraved signature of the bricklayer. The house has four "hidey holes," each large enough to hold several people. Although it is said that Strong built the hiding places as refuge from possible Indian raids, it is possible that he was also worried about bear attacks—a group of bears had come into his first house looking for food, sending his wife and children to a loft for safety. The mansion contains furnishings from the 1800s and some original Strong family pieces; among these are a 1749 tall clock and a ca. 1790 painted fireboard with a beautifully stenciled border.

LOCATION: Route 22A. HOURS: Mid-May through mid-October: 10–5 Friday–Monday. FEE: Yes. TELEPHONE: 802–759–2309.

BRISTOL

Situated near the New Haven River on a plateau at the base of Hogback Mountain is the village of Bristol. In the late-nineteenth century, sawmills along the New Haven produced furniture and caskets, and local cabinetmakers won national renown for their fine work. The Bartlett Plow Manufactory produced equipment for the farmers of the Midwest. The chief architectural sites here are commercial blocks, clustered near the green. The **town hall**—part Queen Anne, part Romanesque Revival—and a **gristmill** also are within the downtown historic district.

VERGENNES

The territorial disputes between New Hampshire and New York were briefly focused here in 1773 when the Green Mountain Boys burned a settlement of Scotsmen established at the behest of a New Yorker. Vergennes was incorporated as a city in 1788 and named for the Comte de Vergennes, the French minister of foreign affairs whose support of America during the Revolution was crucial. It is the nation's smallest city, being only one mile square. What it lacked in size Vergennes made up in energy—by the early 1800s it was a bustling place of iron forges, rolling mills, and sawmills. During the War of 1812, Commodore Thomas Macdonough selected Vergennes as the 1813–1814 winter quarters for his small Lake Champlain fleet. The town's forges produced 177 tons of shot for him and, working with incredible speed, local carpenters built a flotilla for Macdonough, including the twenty-six-gun corvette *Saratoga*, the twenty-gun brig *Eagle*, and ten small gunboats propelled by oars. With these vessels Macdonough defeated the British at Plattsburgh on September 11, 1814—an important victory that thwarted British plans to prolong the war. A **monument** to Macdonough stands in the town green.

Nearby buildings, most of them constructed between 1825 and 1900, reflect Vergennes's industrial prosperity; chief among them are the **Ryan commercial block,** the **Stevens House Hotel,** and **Victorian houses,** all on Main Street; the elegant 1911 **Bixby Memorial Library** stands nearby. **Mill buildings** are preserved below Otter Creek Falls.

FERRISBURG

The Underground Railroad ran through western Vermont, but its operations in this region were less clandestine than those farther south. Perhaps because of a prominent Quaker community, the general sentiment in the region was largely abolitionist. Rowland Thomas Robinson, a Quaker and founder of the Vermont Anti-Slavery Society, used his house as a stop on the Underground

Railroad; escaped slaves worked for wages on his farm and ate with the family. Rowland Evans Robinson, his son, was a nineteenth-century writer and illustrator who chronicled the dialect and folkways of the region in a series of enormously popular stories and essays. His wife, Anna Stevens Robinson, was a portrait painter, and their two daughters were also artists. The 1786 late Federal-early Greek Revival farmhouse where four generations of Robinsons lived is now the **Rokeby Museum** (Route 7, 802–877–3406), furnished entirely with family pieces ranging from the 1780s to the 1890s, including many portraits, landscapes, and genre scenes by this family of artists. Across the road from the museum is a working farm (private) with a round barn, one of only twenty left in the state.

BASIN HARBOR

The history of Lake Champlain and the surrounding region is examined in the **Basin Harbor Museum** (Basin Harbor Road, 802–475–2317) which features historical exhibits and an exact replica of an eighteenth-century *bateau,* based on a wreck found in the lake. The museum supports ongoing underwater research in Lake Champlain, including the exploration of **Arnold's Bay,** about five miles north of Panton, where Benedict Arnold ran five of his ships aground on October 13, 1776, after the battle of Valcour Bay, New York. Arnold—whose treason was to come four years later—delayed a British invasion along Lake Champlain by constructing a small fleet and deploying it brilliantly. The onset of winter prevented the British from continuing their invasion until 1777. After his successful delaying action at Valcour Bay, Arnold beached his vessels north of Panton and set them afire to keep them from British hands. Parts of one ship still lie at the bottom of the lake.

RICHMOND

In 1813 the people of Richmond, a quiet dairy-farming community, built a multidenominational church that looked like no other in the state, but harkened back to the round churches of early Christianity and of early French Protestantism. The **Old Round Church** (off Route 2) actually is sixteen-sided and is topped by an octagonal belfry. It has not been used as a church since 1879 but serves a variety of public functions.

OPPOSITE: *Richmond's striking Old Round Church—which actually has sixteen sides—was constructed in 1813 to serve five denominations.*

An early 1900s photo of the Queen Anne Revival Coach Barn at Shelburne Farms, on the

SHELBURNE FARMS

In the late-nineteenth century the dairy country below Burlington
attracted railroad magnate William Seward Webb, who had married Lila Vanderbilt. The Webbs built a 110-room English cottage–
style manor house on 4,000 acres. Frederick Law Olmsted advised
the Webbs on the landscaping of the grounds. The estate is smaller
now—1,000 acres—and is open to the public; the visitor center is
located in the ca. 1890 **Gate House,** a cottage-style shingle building
once occupied by the Webbs's gatekeeper. **Shelburne House,** the
1889 main house, has been restored with original furnishings and
is operated as an inn. The formal gardens, overlooking Lake
Champlain, are also being restored to their original design. The
five-story **Farm Barn,** which surrounds a central courtyard, currently houses a bread bakery, furniture shop, and offices; restoration is scheduled to begin in the summer of 1989, and a museum
with interpretive exhibits on conservation and agricultural history

estate of railroad mogul William Seward Webb.

will be added. Also notable is the brick Queen Anne Revival **Coach Barn,** now an education center. The complex also includes a working dairy housed in modern buildings.

> LOCATION: Off Route 7, eight miles south of Burlington. HOURS: June through mid-October: 9–5 Daily. FEE: Yes. TELEPHONE: 802–985–3222.

SHELBURNE MUSEUM

The Shelburne Museum houses one of the finest collections of American folk art in the world. It is a complex of thirty-seven buildings, many of them historic structures moved to the museum from other sites in New England. Some of the buildings, which include seven houses, a one-room schoolhouse, a general store, and a railroad station, are furnished in period style; others simply display the immense art and Americana collection of Electra Havemeyer Webb, who, together with her husband, J. Watson Webb

(son of the Webbs of Shelburne Farms), founded the museum in 1947. One of the first structures was a huge horseshoe-shaped barn (constructed from pieces of eleven older barns and two gristmills) built to house the Webb family's collection of carriages and sleighs. Also on the site are a jail, a blacksmith shop, a covered bridge, and the SS *Ticonderoga*. The magnificent collection of quilts, coverlets, and other textiles is housed in the Hat and Fragrance Unit; weathervanes, cigar-store Indians, and other folk art objects are on display in the Stagecoach Inn; and the Colchester Reef Lighthouse is now a gallery of maritime art and ship figureheads. Two modern buildings hold fine collections of paintings and antique furniture.

LOCATION: Route 7, south of Shelburne. HOURS: Mid-May through mid-October: 9–5 Daily. FEE: Yes. TELEPHONE: 802–985–3346.

BURLINGTON

Settled in the early 1770s, Burlington was nearly abandoned during the Revolution, when most of its inhabitants went off to the fighting. But the pioneers returned, to resume building the town on a triple-tiered slope above Lake Champlain. The general plan is still evident, with wharves and warehouses on the shoreline, a business district on the second tier, and residences taking in the whole scene from the top.

Many enterprises went into making Burlington Vermont's largest city. Ira Allen established a shipyard on the Winooski River in 1772. A few years later, he dammed the river and put in sawmills. In 1791, the Vermont legislature called for the establishment of a state university. Accordingly, the University of Vermont was founded here, adding academic affairs to the local business activity. Entrepreneur Gideon King was one of the first to realize the commercial implications of Lake Champlain traffic to and from Canada, and one of the men joining him in exploiting it was John Jacob Astor, the New York fur merchant. Furs and lumber came down from the north woods to markets south and west of Burlington.

Steamboats and the railroads quickened the pace of trade. The *Vermont,* launched in 1809 from Burlington, was the second commercial steamboat in the country, coming two years after Robert

OPPOSITE: *This appliquéd album quilt, from the extensive textile collection of the Shelburne Museum, was made in 1876 to celebrate the nation's centennial by a member of the Burdick-Childs family.*

Fulton made history on the Hudson River with his *Clermont.* Passenger crossings were a popular diversion, and in 1823 when the Champlain Canal opened a path to the Hudson and the sea, Burlington saw the arrival of first-class passenger steamers. The railroad came at mid-century, with the Rutland and Central Vermont lines. The first ran to Boston via Rutland, the second by way of White River Junction.

By 1880, the city had a magnificent courthouse and grand residences (still standing) on fashionable Main, Pearl, and Willard streets. From the city's nineteenth-century boom period are private residences and commercial buildings along Battery Street, Court House Square, South Willard Street, South Union Street, and on the university green.

The square steeple tower of Burlington's 1816 **Unitarian Church** (Church and Pearl streets, 802–862–5630) is topped by a double octagonal spire. The interior gallery is supported by Doric columns. Also on Church Street are the Romanesque **Masonic Temple,** built in 1898 (now converted to offices), and the **Richardson Building,** an 1895 department store and rooming house built in a chateau style.

One of the city's most handsome lakefront houses belonged to railroad executive and county judge Timothy Follett. Known as **Follett House** (63 College Street), the 1840 Greek Revival residence designed by Ammi B. Young now is used for offices. Several of the day's prosperous merchants built their houses on Pearl Street. Still private residences today, they include the **Buell House** at number 303, **Deming House** at number 308, and **Loomis House** at number 342. The **Moore-Woodbury House** (416 Pearl Street), with two late-nineteenth-century elaborations to the 1815 original, once belonged to Urban Woodbury, Burlington mayor and Vermont governor from 1894 to 1896. It is now an apartment house.

University of Vermont

The University of Vermont was founded in 1791 by an act of the state legislature, which endowed the school with a grant of some 29,000 acres of land in parcels all over the state. (Since 1777 the government had been setting aside land for a college in each new town that was chartered—all of these lands were turned over to the new university.) On a smaller but no less important scale, Ira Allen gave the university fifty acres in Burlington for its campus. A statue

The University of Vermont, in Burlington, is graced with buildings designed by several of America's most distinguished architects. McKim, Mead & White's Chapel was built on the college green in 1927.

of Allen stands on the college's **green,** and the **chapel** (1927) is named for him. Designed by the firm of McKim, Mead & White, the chapel rises above the northeast side of the green.

Adjacent to the chapel is the Romanesque **Billings Building,** designed by Henry Hobson Richardson. Originally the library, it was completed in 1885. Richardson called it "the best thing I have yet done." Next door is the Gothic-style **Williams Science Hall.**

Grassmount, the five-bay brick residence of Vermont governor (1823–1826) Cornelius P. Van Ness, at 411 Main Street, is now the university's alumni office. A fraternity occupies the 1891

Queen Anne **Edward Wells House,** at 61 Summit Street. The
original owner hired local woodworker Albert M. Whittekind to
execute intricate carving, inside and out.

LOCATION: Route 2. TELEPHONE: 802–656–3480.

The redoubtable Revolutionary War hero and founding father of
the state, Ethan Allen, is said to be buried at **Greenmount Cemetery** (Colchester Avenue) under a forty-two-foot-tall column,
topped by a statue of Allen. He is depicted at the moment of his
great triumph, the surrender of the British garrison at Fort Ticonderoga. He died in 1789.

East of Burlington, on the Browns River in **Jericho,** is the 1856 **Old
Red Mill** (Route 15, 802–899–3225). Shut down at the turn of the
century, the flour mill is now a museum, with its water-driven
machinery on view.

STOWE

Originally a logging and farming community, Stowe has been primarily a resort since the mid-1800s, when city-bound New Englanders began to flock here for winter sports and mountain air.
The resort is sited between Mount Mansfield (at 4,393 feet the
highest peak in Vermont) and Hogback Mountain. Handsome
commercial and public buildings reflect its prosperity. Among the
most notable within the compact historic district are the **Green
Mountain Inn, Community Church, Carlson Building,** and the
Akeley Memorial Building, housing the **Stowe Historical Society
Museum,** all on Main Street.

The **Fisher Covered Railroad Bridge** spans the Lamoille River east
of **Morrisville.** The 1908 wooden bridge has been strengthened
with steel beams. Its long clerestory is a chimney for locomotive
smoke. **Grand Isle,** in the northern reach of Lake Champlain, is
connected to the mainland of Vermont by ferry and highway. The
abundant wildlife was hunted and fished by Indians, then by settlers of English descent in the late-eighteenth century. Until it was
discovered a century later as a summer resort, Grand Isle was a
small but thriving lake and apple-orchard community.

One of the oldest surviving log cabins in the United States,
built in 1783, is on Route 2 just north of the town of Grand Isle.

The last covered railroad bridge still in regular use in Vermont, the Fisher Covered Railroad Bridge was reinforced with heavy steel beams in 1968 to allow the preservation of the historic wooden structure.

Made of cedar logs, the twenty-by-twenty-five-foot cabin has a half-story loft and a large fireplace at one end. It is called **Hyde Log Cabin** (802–372–8830) after its builder, Jedediah Hyde, Jr., a veteran of the Revolution.

ISLE LA MOTTE

Closer to Quebec than to the Vermont mainland, Isle la Motte is the site of Vermont's first (though not permanent) French settlement. In 1666 Captain de la Motte led 300 men, Jesuits among them, to this small island near the top of the Champlain. To ward off a counterattack from the Mohawk Indians, the French raised Fort Sainte-Anne; the first Catholic mass in the state was celebrated here. Today, the site is marked by **St. Anne's Shrine** (off Route 129, 802–928–3362), which consists of an open-air chapel, a marble statue of Saint Anne, and several small outdoor shrines. A granite statue of Samuel de Champlain marks the spot where he is believed to have landed in 1609. Relics of the island's history are also on display.

The island's rich deposits of black marble were quarried in the late 1800s—the stone was used in the construction of New York's Brooklyn Bridge and Rockefeller Center.

ST. ALBANS

Situated close to Canada, St. Albans, settled just after the Revolution, has been the scene of many illegal escapades and political maneuvers of the type that often beset border towns. When Jefferson's embargo on trade with Britain was in effect from 1807 to the War of 1812, smugglers did a brisk business here, plying various kinds of contraband into and out of Canada. Three Federal officers were killed by gunmen protecting a smuggling craft. In 1837 when French Canadians were plotting a revolt against Britain, St. Albans was one of their rallying places. The most spectacular border incident took place during the Civil War in 1864, when twenty-two Confederate agents (part of a well-organized Confederate terrorist group operating out of Canada) simultaneously robbed all the banks in town, making off with some $200,000. Brought to trial in Canada, the raiders were acquitted on the grounds that their raid was an act of war and not a criminal offense. In 1866 members of an Irish political group, the Fenians, planned to use St. Albans as a jumping-off point for a raid on Canada, but were thwarted by the arrival of federal troops.

The railroads arrived in 1850, and St. Albans became not only an important railroad center but headquarters of the Central Vermont Railroad. Dairy farming, lime processing, and the manufacture of animal feed, maple sugar, and sugar-making equipment added to the economy. The wealth of the town is apparent in monumental public buildings on **Taylor Park,** the **Central Vermont Railroad Headquarters** (Kingman Street), and the large private houses on Main Street.

Occupying an 1861 nine-room school, the **Franklin County Museum** (Church and Bishop streets, 802–527–7933) contains a variety of exhibits depicting aspects of Vermont history: memorabilia of the Central Vermont Railway, winter sports equipment, an Indian canoe, a country doctor's office, and articles relating to the Confederate raid of 1864.

CHESTER A. ARTHUR HISTORIC SITE

Chester A. Arthur was born in 1829. In 1848, after graduating from Union College in New York State, he returned to Vermont to teach at the North Pownall Academy. Two years later, he moved to New York City to pursue a career in law and, later, the civil service. In 1871, President Ulysses S. Grant named him customs collector of the Port Authority of New York. The abuses of the Grant administration had resulted in widespread corruption within the civil service, however, and when the next president, Rutherford B. Hayes, undertook to reform the system, Arthur's appointment was rescinded. When the Republicans nominated James A. Garfield (who had also taught at North Pownall Academy) to run for president in 1880, Arthur was chosen as his running mate to appease an anti-reform faction. A few months after he was elected, Garfield was assassinated and Arthur became president. Against all expectations, he continued the reforms initiated by Hayes and supported the Pendleton Act of 1883, which established the Civil Service Commission. Although Arthur was passed over for nomination in 1884, historians credit him with restoring a measure of dignity to the presidency.

This thirty-five-acre park features a replica of the simple clapboard house where Arthur lived as a child. The building was reconstructed using a photograph of the original; it houses interpretive exhibits about Arthur, his family, and Fairfield County. Also on the site is the ca. 1830 brick church, where Arthur's father preached.

LOCATION: Off Route 36, Fairfield. HOURS: By appointment. FEE: None. TELEPHONE: 802–828–3226.

This modest clapboard house replicates the birthplace of Chester A. Arthur, who became the twenty-first president of the United States when James A. Garfield was assassinated in 1881.

EASTERN VERMONT

OPPOSITE: Autumn in South Woodstock.

To the east and west of the Green Mountains that form
Vermont's great backbone, the land falls away to the flat
valleys of Lake Champlain and the Connecticut River. The
river was the most important corridor of settlement and commerce
in the eighteenth century. Like their neighbors on the eastern side
of the river, the towns were founded by people from Connecticut
and Massachusetts. Puritan and relatively sophisticated, they
looked with some horror on the rough-and-tumble settlements on
the western side of the Green Mountains, the domain of the "awful
infidel," Ethan Allen, and his rowdy cohorts. During and after the
Revolution, towns on both sides of the Connecticut considered
joining together to form their own state. The plan was promoted
by the founder of New Hampshire's Dartmouth College, Eleazor
Wheelock. Alarmed that the new republic of Vermont might lose
its eastern flank, the Allen brothers decided to hold the 1777
constitutional convention at an eastern locale, in Windsor. Although the Allens and their Green Mountain Boys were not active
in eastern Vermont, one town, Irasburg, was named after Ira Allen
in recognition of his role in the founding of the state.

In the nineteenth century the Green Mountains yielded a
harvest of stone. Granite was quarried in Bethel, Mount Ascutney,
Derby, and Woodbury; soapstone in Springfield; and slate in Fair
Haven. Northeastern Vermont is still a place apart—known as the
Northeast Kingdom, a name first applied to the region in the
1930s. Isolated and still largely undeveloped, this mountainous,
forested territory is partly owned by paper companies. Many of the
towns are unincorporated.

This chapter begins in the Northeast Kingdom at the Canadian border and descends south to St. Johnsbury, Montpelier, Barre,
and then along the Connecticut River to Brattleboro.

NORTHEASTERN VERMONT

North of the Green Mountains are eighteenth-century settlements
that would develop into lumber towns in the nineteenth century—
Troy, Irasburg, Coventry—tied to the south by railroads. One of
the more isolated of these was **Brownington.** Virtually the entire
village is a historic district. Notable within it is the **Old Stone House
Museum** (802–754–2022), a four-story school built of granite
blocks in the 1830s by the Reverend Alexander Twilight, one of

An 1876 lithograph depicting Brattleboro, along the Connecticut River (detail)

America's first black college graduates. The museum displays tools, furniture, and household items, and is operated by the Orleans County Historical Society.

Above Brownington is Lake Memphremagog—"Beautiful Waters" to the Indians who crossed it in birch canoes. **Newport,** the border city on the western bank, grew into a thriving lumber town, railroad center, and a resort favored by Americans and Canadians. Recalling the town's late-nineteenth-century heyday are the **Goodrich Memorial Library** (802–334–7902), and the old **Federal Office Building** (now a state office complex), both on Main Street. A 1905 railroad car is part of the permanent exhibits of industrial machinery and equipment at the **Old Colony Maple Sugar Factory** on Bluff Road outside of Newport (802–334–6516).

Across the lake, the international border line runs along the maple-shaded streets of **Derby Line** straight through the **Haskell Free Library and Opera House** (Caswell Avenue, 819–876–2471), donated to the communities of Derby Line and Rock Island, Quebec, just after 1900 by patron Martha Stewart Haskell.

Eastward, the border dips into valleys, climbs hills, and levels out on large plains, almost always in view of water—northern

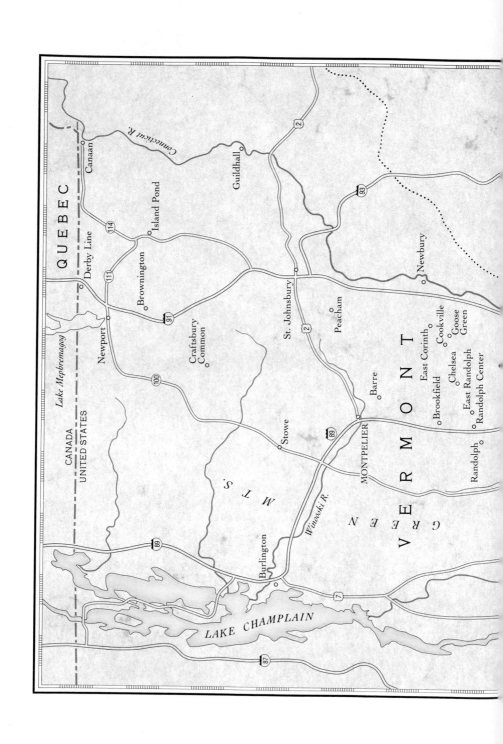

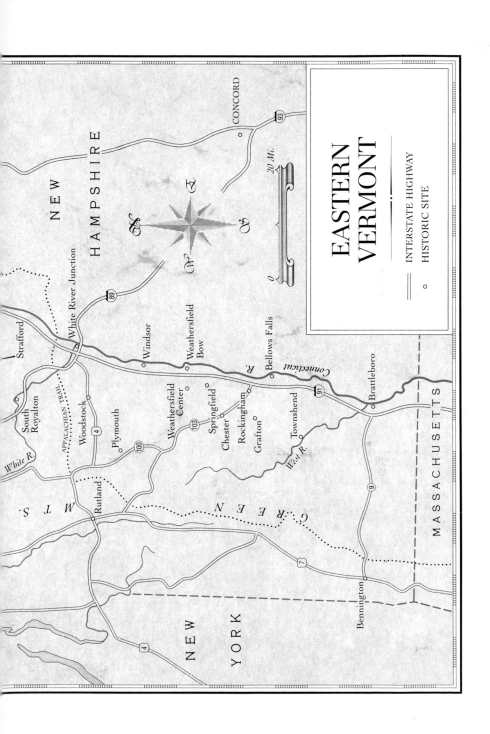

EASTERN
VERMONT

INTERSTATE HIGHWAY
HISTORIC SITE

CONCORD

NEW HAMPSHIRE

20 Mi.

White River Junction

Strafford

South Royalton

APPALACHIAN TRAIL

White R.

Windsor

Weathersfield Bow

Weathersfield Center

Woodstock

Plymouth

Springfield

Chester

Rockingham

Grafton

Bellows Falls

Connecticut R.

West R.

Townshend

Brattleboro

MASSACHUSETTS

M T S.

Rutland

G R E E N

Bennington

NEW YORK

Headmaster Alexander Twilight built the 1836 Old Stone House as a dormitory for Browning-ton Academy after the school's trustees refused to do so; local legend has it that he quarried the granite himself. Twilight was without doubt a remarkable man, serving as the headmaster of the school for twenty-one years and in the Vermont state legislature for two. Middlebury College claims him as the first black college graduate in the United States.

Vermont is rich in streams, ponds, and small lakes. The highest elevations of Vermont's "Northeast Kingdom" look west to the Adirondacks, south to the Green Mountains, and east to the Connecticut River and the White Mountains of New Hampshire. Before the railroads **Canaan** was a stage stop on the river valley route from Franklin, New Hampshire, to Montreal. **Ward Library** (Park Street, 802–266–8676), the 1846 house of abolitionist Fernando C. Jacobs, was known for years as Jacob's [sic] Stand, being the northernmost hideout on the Underground Railroad.

The midpoint between Montreal and Portland, Maine, **Island Pond** became one of Vermont's vital economic links when the Grand Canadian Trunk Railway first came to this forest town in 1853. The 1903 **depot** is made of native timber and granite, as are other commercial buildings within the small historic district.

Guildhall is the oldest community in northeastern Vermont, settled in 1764. Early houses and public buildings, including the

Greek Revival **Essex County Court House** and **Guild Hall,** a portion of which dates from 1795, surround the small green, which leads to the Connecticut River.

CRAFTSBURY COMMON

This classic hilltop village is named after Revolutionary Colonel Ebenezer Crafts, who founded Craftsbury proper in 1788 (Crafts' son Samuel was governor of Vermont from 1828 to 1831). Eighteenth-century gravestones dot the iron-fenced **cemetery** at the west end of the village. The **United Church of Craftsbury, Craftsbury Academy,** and the **Craftsbury Public Library** face the large green common, surrounded by a white wooden fence.

ST. JOHNSBURY

A quiet farming village settled by Rhode Islanders in 1786, St. Johnsbury landed on New England's industrial map in 1823 when two brothers, Thaddeus and Erastus Fairbanks, established a small iron foundry here. Thaddeus was an inventor and won his first patent for a cast-iron plow. The family soon specialized in the manufacture of scales, from the smallest (for measuring doses of medicine) to the largest platform (which could hold railroad cars).

Maple sugaring also enlivened the local economy. Exhibits at the **Maple Grove Maple Museum** (East of town on Route 2, 802–748–5141) illustrate the process and history of indigenous maple sugaring. By 1850 three railroads served the town, including the 1883 **Canadian-Pacific Depot** (Depot Square, 802–748–4401).

On and near Main Street are St. Johnsbury's most important buildings, many of them built by the Fairbanks family. Among them are the **Fairbanks Block,** distinguished by fancy brickwork and **Brantview,** a Queen Anne house at the foot of Main Street designed by Lambert Packard, a Vermont architect, for William P. Fairbanks in 1883. **St. John the Evangelist** and **North Congregational** churches, both Packard creations, contrast sharply with the Neoclassical **South Congregational Church** farther down Main Street at number 11. The **Fairbanks Museum and Planetarium** (Main and Prospect streets, 802–748–2372), founded by industrialist Franklin Fairbanks in 1889, occupies a towered, Romanesque building of red sandstone, also the work of Lambert Packard. The **Caldedonia County Courthouse,** at 27 Main Street, faces a monument to Vermont's Civil War soldiers.

The St. Johnsbury Athenaeum, one of many local benefactions of the Fairbanks family, incorporates a library and a gallery containing a significant collection of American paintings.

St. Johnsbury Athenaeum

The town's library and art museum are housed in another Fairbanks legacy, the Athenaeum. The library, built in 1871, still contains many of the original books. Wooden spiral staircases lead from the main floor to graceful balconies, and the main reading room has retained its original gas chandeliers (now converted to electricity). The gallery, which was added in 1873, houses an excellent collection of Hudson River School paintings as well as copies of old master paintings commissioned by Horace Fairbanks. The centerpiece of the collection is Albert Bierstadt's *Domes of the Yosemite;* the 116-by-180-inch painting takes up the entire back wall of the gallery and is lit from above by a skylight. The building may actually have been designed to accommodate the painting.

LOCATION: 30 Main Street. HOURS: June through August: 9:30–8 Monday and Wednesday, 9:30–5 Tuesday, Thursday, Friday, 9:30–2 Saturday. September through May: 9:30–8 Monday and Wednesday, 9:30–5 Tuesday, Thursday–Saturday. FEE: None. TELEPHONE: 802–748–8291.

Below St. Johnsbury is the town of **Peacham.** With its apple orchards and stately white houses, it is among the most picturesque towns in a state famous for them. The white clapboard **Congregational Church** was built in 1806.

MONTPELIER

The name of Vermont's capital was apparently the whim of Francophile Jacob Davis, a veteran of the Revolutionary War who led a band of settlers to this Green Mountain gap in 1788. Davis and his fellow pioneers cleared land along the Onion River, cutting paths that became State and Court streets. Seat of Vermont's government since 1805, the city is dominated by the capitol's gleaming gold dome.

Vermont State House and State Complex

The present statehouse was designed by Thomas Silloway and built in 1857 to replace the capitol designed by Ammi B. Young in 1833. Young's capitol was destroyed by fire; however, Silloway incorporated the Doric portico, which is derived from the ancient Greek temple of Theseus. The exterior is of Vermont granite. Interior details are rich, particularly the molded plaster ceilings in the Governor's Office, Representatives' Hall, and Senate Chamber, and the black marble on the lobby floor, quarried from Isle la Motte. Fine granite from Millstone Hill in nearby Barre also was used in the state house.

LOCATION: 115 State Street. HOURS: 8–4 Monday–Friday. FEE: None. TELEPHONE: 802–828–2228.

The capitol is the centerpiece of a complex that includes the **Supreme Court Building** and the **Pavilion Building** (109 State Street), now a state office building. The Pavilion is a 1970 copy of its 1876 predecessor, which, as a hotel, was the center of the city's social and political life. The first floor of the building is given over to the Vermont Historical Society's **Vermont Museum** (802–828–2291), in which permanent and rotating exhibits illustrate Vermont's way of life from prehistory to the present day. Montpelier's

OVERLEAF: *The Vermont State House was built in 1857, incorporating the portico of an 1833 capitol that had burned down. Atop the golden dome is a statue of Ceres, the Roman goddess of agriculture.*

residential and commercial districts contain many attractive Victorian buildings, including **city hall,** the Gothic, all-granite **Christ's Church, Washington County Court House,** and the **Blanchard and Walton commercial blocks.**

BARRE

Since the early 1800s more than 100 quarrying companies have harvested Barre's granite and marble deposits. The business was local for many years, but in 1875, when the Central Vermont Railroad connected the town to southern markets, Barre's economy boomed—and the population more than tripled in the following decade. Scotsmen, Scandinavians, and Italians arrived, already skilled in stonecutting. Barre became as rambunctious as a logging town, with no shortage of pubs and saloons to serve the male working population.

In construction and detail, buildings in downtown Barre reflect extravagant use of the native stone, to particularly graceful effect in the 1899 **Barre City Hall,** which contains the local opera house, and the 1924 **Soldier and Sailors Memorial** in City Park. The 1899 **Robert Burns monument,** in front of the Spaulding School, is also carved from local granite. The abbeylike **Episcopal Church** and **Aldrich Public Library** (housing the **Barre Museum**) are on the park. The museum (6 Washington Street, 802–476–7550) has permanent exhibits on the history of the town and the granite industry, as well as rotating exhibits on various subjects. Barre's **Rock of Ages Company** (Main Street in Graniteville, just outside Barre, 802–476–3115) still harvests a twenty-acre quarry, and its massive operations are open to the public. Many of Barre's stoneworkers are buried in **Hope Cemetery** (Upper Merchant Street), their headstones and monuments a testament to the skills of the local craftsmen.

NEWBURY

On the **town common** stands the **Jacob Bayley Monument,** honoring one of the men who founded the town in the 1760s and who played a significant role in the development of this region of the state. A vocal Patriot, Bayley was nearly arrested by the British while plowing his fields, but a friend warned him of the approaching patrol and he escaped. Across the common from the monument are the **Methodist Church** and a marker for the Newbury

Seminary, which operated from 1834 to 1868. It was the first Methodist theological school in the country. The town's **Congregational Church,** with its white siding, tall spire, and portico, was built in 1856, replacing an earlier one that had burned. The congregation, organized in 1764, was the second in Vermont. A half-mile north of the church is **Oxbow Cemetery,** with many markers dating to the 1700s.

To the west, where the terrain turns mountainous and streams run a little faster, is **Brookfield,** a former milltown (the power came from nearby Sunset Lake) with a manufacturing specialty—pitchforks, in this case. Brookfield's library was established in 1791. What may look like the earliest houses in the village were actually built as taverns. Sunset Lake boasts an unusual "pontoon" bridge, a floating platform buoyed by wooden barrels. The **Historical Society of Brookfield** (Ridge Road, Brookfield Center) occupies an 1835 house and displays pitchforks along with other farm tools, boot dryers, and a washing machine patented in 1861—all made in Brookfield—and local furniture and clothing.

RANDOLPH

The railroad came to Randolph in 1848 to take the village's produce and manufactured products to market. The resulting nineteenth-century development of downtown Randolph is apparent in the Italianate **Central Vermont Railway Depot,** the Second Empire **DuBois and Gay commercial block,** other commercial buildings in the Italianate and Queen Anne styles, and the Gothic Revival **United Church of Randolph. Chandler Music Hall** was built in the early 1900s and is still used for the performing arts. The **Randolph Historical Museum,** located on the second floor of the Village Building (Salisbury Street, 802–728–5398), preserves the town's drugstore and soda fountain, in operation from 1893 to 1958, as well as tools, signs, and other items from the area.

STRAFFORD

East of Randolph is the small village of Strafford. The **town hall** was built on the town green in 1799, the year the farming and dairy community was founded in the Ompompamoosuc River valley.

Justin Morrill Homestead

This two-story Gothic Revival house was built by Justin Morrill, who served in both the House of Representatives and the Senate. The son of a blacksmith, Morrill was forced to leave school at age 15 and work as a store clerk. He soon had a store of his own and was so successful that he was able to retire at age 38, to lead the life of a country gentleman. He was elected to the House in 1854 and the Senate in 1866, where he sponsored the Land-Grant College Acts of 1862 and 1890.

Morrill began building his house in 1848, the year he retired; it was completed in 1851. The seventeen-room frame house is painted pink to imitate sandstone, and is embellished with elaborate carved details. Family antiques, paintings, murals, and decorative objects are on display.

LOCATION: Strafford Village. HOURS: June through mid-October: 9:30–5:30 Wednesday–Sunday. FEE: Yes. TELEPHONE: 802–828–3226.

SOUTH ROYALTON

South Royalton grew as a freight depot when the Vermont Central came through in 1848. Around Village Park, houses were built in the popular revival styles of the Victorian period—late Greek Revival, Queen Anne, and Italianate. Those styles also are seen in the 1886 **Railroad Station and Baggage House** and the two-story brick **commercial block,** built in 1887. The centerpiece of the park is an ornate bandstand dating from the 1880s; the park also contains a granite arch that stands as a memorial to Hannah Handy, who rescued nine children from British-led Indian raids in 1780.

The Mormon prophet Joseph Smith was born on a farm in the hills east of Royalton in 1805, and spent his first decade there. His family moved across the border into New York in 1816, during a period of evangelistic revivals. As a young man, Smith had the visions that led him to establish the Church of Jesus Christ of Latter-Day Saints. The monolithic **Joseph Smith Monument** (Dairy Hill Road, 802–763–7742) of Barre granite marks the Smith property and a chapel, museum, and visitor center stand on the site of the family farmhouse.

OPPOSITE: *The Justin Morrill Homestead, built in the 1840s by the Vermont congressman and senator who sponsored the Land Grant College Acts, is furnished with many original Morrill family pieces.*

President Calvin Coolidge was born in this modest dwelling on July 4, 1872. After many

PLYMOUTH NOTCH

This village, administered by the state of Vermont, is best known for the **Coolidge Birthplace,** a modest five-room frame house attached to the village's general store. The thirtieth president was born in the downstairs bedroom on July 4, 1872. When he was 4 years old, the family moved to a larger house, now known as the **Coolidge Homestead.** It is here that Coolidge assumed the country's highest office. Colonel John Coolidge administered the presidential oath to his son on August 3, 1923, at 2:47 AM—President Warren G. Harding had died a few hours before.

The Coolidge family had lived in the shadow of the Green Mountains for generations. Coolidge attended Plymouth's school, and stones from that first structure went into the foundation of the present **One-Room Schoolhouse.** Schoolteacher Carrie Brown,

alterations, the Coolidge Birthplace was restored to its 1872 appearance in 1968.

who greatly influenced the young Calvin, married his widower father in 1891. Coolidge began his political career in Massachusetts, where he became mayor of Northampton after attending Amherst College; in 1919 he was elected governor of that state. In 1920, he and Harding defeated James Cox in the presidential election. Coolidge was home visiting Plymouth when he became president—no other president has been sworn into office at his ancestral home. Plymouth Notch includes the Coolidge compound of houses and barns and its surrounding village, touched only by preservationists and restorers since the late-nineteenth century. Six generations of Coolidges, including the president, his father, mother, and stepmother, are buried in **Plymouth Cemetery**.

LOCATION: Off Route 100A. HOURS: June through mid-October: 9:30–5 Daily. FEE: Yes. TELEPHONE: 802–828–3226.

WOODSTOCK

Settled in 1765, Woodstock is situated between hills on the Ottaquechee River. Almost from the beginning, the town seemed rar-
efied—from Massachusetts and Connecticut came professionals,
scholars, and superior craftsmen. Around the oval **green** were the
shops of hatters, tailors, silversmiths, jewelers, cabinetmakers, and
weavers. Literate Woodstock had bookbinders and publishers and,
by the 1850s, five weekly newspapers. Musical instruments were
made here—flutes, pianos, and violins. Four bells cast by Paul
Revere survive in Woodstock; three of these still ring from local
steeples while the fourth is displayed at the **Congregational
Church** on Elm Street. From 1827 to 1856, Woodstock boasted the
state's premier medical school.

Virtually all structures in the village date to the nineteenth
century, from the houses and public buildings on the green (still
dominated by the octagonal tower of the 1855 **Windsor County
Courthouse**) to the rows of stone business buildings north of it.
The **Woodstock Historical Society** occupies the 1807 **Dana House**
(26 Elm Street, 802–457–1822). Built for merchant Charles Dana
in 1807, the house remained in the family until 1943. It displays
furniture, silverware, and china dating from the periods of the
Dana family's occupancy. Nearby is the ca. 1806 **First Congregational Church** (Elm Street at Pleasant).

Vermont congressman, linguist, lawyer, conservationist, ar-
chaeologist, and diplomat, George P. Marsh grew up in Woodstock, in an 1807 brick and frame Federal house (54 Elm Street,
private). When Robert Mills's original design for the Washington
Monument in the national capital was put aside, Marsh recom-
mended the monument be an obelisk and, from his diplomatic post
in Rome, sent the engineers accurate measurements of an ancient
example. On the town green is the 1804 **Ottaquechee D.A.R.
House,** which displays toys and railroad memorabilia.

At the edge of the village, the **Billings Farm and Museum**
(Route 12 and River Road, 802–457–3555) is a working farm that
demonstrates nineteenth-century agricultural methods.

WINDSOR

Popularly known as the birthplace of Vermont, Windsor is the
home of the **Old Constitution House** (Route 5, 802–828–3226),
the eighteenth-century tavern where representatives met in 1777

The Windsor-Cornish Covered Bridge, the longest in the United States, connects Vermont and New Hampshire.

to adopt Vermont's first constitution. The convention was a dramatic one, seven days in duration; on July 8, the day of adjournment, the delegates received news of the costly American rearguard action at Hubbardton. The first legislature met in Windsor in March 1778, and remained independent until 1791, when Vermont became the fourteenth state.

The Georgian-style wooden building no longer stands on its original site, having been moved twice to accommodate downtown expansion. The interior is currently (1988) being renovated; a major interpretive exhibit, with mounted displays and period rooms, will be installed. One artifact that will remain is the tavern table on which, according to tradition, the constitution of the Vermont Republic was written.

The manufacture of firearms became an important local industry in the mid-nineteenth century, and this, in turn, led to important developments in standardization and mass production. In 1846 a local firm built an armory and machine shop to produce rifles with interchangeable parts—a new technology at the time. The company's exhibit at the Crystal Palace Industrial Exhibition in London in 1851 led to widespread interest in the system, and soon the Windsor factory was exporting machine tools and finished products to England. The building—a three-story structure made, ironically, of handmade bricks—now houses the **American Precision Museum** (South Main Street, 802–674–5781), which traces the history of manufacturing by displaying various products, such as rifles, typewriters, engines, and even an automobile, together with the tools used to make them.

Alexander Parris designed the classic **St. Paul's Episcopal Church** (State and Court streets, 802–674–2926) on a monumental scale; the two-story brick church, built in 1822, has round-arched windows that conceal the actual interior height, and the gabled roof is topped by a dome-capped, tiered bell tower. The 1798 Federal-style **Old South Congregational Church** (Main Street, 802–674–5087) is attributed to Asher Benjamin. Windsor's Italianate **U.S. Post Office** (Main Street, 802–674–5822), designed by Ammi Burnham Young in 1857, is the oldest active post office–courthouse in the country.

The houses of Windsor encompass a wide range of architectural styles, from the simple Federal-style **Skinner House** (Main Street, private) built in 1820, to the gingerbread-rich **McIndoe House** (Court Street, private), an 1849 Gothic Revival cottage noted for the elaborate decorative elements and details that seem to animate its exterior. The ca. 1785 **Nathaniel Leonard House** (Main Street), a Federal-style wood-frame house with a gabled roof and a Palladian window, was partially destroyed by fire in 1881 and restored in 1919; it is now used as a Masonic lodge.

Merino sheep, prized for their thick white fleece, were introduced into Vermont south of Windsor at **Weathersfield Bow,** named for its location at a crook in the Connecticut River. William Jarvis, U.S. consul to Portugal during the first decade of the nineteenth century, returned to his native Vermont in 1811 with a large flock of the sheep (acquired at distress prices during the Peninsular War). The ensuing wool production added substantially to the state's economy.

West of the river is **Weathersfield Center.** Its Federal-style **meetinghouse** was built in 1821 to replace an earlier one that had

OPPOSITE: *The Federal-style Weathersfield Meetinghouse, built in 1821, was remodeled forty years later to accommodate both church and state. The first floor was used for town meetings and the second by the Congregational Church.*

been destroyed by fire. The two-story building served public and
religious functions—town meetings on the ground floor, Congregational services on the second. In 1985 the building was gutted by
fire but has been meticulously restored. The first pastor of the
church lived nearby in the **Reverend Dan Foster House** (802–263–
5239), which now houses the historical society's museum. It was built
during the Revolution and expanded in 1787, 1825, and 1888.

SPRINGFIELD

The early industrialization of Springfield has been credited to
Isaac Fisher, who came from New Hampshire in 1808 and bought
frontage along the Black River for mills and foundries. Although
no longer water driven, some of the mills still operate on the Black
River, along with more recent machine tool companies.

In the 1750s, Abenaki Indians shared the valley with English
and French settlers; together they harvested the forest, fished, and
worked a generally good soil. Further settlements grew up along
the Springfield section of the **Crown Point Military Road,** blazed
across Vermont in 1759 to connect the Connecticut River to Lake
Champlain.

A photo of the Old Tavern Inn, Grafton, as it looked in 1885, from the collection of the
Grafton Historical Society.

In 1790 those first settlers built **Eureka Schoolhouse** (east of Springfield on Route 11, 802–828–3226), one of Vermont's few surviving eighteenth-century public buildings, and the state's oldest one-room schoolhouse. Adjacent to it is the **Baltimore Covered Bridge,** built over Great Brook in 1870, tying Springfield to the smaller town of Baltimore.

Springfield's second generation built a sawmill on the falls, then gristmills, cotton mills, and a foundry. By the late-nineteenth century a third of the town's population came from Eastern Europe.

CHESTER VILLAGE

This town suffered religious factionalism early in its life, in 1785, with Congregationalists isolating themselves in the north end of town (now known as **Stone Village**), and the Baptists taking over the south. The buildings in the Stone Village area—which consists of a single street—are, indeed, of stone. The work probably was executed by Scottish stonemasons in the early nineteenth century.

Many fine buildings are in the **Chester Village Historic District,** particularly the Italianate **Fullerton House** (now converted to an inn) on the common.

GRAFTON

This virtually unspoiled nineteenth-century village boasts two steepled churches—the 1833 **Brick Meeting House** and the nearby **Baptist Church** (both on Main Street), notable for its Sandwich glass chandeliers. In 1790 the first of six dams was built along Saxtons River; by 1824 the dams furnished power to more than a dozen mills. A large woolen mill was built in 1831 to process the wool yielded by Grafton's 10,000 merino sheep.

From 1825 to 1900 one of the country's largest soapstone quarries brought much prosperity to Grafton, as did the manufacture of carriages, sleighs, butter churns, fine fishing rods, and violins. Logging, dairying, and the production of cheese and maple syrup were also important industries here.

The **Grafton Historical Society Museum** (Main Street, 802–843–2388) displays a fine collection of local artifacts and more than 500 old photographs. The **Old Tavern Inn** (Main Street) was built in 1801. The Grafton cornet band has played on the green every summer Sunday evening since 1867.

BELLOWS FALLS

A variety of Native American groups knew the area of Bellows Falls before its settlement in the 1780s and left stone carvings on the rock walls of the falls of the Connecticut River. When the light is right, the **petroglyphs** are visible downriver from the **Vilas Bridge.**

In order to develop commercially the river had to be made navigable, and in 1792 settlers began construction of a canal. Completed in 1802, the canal was one of the first in the nation. For a half century, barges, rafts, and then steamers made their way to and from the town's mills and other businesses. When the railroad came to Bellows Falls in 1875, the canal became less important for transportation but more important for hydroelectric power. It was enlarged in the 1870s and again in the late 1920s to its current width of 125 feet. The power station built in 1928 is still in use.

The 1831 **Adams Old Stone Grist Mill** (Mill Street, 802–463–3706) preserves its original machinery. The mill was water powered until 1926, when it was electrified; it ceased operations in 1956. The building also houses exhibits on the region's history and locally made churns and creamery equipment.

A small rag-paper mill that went up in 1802 marked the beginning of a major industry—seventy years later, the state's first pulp mills were in operation and Bellows Falls was home of the International Paper Company. A landmark of industrial Bellows Falls is the 1925 crenellated clock tower on the town hall.

The town gained a famous resident in 1867 when local businessman Edward H. Green married financier Henrietta Howland Robinson. Born in New Bedford, Massachusetts, in 1835, "Hetty" inherited the family fortune made in the China trade, and increased her holdings tremendously as a crackerjack operator on Wall Street. (It has been said that she learned about finance as a youngster when she read the business pages aloud to her grandfather.) She had a reputation as a miser—detractors called her "The Witch of Wall Street."

Hetty Green's desk is in the **Rockingham Free Public Library** (65 Westminster Street, 802–463–4270), as well as Indian artifacts, antique dolls and a dollhouse, locally made farm machinery, and other articles relating to local history.

OPPOSITE: *With a certain slant of light, mysterious Indian petroglyphs are visible on the rocky banks of the Connecticut River below the Vilas Bridge in Bellows Falls.*

North of Bellows Falls in the small village of **Rockingham** is a hilltop **meetinghouse** (off Route 103) built in 1787. South and west, on Route 30 in **Townshend,** is the longest wooden highway span within Vermont, the **Scott Covered Bridge,** spanning the West River. The original section was built by Vermont engineer Harrison Chamberlain in 1870 and is 166 feet long. As the bank eroded, the bridge was lengthened; it is now 276 feet long. Between 1894 and 1910, Chamberlain's colleague, James Otis Follett, became known for his arched stone bridges, four of which are near Townshend, off Route 30.

BRATTLEBORO

The land on which modern Brattleboro stands was bought at auction in 1718 at a price of approximately one farthing an acre by a group of Massachusetts notables that included the lieutenant governor, William Dummer, and financier William Brattle. Although the town was later named for him, Brattle never was to see it. In 1724 a blockhouse, called Fort Dummer, was built on the bank of the Connecticut River and became the first permanent British settlement in what is now Vermont.

Various industries have thrived here: cotton weaving, woolen milling, bottling, printing, and the manufacture of paper, organs, and wood products. In 1845 D. Robert Wesselhoeft established a hydropathic center here, treating a variety of illnesses with Brattleboro mineral water. Downtown Brattleboro reflects the range of nineteenth-century architectural styles and the scale of building associated with industrial prosperity.

Among the local historical exhibits in the **Brattleboro Museum and Art Center** housed in the 1915 **Union Railroad Station** (Main and Vernon streets, 802–257–0124), are organs made by Jacob Estey, whose 1855 company became the country's largest manufacturer of pipe organs. Seven of the Estey factory buildings stand on Birge Street. The collections in the **Brooks Memorial Library** (224 Main Street, 802–254–5290) include nineteenth-century Vermont arts and crafts, paintings, and furniture.

Brattleboro cultivated artistic and literary talent. Rudyard Kipling built a house (private) in nearby **Dummerston,** where he lived from 1892 to 1896 and wrote *The Jungle Book* and *Captains Courageous.* Accomplished natives included Richard Morris Hunt, the society architect who designed some of the most opulent mansions

The severe 1781 Rockingham meetinghouse, north of Bellows Falls, is the earliest public building that survives in nearly original condition in Vermont.

of the Gilded Age, and his brother, William Morris Hunt, a noted portrait painter. (The brothers sometimes shared clients, one designing their palatial houses, the other painting their portraits.)

Another Brattleboro-born architect, William Rutherford Mead, joined in partnership with Charles McKim and Stanford White in 1879 to create the famous firm of McKim, Mead & White. Mead's older brother, Larken G. Mead, Jr., was a sculptor who designed the figures on Abraham Lincoln's tomb in Springfield, Illinois, a statue of Ethan Allen for the Vermont state capitol, another statue of Allen for the national Capitol, and the tomb monument for the robber baron Jim Fisk, who is buried in Brattleboro.

PORTSMOUTH
AND
SOUTHEASTERN
NEW
HAMPSHIRE

OPPOSITE: *Of all the houses in Portsmouth in the late eighteenth century, George Washington claimed that Colonel John Langdon's ". . . may be esteemed the first."*

"Air pure and salubrious; the country pleasant, having some high hills; the rivers well stored with fish . . . meadows full of timber-trees"—thus did an explorer glowingly describe the land that would become New Hampshire. The pure air apparently did prove salubrious to the settlers, often said to be pugnacious and the toughest of New England. New Hampshire is known as the Granite State not just for the plentiful bedrock, but for the character of its people, who, early on, survived more than their share of disillusion as they discovered the harsh truth behind the optimistic promises of sea captains and entrepreneurs.

The European settlement of New Hampshire began at the mouth of the Piscataqua River, which had been explored, on separate occasions, by Martin Pring (in 1603), Samuel de Champlain (1605), and Captain John Smith (1614). All found the spot suitable for settlement—Pring noted its "goodly groves and woods and sundry sorts of beasts." The first settlers were not seekers of religious or social freedom, but colonists dispatched from England by merchants to establish a profitable trade in furs and fish. In 1620 Sir Ferdinando Gorges persuaded royal officials to create a Council of New England that would control the territory between the fortieth and forty-eighth parallels. The Council granted patents to many commercial ventures, notably three run by Gorges, by David Thomson, and by Sir John Mason. In 1623 Thomson himself led a small group of about a dozen settlers to Odiorne's Point on the Piscataqua, only to find that he had vastly overestimated the ease of life in New England. A man who visited Odiorne's Point in 1624 wrote a sarcastic letter back to England: "I will not tell you that you may smell the corn fields before you see the land, neither must men think that corn doth grow naturally (or on trees), nor will the deer come when they are called or stand still and look on a man until he shoots him . . . which is no truer than that the fowles will present themselves to you with spits through them." Thomson left after four years for Boston, where he died.

New Hampshire owes its name to another of its early would-be developers, John Mason, who obtained a patent to the land between the Merrimack and the Piscataqua Rivers in 1629. He never laid eyes on it, but named the region after his home county of Hampshire. (The boundaries of his patent more or less define New Hampshire's present eighteen-mile-long coastline.) Mason and Gorges founded the Laconia Company to establish settlements along the Piscataqua and trade with the Indians for furs. When no

An early photograph of Congress Street, Portsmouth, between 1890 and 1895. Once a residential area, the street succumbed to commercial interests after the Civil War.

profits ensued the merchants ordered the settlers to switch to fishing; but the colony still struggled. Just as the colonists were hoping for a fresh infusion of cash, Mason died, and the Laconia Company was subsequently dissolved. Some of the Piscataqua settlers dispersed to Maine and Massachusetts, but a group at Strawbery Banke, the future Portsmouth, hung on and thrived.

The Piscataqua settlers built squared-log cabins, simple meeting houses that doubled as town hall and church, and mills to saw wood and grind grain. The lumbermen among them harvested the forests and sold valuable white pine timber to carpenters and shipbuilders in the coastal towns. Shippers exported the timber, and fur pelts, in an increasingly profitable trade with Britain and the West Indies.

Until 1675 there were only four towns in New Hampshire— Portsmouth, Dover, Exeter, and Hampton. In 1641 Massachusetts Bay Colony asserted its control over them. In 1679 New Hampshire was split off as a separate colony; briefly came under Massachusetts rule again; and was permanently separated in 1692. However, both colonies were ruled by a single governor until 1741.

New Hampshire's growth was slow in the seventeenth and early eighteenth centuries, hindered in large part by the resistance of the Indians to white encroachment. Incited by the French, Abenaki and Pennacook Indians killed many settlers along the Cocheco River in 1689 and at Salmon Falls and Exeter the following year. In the 1690s Portsmouth and Dover were repeatedly raided. This stage of the fighting ended with a treaty in 1713, but the fighting was renewed in "Governor Dummer's War" of the 1720s. Intent upon driving the Indians out once and for all, the provincial government offered high bounties to Indian hunters who could present a scalp. The grim policy worked: by 1730 there were few natives left in the Piscataqua and lower Merrimack regions to contest white settlement.

Around that time an important new group of settlers arrived. Several hundred Scotch-Irish Presbyterians, originally invited to settle in Massachusetts, opted for southern New Hampshire when they found that the Puritans expected them to convert to Congregationalism. They settled along the Merrimack Valley, founded the town of Londonderry, and prospered from the home manufacture of very high-quality linen. In the mid-1700s prosperity was spreading across the colony. Agriculture flourished, and was given an additional boost by the French and Indian War, when New Hampshire farms profited from sales to the British army. Meanwhile, Portsmouth merchants carried on a lucrative business in lumber and, particularly, in selling pine masts.

New Hampshire's highly disputed border with Massachusetts was finalized in 1741, but a further ambiguity remained to the west. Governor Benning Wentworth granted lands on the western side of the Connecticut River—territory, known as the New Hampshire Grants, that is now Vermont. By 1764 Wentworth had granted 131 towns across the river, only to have New York assert its claim to the region and begin granting towns. The confusion of claims and grants was not sorted out until Vermont was admitted as a state in 1783.

No Revolutionary War battles were fought in New Hampshire, but the colony provided two of the Revolution's important military leaders, John Stark and John Sullivan. The latter was one of the commanders in a pre-Revolutionary raid on Fort William and Mary, outside Portsmouth, in which the Americans, without firing a shot, made off with a large amount of supplies. In the war itself Sullivan commanded forces at battles in Pennsylvania and Rhode

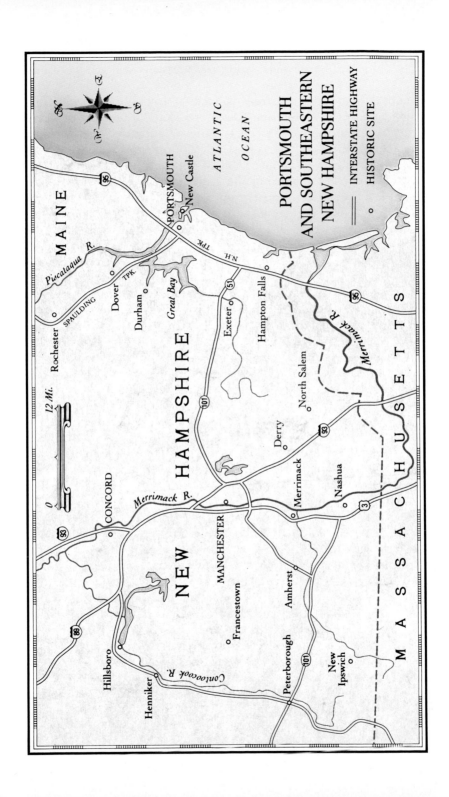

PORTSMOUTH
AND SOUTHEASTERN
NEW HAMPSHIRE

INTERSTATE HIGHWAY
HISTORIC SITE

ATLANTIC

OCEAN

MAINE

Piscataqua R.

PORTSMOUTH
New Castle

N.H. TPK

SPAULDING

Rochester

Dover TPK

Durham

Great Bay

Exeter

Hampton Falls

NEW HAMPSHIRE

North Salem

Merrimack R.

12 Mi.

0

Derry

CONCORD

Merrimack R.

Merrimack

Nashua

MANCHESTER

MASSACHUSETTS

Francestown

Amherst

Hillsboro

Peterborough

Henniker

Contoocook R.

New
Ipswich

Island, and conducted a controversial "search-and-destroy" campaign against the Iroquois in New York. Stark, whom the military historian John Elting described as a combination of "New England cantankerousness with Scots-Irish contentiousness," played a large role in the Battle of Bunker Hill in Boston. In that contest the British succeeded in ousting the Americans from their fortification, but at a terrible cost. Having ordered his men to march to Bunker Hill at a regular pace despite a heavy British bombardment, Stark was urged by one of his officers to quicken the pace. In response, as the officer later recalled, "With a look peculiar to himself, he fixed his eyes on me and observed with great composure—'Dearborn, one fresh man in action is worth ten fatigued.'" Stark is also remembered for a remark to his men before the Battle of Bennington in New York: "There, my boys, are your enemies—We'll beat them before night, or Molly Stark will be a widow."

New Hampshire's role in the ratification of the Constitution was the decisive one. It was the ninth state to vote its approval, providing the two-thirds majority needed for ratification. At the birth of the republic New Hampshire was itself a house divided—the old colonial towns along the coast and just inland were isolated from the settlements on the Merrimack and the Connecticut, and from the northern frontier. In addition, the Portsmouth merchants were distrusted by the farmers of the interior. Sectional tensions and jealousies were such that the state could not decide on the location of its capital until 1806.

One of the country's most important political figures of the nineteenth century, Daniel Webster, was born in New Hampshire in 1782. After attending Phillips Exeter Academy and Dartmouth College, Webster began a law practice first in Boscawen, then in Portsmouth. As counsel to many corporations, he became rich. He represented Massachusetts in the U.S. House and Senate, and served as Secretary of State under presidents Harrison, Tyler, and Fillmore. A lifelong defender of the Union, and a superlative speaker, he became a Northern hero. In his January 1850 debates with Senator Hayne of South Carolina he attacked the states' rights theory with the memorable phrase, "Liberty and Union, now and forever, one and inseparable." However, his willingness to compromise on the slavery issue was not popular in New England.

The state remained largely agricultural in the first half of the 1800s, but by the mid 1800s thousands of farmers were abandoning their rocky fields for richer lands in the West. In the 1860s the state's population actually began to shrink. After the Civil War, industry surged as agriculture declined markedly (in the middle decades of the century the acreage under cultivation fell by 20 percent). Mills produced miles of woolen and cotton goods every day, and shoe factories operated in overdrive. The old colonial towns of Dover and Exeter, as well as newer settlements such as Keene and Nashua, grew into small mill cities.

The behemoth of New Hampshire industry was Manchester, site of the massive Amoskeag Manufacturing Company operations, which produced mainly cotton cloth but also machinery, locomotives, fire engines, and other items. As were Lowell and Lawrence farther down the Merrimack River in Massachusetts, Manchester was completely a company town, owned by Bostonians. Virtually all aspects of life in the town were determined by the company's planners. A strike in 1922, followed by several years of declining profits, led to the closing of the huge Amoskeag mills. New Hampshire's other mills were also closing, faced with competition from the South. Agriculture also continued its decline in the early decades of the twentieth century: by the 1930s only a little over ten percent of the populace was involved in farming. The economic decline began to reverse itself, however, in the 1960s, with a boom in recreation and manufacturing.

New Hampshire's historic heritage is reflected in well-planned towns and the formal designs of their churches, government buildings, and private houses—New Hampshire's early Colonial and Federal architecture ranks with the finest in New England. And its old mill buildings, in such towns as Salmon Falls, Dover, and Newmarket, often made of native brick that ranged from salmon to dark red in color, are landmarks as important to New Hampshire's past as the celebrated frame houses and spired churches.

This chapter covers the southeastern portion of New Hampshire, focussing on the original colonial settlements and on the manufacturing centers along the Merrimack. It begins in Portsmouth, and traces a loop through Nashua and Manchester, detouring briefly to the west, and ending with Concord.

Located at the mouth of the Piscataqua River, on the Atlantic coast, Portsmouth became a

PORTSMOUTH

Located at the mouth of the Piscataqua River, one of the finest natural harbors on the east coast, Portsmouth was preeminent in the economic and political affairs of colonial New Hampshire. The first settlements, funded by English merchants and led by John Mason and Sir Ferdinando Gorges, were established in the 1620s and 1630s. The company's high hopes for making a quick profit from the sale of furs and fish were not realized. Mason wrote, "I have disbursed a great deal of money in the plantation, and never received one penny." After Mason's death in 1635 the company ceased to support its operations on the Piscataqua; some settlers returned to England, some dispersed to other points on the New England coast, but others decided to continue.

In its early years Portsmouth was a refuge for religious dissenters and common criminals from Puritan Massachusetts, whose authorities complained that the settlement attracted "desperately wicked" characters and welcomed "all such lewd persons as fled from us to them." John Winthrop accused one colonial leader of living "very wickedly in whoredom, drunkenness and quarelling."

major shipbuilding center soon after its founding in the 1620s.

Able-bodied workers, regardless of religious beliefs or criminal pasts, were always in demand on the Piscataqua, a busy scene of shipbuilding from the 1630s into the nineteenth century. The profusion of timber in the forests that ran right to the sea enabled shipwrights to produce trading vessels far cheaper than European shipyards. By the early 1700s British shipyards were feeling a marked decline in their business, leading their shipwrights to emigrate to the colonies, including Portsmouth. Timber was also shipped to the British colonies in the West Indies, along with agricultural products. But among the most important of Portsmouth's commodities were masts for the Royal Navy. The nearby forests produced straight, tall pines—3 to 6 feet in diameter and up to 200 feet in height—ideally suited for masts. As these behemoths took five to ten centuries to reach that height and girth, they were not a readily renewable resource and had to be harvested with care. Royal officials scoured the woods, placing the king's mark on mast trees and imposing heavy fines on anyone who felled one without authorization. Profits from the sale of masts, ships, fish, furs, and other goods created a wealthy trading class in Portsmouth.

The seventeenth-century Richard Jackson House.

A tight little aristocracy of loyalists revolved around the royal governor. John Adams referred to "the pomps and vanities and ceremonies of that little world, Portsmouth." But the middle class of tradesmen and artisans, as well as the laboring class were firmly in support of independence. Although the Revolution destroyed Portsmouth's trade with England and the West Indies, business subsequently revived, and the town enjoyed several decades of prosperity. Portsmouth declined as fortunes were being made from manufacturing along the rivers of the interior.

Despite an 1813 fire that destroyed many of the oldest buildings, Portsmouth preserves handsome vestiges of its eighteenth- and early-nineteenth-century heyday.

Richard Jackson House

The state's oldest residence surviving in its original form, the Richard Jackson House is a weathered saltbox named for the shipwright who built it ca. 1664. His descendants lived here for nearly three centuries, adding a lean-to on one side and a wrap-around addition on the other. The central, oldest portion of the house is immediately recognizable by its seventeenth-century windows, which have been reconstructed and fitted with leaded glass.

The old-style windows are much smaller than those in the additions. The house, a study property of the Society for the Preservation of New England Antiquities, is not furnished.

LOCATION: Northwest Street. HOURS: By appointment. FEE: Yes. TELEPHONE: 617–227–3956.

Wentworth-Coolidge Mansion

This house was the seaside home of the first royal governor, Benning Wentworth (his term was from 1741 to 1766), who wrote "The place of my residence is within a mile of . . . the harbor . . . and no vessel can come into port without coming into my sight, which . . . has contributed in great measure to the chastity of the port." The governor's brother, Mark, carried on a brisk business in masts, selling them to all comers "at his own price." One large parlor was used as the council chamber for the provincial government. The fireplace in that room is flanked by a sculptured pair of comely women with half-bare breasts. Some original Wentworth pieces are in the house: a punch bowl (invitations to the house always mentioned a toast to the king's health), some Chinese export porcelain, and a late-eighteenth-century spinet. The wallpaper in the parlor and a bed chamber is original, a 1740s pattern put up in the 1750s;

The Wentworth-Coolidge Mansion, home of New Hampshire's first royal governor, Benning Wentworth, in the 1750s. It is one of the few colonial governors' residences to survive unchanged.

the old colors, gold and crimson, of the costly flocked damask paper have faded. The lilacs on the grounds were the first in the country—brought by the governor from England.

In 1885 the house was purchased by J. Templeman Coolidge (no relation to the president), whose father-in-law, the eminent historian Francis Parkman, came to the house in the summer to write. One room has been furnished to the period of the 1880s. The exterior colors—dark mustard and dark green—were chosen in the nineteenth century.

LOCATION: Little Harbor Road. HOURS: Memorial Day through mid-June: 10–5 Saturday–Sunday; mid-June through August: 10–5 Daily. FEE: Yes. TELEPHONE: 603–436–6607.

MacPheadris-Warner House

Portsmouth's oldest brick residence, this three-story, fourteen-room house was built ca. 1716 by John Drew for Captain Archibald MacPheadris, who married into the Wentworth family. The bulk of the house—the red brick walls are eighteen inches thick—is lightened by the doorway and windows, perfectly ordered in the Georgian style. The roof has been remodeled; it was once two parallel gables, in an M shape.

The house's remarkable feature is the painted murals in its stair hall. Dating to about 1720, they may be the oldest such paintings in the country still in their original setting. The subject matter of the murals is puzzling in its variety: They depict a British soldier on horseback; two Mohawk Indians (these portraits were apparently not made from life but were copied from engravings made in England when four Mohawks visited the queen); the biblical episode of Abraham's intended sacrifice of his son Isaac, interrupted by the appearance of an angel; and an allegorical scene of hawks attacking a chicken. The murals, covered with wallpaper, were discovered in 1852 and restored several times, most recently in 1988. A ceiling mural may be hidden under a coat of paint.

The house preserves some original family furnishings, such as a set of six chairs made about 1810, books from the 1740s, a coverlet of the 1760s, and a silk dress given to Sarah Warner by the wife of John Wentworth, the royal governor.

LOCATION: 150 Daniel Street. HOURS: June through mid-October: 10–4:30 Tuesday–Saturday. FEE: Yes. TELEPHONE: 603–436–5909.

Moffatt-Ladd House

This three-story Georgian residence, topped by a captain's walk, was built in 1763 by John Moffatt and occupied by the same family until 1913. Because two inventories were made of the objects in the house, in 1768 and 1786, this is one of the best-documented Colonial residences in the state. It is furnished with eighteenth- and early-nineteenth-century items, many of them original to the house, such as silver, jewelry, clothing (including wedding dresses), family portraits (one by Gilbert Stuart), and eight samplers. A set of Chinese Chippendale chairs, bench, and settee on display was purchased by the Moffatts at an auction of the belongings of Governor John Wentworth. The carving on the staircase is especially fine. The garden at the rear of the house retains its nineteenth-century arrangement, with arbors and beehives. Also on the grounds are a coach house and counting house (the family was in the shipping business), displaying shipping artifacts, a telescope, and an early wall safe.

LOCATION: 154 Market Street. HOURS: Mid-June through mid-October: 10–4 Monday–Saturday, 2–5 Sunday. FEE: Yes. TELEPHONE: 603–436–8221.

The 1763 Moffatt-Ladd House contains an elegant carved staircase and many original furnishings.

Governor John Langdon House

John Langdon was one of the most prominent New Hampshire men of his day. He served as president of the state, as its governor, and as a U.S. senator. He made his fortune during the Revolution in shipbuilding and privateering, thanks in part to his position as the government's agent for procuring new ships and for distributing the goods captured by privateers. It is often noted that he financed several military campaigns out of his own pocket—but he was always careful about getting repaid. In 1783 work began on this grand residence.

The house was admired by George Washington, an astute judge of architecture and the status it implied, who was a guest here in 1789. In his diary he wrote that among Portsmouth's houses, "Col. Langdon's may be esteemed the first." Langdon's house clearly was a statesman's, from the monumental exterior enhanced by gardens to the exquisitely carved interior woodwork. The drawing room fireplace is a particularly fine example of late-eighteenth-century woodworking. Langdon descendants have furnished the house with antiques of the period; it is now a property of the Society for the Preservation of New England Antiquities.

LOCATION: Off Route 95. HOURS: June through mid-October: 12–5 Wednesday–Sunday. FEE: Yes. TELEPHONE: 617–227–3956.

John Paul Jones House

While his ship *America* was being readied in October and November 1782, John Paul Jones stayed in the commodious house of Sarah Purcell, who was operating it as an inn after the death of her husband. The master carpenter who built it in 1758 may have been the mulatto Hopestill March, renowned in the Portsmouth area for his fine gambrel-roofed houses. The house and its exhibits are the property of the Portsmouth Historical Society.

LOCATION: 43 Middle Street. HOURS: July through August: 10–4:15 Monday–Saturday, 1–4:15 Sunday. FEE: Yes. TELEPHONE: 603–436–8420.

OPPOSITE: *Exquisitely carved interior woodwork graces the Governor John Langdon House, built in 1784 by the wealthy Portsmouth merchant and statesman.*

Rundlet-May House

A farm boy named James Rundlet moved from Exeter to Portsmouth in the 1790s and amassed a comfortable fortune as a merchant. To proclaim his success in this town of aristocratic airs, he built an elegant three-story house with extensive gardens on an artificial terrace eight feet above the level of Middle Street. Located in a then-unfashionable, indeed, almost empty, part of town, the house stirred envy and disdain in the hearts of some townspeople, who predicted that the Rundlets would fall as fast as they had risen. But the house remained in the family for four generations until it was given to the Society for the Preservation of New England Antiquities. Rundlet's careful accounts show that he imported wallpaper from England but preferred locally made furniture, resulting in the house's fine collection of Portsmouth's Federal furniture.

LOCATION: 364 Middle Street. HOURS: June through mid-October: 12–5 Wednesday–Sunday. FEE: Yes. TELEPHONE: 617–227–3956.

The **Wentworth-Gardner House** (140 Mechanic Street, 603–436–4406) is another of Portsmouth's fine Georgian residences, built by Elizabeth Wentworth as a wedding present for her son, Thomas. It has eleven fireplaces and is celebrated for its hand-painted wallpapers and graceful carvings—woodworkers are said to have labored on cornices and pilasters the entire year of 1760. The pineapple within the entrance pediment is a symbol of welcome.

Portsmouth's 1804 **Athenaeum** (9 Market Square, 603–431–2538), housed in a fine Federal building, contains collections of books, early manuscripts, and other historical documents; portraits of important local figures (two painted by Samuel F. B. Morse); Indian artifacts; ships' models; and curiosities from around the world brought home by seamen.

The **Portsmouth Public Library** (8 Islington Street, 603–431–2007) was built as a private boys' school, the Portsmouth Academy, in 1809. Once thought to be the work of Charles Bulfinch, the building was designed by James Nutter, who also did the interior of St. John's Church. The brick structure has housed the library since the 1890s.

The brick **St. John's Church** (101 Chapel Street), built in 1807, stands on the site of its 1732 predecessor, Queen's Chapel. Portsmouth's first church, also Anglican, was built a century earlier at the southwest corner of Court and Pleasant streets. After the Revolution, Queen's Chapel was rechristened St. John's; it was de-

The 1804 Portsmouth Athenaeum contains a variety of curiosities brought home by seafaring adventurers and traders.

stroyed by fire on Christmas Eve 1806. Surviving the blaze are the altar, now known as the Credence Table, in the chancel; the baptismal font; and the box pews in the south gallery. The church's Brattle organ, imported to Massachusetts from England before 1708, is the oldest operating pipe organ in the United States. Plaques on some pews commemorate former parishioners such as Daniel Webster. On display is a rare 1717 Vinegar Bible, so named for a misprint of "vineyard." Royal Governor Benning Wentworth is buried in the churchyard.

The 1826 **South Church** (292 State Street) was designed and constructed by Jonathan Folsom, a local contractor, church builder, and stonemason. Built in massive proportions with two-foot-thick granite walls and in Greek Revival style, this building is one of the first in New England to utilize a truss roof and hung ceiling.

Strawbery Banke

Settled in 1630, this ten-acre site was established as a plantation compound by the English. Originally named for the abundance of wild berries growing along the shores of the Piscataqua River, the settlement was renamed Portsmouth in 1653 and became a thriving waterfront neighborhood during the seventeenth and eighteenth

centuries. Rescued from many years of neglect, the area is now an outdoor history museum, with ongoing archaeological excavations. Collections include ceramics and other decorative objects, household furnishings and implements, artifacts from the settlement's earliest period, and books and other scholarly materials relating to the history of the compound. Functioning crafts shops include a cooper at the **Dinsmore Shop,** a weaver at **Shapley-Cotton House,** potters at **Cotton Tenant House,** a cabinetmaker at **Peacock House,** and boat builders at the **Boat Shop.** An exhibition on early tools and craftmanship is in the **Lowd House.** Seventeenth-century construction techniques are on view in **Sherburne House.**

There are forty-two historic houses from the 1600s to the 1900s, most of which stand on their original foundations. Seven are furnished to illustrate different time periods in Strawbery Banke's history: the 1850s **Goodwin Mansion,** home of Governor Ichabod Goodwin; **Chase House** (1790–1830); **Wheelwright House** (1780s); **Walsh House** (spanning 1790–1830); **Pitt Tavern** (ca. 1800); the **Thomas Bailey Aldrich House,** a 1908 restoration of a mid-nineteenth-century home; and the **Drisco House,** in which domestic life in the 1790s is contrasted with that of the 1950s. Gardens include the vegetable and herb beds of the 1695 **Sherburne House**. The elaborate **Victorian Garden** of the Goodwin Mansion, the special domain of Mrs. Sarah Parker Rice Goodwin, is planted today according to her detailed 1862 diaries and sketches.

LOCATION: Marcy Street. HOURS: May through October: 10–5 Daily. FEE: Yes. TELEPHONE: 603–433–1100.

The most historically significant commercial buildings in Portsmouth are the wood-frame and brick warehouses along the waterfront. While outfitting the *Ranger,* John Paul Jones used the **Sheafe Warehouse** (Mechanic Street at Prescott Park). The warehouse, framed and shingled about 1705, is now a museum of folk art, featuring wooden sculptures of wildlife and boats and a replica of a gundalow, a flat-bottomed boat used to transport cargo on the river during the nineteenth century.

NEW CASTLE

New Castle, off the coast on Great Island, was first settled in 1623 and received its royal charter in 1693. An early provincial capital, the town was scattered with simple fishermen's cottages as well as

OPPOSITE: *Strawbery Banke, a ten-acre outdoor history museum commemorating Portsmouth's long history, re-creates the appearance of a colonial settlement.*

the elegant houses of the Frost, Pepperrell, and Jaffrey families. English loyalists realized the island's strategic importance early on and built a redoubt on a rocky point there in 1632. A timber blockhouse was added in 1666; in 1692, cannon and military stores were brought in from England and a breastwork erected to protect them. The fort was named Fort William and Mary in 1694, in honor of the king and queen, and was the scene of one of the first overt acts leading to the Revolution: On December 13, 1774, Paul Revere brought the message from Boston that the British were on their way with reinforcements; the following day, the Portsmouth colonials (led by Major John Langdon) raided the fort and removed approximately five tons of gunpowder from the magazines. The next day, Major John Sullivan led them in a second raid. Some of the guns and powder taken from the fort were sent on to Patriots at Bunker Hill. New Hampshire gave the facility to the United States government in 1791; the fort was renamed **Fort Constitution** five years later. The site consists of the ruins of the seventeenth-century walls and later constructions.

A very different attraction in New Castle is **Wentworth-by-the-Sea** (Wentworth Road, private), a resort hotel built at the height of the Victorian era. Since 1874, its verandas and mansard towers have looked out to the **Isles of Shoals.** Four of the nine isles belong to New Hampshire, five to Maine. Dotted with weathered cottages, stone churches, fishing shacks, and inns, the rocky little islands were strategically important to colonists, pirates, and fishermen.

Toward the coast from Exeter, **Hampton** and **Hampton Falls** (incorporated separately in 1726) preserve many eighteenth- and nineteenth-century houses along and off Route 1. At the center of Hampton Falls is the **First Congregational Society Unitarian Church**, built in 1843 in the form of a small Greek temple.

EXETER

Exeter lies on the Squamscott River at the southeastern point of an irregular box shape it forms with Dover, Portsmouth, and Hampton. Together the towns share New Hampshire's richest Revolutionary history. Like Dover, Exeter is inland, but only just, and its access to the sea bestows a coastal air. It was founded in 1638 by Reverend John Wheelwright, who was expelled from Boston by the

Fort Constitution, originally named Fort William and Mary, the site of one of the first overt acts leading to the Revolution.

Massachusetts General Court for "contempt and sedition." His "sedition" had been to publicly disagree with the Puritan church on a theological matter. Wheelwright and some followers secured a large tract of land here (thirty miles square) from the Squamscott Indians and established an independent government. In 1643, when the majority of the townspeople decided to seek annexation by Massachusetts, Wheelwright left for Maine.

As the town grew in the eighteenth century, prospering from fishing and lumbering, it retained its independent spirit. Like many coastal towns, Exeter profited from the sale of masts—legally to the Royal Navy and illegally to every other shipbuilder. When royal agents visited Exeter in 1734 to reassert the official monopoly on the colony's masts, the townspeople burned the ship. As the Revolution neared, it was common to see British officials burned in effigy on the Exeter green. In 1775, New Hampshire moved its capital from loyalist Portsmouth to more patriotic Exeter. In 1776 the Provincial Congress adopted the first independent state constitution, making New Hampshire the first of the thirteen colonies. Throughout the Revolution, the state's Legislative Assembly met at the **Exeter Town House,** its site marked at Court and Front streets. The current **Town Hall** (Front Street) dates from 1855.

Gilman Garrison House

For decades after its construction in the 1650s or 1660s, this fortified refuge was a garrison, built by John Gilman near his sawmill.
The door of the house was protected by a portcullis, metal bars that
could be dropped in front of the door to bar entrance. The house
was constructed of massive logs, some of which show the marks of
Gilman's sawmill. One of the first-floor rooms was a fort within a
fort—its ceiling is as thick as its walls—so that if attackers managed
to break into the house the defenders would have a fall-back. Peter
Gilman, grandson of John Gilman, was a brigadier general in the
New Hampshire militia in the expedition against Crown Point in
1745. He made additions to the house in 1725 and again in the
1770s. His remodeling, in a more formal Georgian style, is in sharp
contrast to the old portions of the house. The house, one of the
oldest in New Hampshire, is a property of the Society for the
Preservation of New England Antiquities.

> LOCATION: 12 Water Street. HOURS: June through mid-October:
> 12–5 Tuesday, Thursday, Saturday, Sunday. FEE: Yes. TELEPHONE:
> 617–227–3956.

Cincinnati Hall

Also known as the **Ladd-Gilman House,** the 1721 building is
owned by the New Hampshire chapter of the Society of the Cincinnati, a group composed of descendants of Revolutionary officers.
The house, the state treasury from 1775 to 1782, displays an
important collection of historical papers, including documents
signed by Washington, Lafayette, and John Hancock. Memorabilia
of the Gilman family and of others who served in the Revolution
with them are also exhibited. Colonel Nicholas Gilman, Sr., was the
treasurer and receiver general of the state in 1775. Captain Nicholas Gilman, Jr., held a high post on George Washington's staff and
participated in many major campaigns of the war. The room used
as the treasury during the Revolution is restored.

> LOCATION: 1 Governor's Lane. HOURS: May through October: 12–5
> Tuesday, 12–5 Sunday. FEE: Yes. TELEPHONE: 603–772–2622.

As trade and commerce quickened after the Revolution, **Front
Street** became Exeter's fashionable address. A number of fine
Federal houses survive along that tree-shaded street. Among them

are the 1809 **George Sullivan's House** (4 Front Street), now converted to apartments and offices; the 1826 **Gardner House** (12 Front Street, private); and the 1815 **Perry-Dudley House** (14 Front Street, now offices). The Federal style gives way to the Greek Revival at number 81, the **Otis-Gorham House,** built in 1820 as a residence with office attached. Also on Front Street is Exeter's 1798 **Congregational Church** at number 21 and the 1831 **Granite Bank.** At **65 High Street,** where it was moved from beside the Town Hall, is an exceptionally handsome early-nineteenth-century house (private) designed by Ebenezer Clifford.

An important part of Exeter's post-Revolutionary development was **Phillips Exeter Academy,** founded in 1781 by John Phillips. Having joined his brother in endowing an academy in his hometown of Andover, Massachusetts, Phillips determined to do the same for his adopted Exeter. The college preparatory school's campus, composed of more than 100 buildings, lies on both sides of Front Street. All except one of the academy's buildings date to the late nineteenth or early twentieth century. The academy's ornate English Gothic church was built in 1897.

NORTH SALEM
America's Stonehenge

Once known as Mystery Hill, this thirty-acre archaeological site—dated to about 1000 B.C., it is among the oldest man-made complexes in North America—has confounded scholars and delighted other visitors. The stone slabs, chambers, tunnels, and wells seem to have been arranged as a great outdoor astronomical facility, used to observe stars and chart the seasons. Or it may have been used for other rituals: One slab, weighing nearly five tons and standing on stone legs, is known as the Sacrificial Table, etched with channels that might have conveyed blood into stone receptacles. Many guesses have been made about its builders, obviously strong, clever, and numerous: ancient Greeks or Phoenicians, medieval explorers, North American Indian tribes, aliens from another planet. In the nineteenth century, the stones may have been put to practical purposes—according to local legend, a cobbler who lived nearby used chambers in an elaborate liquor-distilling operation and to shelter runaway slaves.

OVERLEAF: *Most of the buildings at Phillips Exeter Academy date from the late nineteenth and early twentieth centuries.*

DERRY

Scotch-Irish families settled here, east of Beaver Brook, in the early 1700s. They cultivated potatoes, and their linen making was the first of Derry's manufacturing enterprises (later came shoes, woolens, and hats). Derry's **Pinkerton Academy** (Route 93), named for the Scotch-Irish family that founded it in 1814, remains a premier educational institution. The original wood-frame **Old Academy** was the school's sole building until 1887, when officials built a high-towered Romanesque companion next to it. Pinkerton's most famous alumnus is Admiral Alan B. Shepard, Jr. (class of 1940), the first American in space. Pinkerton's best-known teacher, on faculty in the early 1900s, was the poet Robert Frost. Born in California in 1874 to New Englanders, Frost moved back East with his family when he was 10 years old to live at the place, south of Derry, preserved as the **Robert Frost Farm** (off Route 28, 603–432–3091). "Stopping by Woods on a Snowy Evening" is one of the works Frost set in the Derry countryside.

Home to Robert Frost from 1900 to 1911, this farm in Derry allowed the young poet the "time and seclusion" to develop his poetic voice.

MANCHESTER

The history of New Hampshire's largest city is interwoven with the textile industry on the Merrimack River. But long before the falls turned industrial wheels, Manchester was a gathering place for Algonquian Indians, who trapped and fished here. Early in the 1700s, Archibald Stark, the father of Revolutionary War general John Stark, bought land in Londonderry. Here his famous son, a Rogers' Ranger in the French and Indian War, was born in 1728, in the northwest section of Londonderry called Derryfield. A memorial to the hero stands in **Stark Park** on North River Road. Derryfield became Manchester in 1846.

After the Revolution a growing milling industry began to attract thousands of immigrants—French-Canadian, Greek, Polish, Italian, Turkish, and English. The **Amoskeag Manufacturing Company** grew out of a small mill built on Amoskeag Falls in 1805 by New Ipswich's Benjamin Prichard. It attracted investors in Boston and New York, who incorporated a new company in 1831. The red-brick mill buildings, put up between 1838 and 1910, stretch for a mile along the east bank of the Merrimack River in downtown Manchester. The grimness of the long brick walls is relieved somewhat by granite trim and by ornamented stair towers.

In the nineteenth century the Amoskeag company owned nearly all of the land in the city and in 1838 drew up a master plan for development. It built housing for its workers, gave land for churches and cultural centers, and regulated private development. In addition to its weekly output of 4 million yards of cloth, the company produced its own machinery, bricks, locomotives, fire engines, and, during the Civil War, muskets. By the beginning of the twentieth century, Amoskeag claimed to be the largest textile mill in the world, employing 17,000 people. But not even the great Amoskeag company was immune to the various factors that led to the demise of New England textile milling—a drop in demand for cotton with the coming of rayon in the 1920s, labor disputes, and competition from southern mills. In 1936, more than a century after it had opened, the Amoskeag Manufacturing Company filed for bankruptcy. But other manufacturing developed, some of it in heavy machinery, putting people back to work and the mill buildings back in use. Information on tours of the Amoskeag Mills is available at the **Manchester Historic Association** (129 Amherst Street, 603–622–7531).

The city of Manchester straddles the Merrimack River, which provided power for the Amoskeag

Manchester's nineteenth-century prosperity is reflected in several impressive buildings, including its **City Hall,** an 1845 Gothic Revival edifice (Elm and Market streets); the towered, Romanesque **Webster Street Fire Station,** built in 1887 on Webster at Chestnut Street; and the 1874 **Ash Street School,** whose pair of mansard-roofed towers give it a storybook air (Ash at Bridge Street). **Grace Episcopal Church** (106 Lowell Street), designed in 1860 by Richard Upjohn, and the **Alpheus Gay House,** the 1870 villa of one of the city's prominent men (Myrtle and Beech), are also of note.

MERRIMACK

The Merrimack River meets the Souhegan below Manchester, and Merrimack, compared with its northern neighbor, developed modestly as a mill town. It was the hometown of Matthew Thornton, born in 1714, when Merrimack was known as Dunstable. Thornton, Revolutionary soldier and signer of the Declaration of Indepen-

Mills, in the foreground.

dence, presided over the Provincial Congress in 1775. His grave **memorial** is across from the **Thornton homestead** (private) on Daniel Webster Highway in the Thornton's Ferry district.

NASHUA

A fur-trading post turned mill town, Nashua lies on the hilly western bank of the Merrimack. The Nashua River, which runs through the city, drove gristmills as early as 1700 and textile mills in the 1820s. The **Nashua Manufacturing Company,** a Romanesque complex of brick and stone, extends along the aptly named Water and Factory streets. Through the nineteenth century, Nashua developed other manufacturing industries, and the diversity of its international population matched that of Manchester.

Fine Victorian residences, all privately owned, may be seen on Concord Street: the **Shattuck-Tolles House** at number 65 and the **Elijah Shaw House** at number 85, both built in 1890; the 1879

Dana King House at number 47; the **Samuel Dearborn House** at number 6, built in 1886; and the **F. D. Cook House,** built in the Shingle style in 1889. The villa-style, 1856 **George Stark House,** at Concord and Manchester streets, now contains offices. Its wooden construction softens the Italianate styling, usually executed in stone. The white clapboard **Abbot-Spalding House** (5 Abbot Street, 603–883–0015), finished with red brick ends, was built by lawyer Daniel Abbot in 1804; it is owned by the Nashua Historical Society.

Among the city's public buildings are the Romanesque **First Church,** erected in 1893 on Library Hill, and the **John H. Hunt Memorial Building,** built as the Main Street library in 1902. The **First Unitarian-Congregationalist Society** church, with a portico overlooking Concord and Grove streets, may be the work of architect Asher Benjamin, who in 1825 had been commissioned by the Nashua Manufacturing Company to lay out new city streets.

Heading northwest from Nashua, travelers dip into one green valley after another, white church steeples visible from one village to the next in **Hollis, Milford, Wilton,** and **Greenfield.**

Northeast from New Ipswich, Route 101 leads through a long valley that grew in population through the eighteenth century with the increasing stagecoach traffic on the Boston Post Road. In **Amherst,** near the Bedford border, is the **Birthplace of Horace Greeley,** a small one-story frame house (just off Route 101 on Horace Greeley Road, private). Greeley, the legendary newspaperman who founded the New York *Tribune* in 1841, was born here in 1811 and brought up on the Puritan simplicity and discipline he considered the great heritage of his home state. As a newspaperman he was a foe of slavery and an advocate of granting free land in the West to farmers and to new colleges. His name is forever linked with the phrase "Go West, young man, and grow up with the country," which appeared in his July 13, 1865, editorial in the *Tribune*. (Greeley had actually found those words in an 1851 editorial in an Indiana paper—he freely acknowledged his borrowing.) Greeley went on to become a congressman and presidential candidate. He ran against Grant in 1872 on the ticket of the newly formed Liberal Republican Party and garnered 2,800,000 votes, more than 40 percent.

OPPOSITE: *Nashua's 1893 First Church, a substantial example of the Romanesque style.*

NEW IPSWICH

A group of settlers arrived here from Ipswich, Massachusetts, in 1738; by the end of the eighteenth century, the town had a population of about 1,000. Most of them were farmers, but factories turned out potash, linseed oil, glass, and other products. In 1803 a cotton mill, probably the first in the state, was built here; Benjamin Prichard, a carpenter who helped with its construction, later started the great textile factory on Amoskeag Falls in Manchester. In 1810, Peter Wilder brought in another local industry with his chair and stool factory. The 1875 **Columbian Mill** rises above the Souhegan, on a site of two earlier mills; the cotton-processing complex includes a picker house and storage facility.

Barrett House

One of New Ipswich's leading industrialists, Charles Barrett, gave his son this great hilltop estate as a wedding present. The property includes a three-story main house, a summer house, and extensive grounds. It is now administered by the Society for the Preservation of New England Antiquities. The facade of the three-story, Federal-style main house, built in 1800, features four pilasters and a handsome doorway topped by a pediment. Inside are many of the original furnishings given to the young Barretts by the bride's father, including portraits and musical instruments.

LOCATION: Main Street. HOURS: June through mid-October: 12–5 Thursday–Sunday. FEE: Yes. TELEPHONE: 617–227–3956.

FRANCESTOWN

Named for the wife of Governor John Wentworth, last royal governor of New Hampshire, Francestown was incorporated in 1752. The first and only industry to speak of was soapstone quarrying; an enormous deposit of the mineral was discovered by accident in 1794. Francestown soapstone was used in the manufacture of sinks, hearths, mantels, and water pipes. On the common, next to the **Old Meeting House,** is a **memorial** to Levi Woodbury (1789–1851), a Francestown native who served as state legislator, judge, governor, U.S. senator, treasury and naval secretary, and Supreme Court justice. Woodbury's **birthplace** (private), across the street, is in the Federal style, with pilastered doorways and elaborate stencilwork; among the eighteen rooms is a ballroom.

The nineteenth-century Contoocook Mills, Hillsboro.

HILLSBORO

This town, known primarily as the boyhood home of President Franklin Pierce, also has an industrial past. The **Contoocook Mills** (Bridge Street), begun in 1828 on the riverbank near the center of town, operated grist- and sawmills and cotton and wool manufacturing through the nineteenth century. The library and community center occupy the **Governor John B. Smith House** (School and Myrtle streets), a local landmark since its construction in 1892. Architectural details are intricate, from the molded chimney and irregular windows to the wooden carvings inside the house.

The Franklin Pierce Homestead

General Benjamin Pierce, Revolutionary War hero and twice governor of New Hampshire, finished his family's large, two-story Federal house below Hillsboro in 1804, just six weeks after the birth of his son on November 23. The general's son Franklin—the seventh of eight children—would become the fourteenth president of the United States and the only New Hampshire man to occupy the White House.

A Currier and Ives lithograph of the Franklin Pierce Homestead.

After studying law at Bowdoin College in Brunswick, Maine, Franklin returned to New Hampshire to join the ranks of the state's other political leaders—Daniel Webster, Isaac Hill, Levi Woodbury, Horace Greeley, and Salmon P. Chase, many of whom would visit the Hillsboro house. He won his first election at the age of 25, serving in the state legislature when his father was governor. At the outbreak of the Mexican War he enlisted in the state militia as a private, later being appointed colonel, and then general, by President Polk. He met Jefferson Davis at that time and formed a lifelong friendship with the future president of the Confederacy. The politics of the two were compatible—Pierce, in the rough political parlance of the day, was a "doughface," a northern man of southern principles. In 1852 a divided Democratic Party nominated him for president; his campaign biography was written by his

old friend from Bowdoin, Nathaniel Hawthorne. Pierce won, but his was not a popular presidency—one of his critics said that he managed to further divide not only North and South but also industry and agriculture, town and country. In 1854, as president, he signed the Kansas-Nebraska Act, which opened the territories north and west of Missouri to slavery.

The Pierce home, restored to the period of the late 1830s, is typical of Federal houses in this section of New Hampshire, only grander, with a ballroom, French scenic wallpaper depicting the Bay of Naples, and particularly handsome pedimented doorways.

LOCATION: Near the junction of routes 9 and 31 in Hillsboro. HOURS: June, September, October: 10–4 Friday–Saturday, 1–4 Sunday; July through August: 10–4 Saturday, 1–4 Sunday. FEE: Yes. TELEPHONE: 603–478–3165.

HENNIKER

The charming pirate tale of "Ocean-Born" Mary is told in this landlocked village. According to the story, Mary was born at sea to a couple emigrating from Ireland in 1720. Pirates captured their ship, then took kindly to the young parents and their baby girl. The pirate captain promised safe passage if they would name the child after his deceased wife, Mary. He gave the couple a bolt of brocaded silk, asking that the girl wear it on her wedding day. Years later, "Ocean-Born" Mary, who grew up in Londonderry, did indeed have her wedding gown made of the pirate captain's silk. She and her husband, James Wallace, moved to Henniker, where she died at the age of 94. She is buried in the cemetery behind the town hall.

CONCORD

First settled around 1733, Concord was originally named Rumford. The colonies of New Hampshire and Massachusetts had both issued grants to settlers in this place. This confusion of sovereignty wended its way through colonial and English courts until the king decided in 1741 that New Hampshire owned the town. Perhaps to symbolize that the dispute had been settled amicably, the town was renamed Concord.

State House

After the Revolution the state legislature met at various times in eight different towns, delaying designating a permanent capital because any choice would inevitably annoy one region of the state or another. In 1806, at last, Governor Langdon urged the legislature to settle at Concord. State records were transported to the town in 1808, but there was as yet no capitol, something of an embarrassment—in 1814 a committee pointed out to the legislature that New Hampshire was the only state that did not have a capitol building. The lack was soon remedied. The people of Concord donated land and granite, which was transported to a state prison where convicts worked it into blocks; the cut stone was then hauled to the building site in oxcarts. Despite the undoubted reluctance of the forced labor that produced the raw material, the

OPPOSITE: *The New Hampshire legislature still meets in its original chambers in the 1819 State House in Concord.*

foundations were pronounced to be "a specimen of workmanship, not deficient in beauty, and in strength not exceeded by any work of the kind" in the nation.

The original structure, completed in 1819, was a simple and dignified Federal design with a central pavilion flanked by wings and topped with a tower. It was enlarged and remodeled by the Boston architect Gridley J. F. Bryant in the 1860s. He added a third story and the mansard roof, as well as the two-story portico to the front, and replaced the tower with an octagonal, domed cupola, transforming the Federal building into a more stylish expression of the Second Empire mode. A 1910 addition by architects Peabody and Stearns doubled the amount of space in the building; this addition houses the executive chambers and legislative offices. After its early era of wandering the state, the legislature has exhibited a marked reluctance to change its quarters: It has met in the same room since 1819, a record unparalleled in the nation.

LOCATION: Main Street. HOURS: 8–4:30 Monday–Friday. FEE: None. TELEPHONE: 603–271–2154.

The **New Hampshire Historical Society Museum and Library** (30 Park Street, 603–225–3381) occupies a Neoclassical building of white granite, the gift of businessman and philanthropist Edward Tuck. On permanent display are a Concord coach and other examples of local craftsmanship. The museum frequently hosts traveling historical exhibits. One of the most famous artifacts of the Old West—the stagecoach—was a Concord product. Concord Coaches were manufactured by Abbot, Downing & Company at a factory (now demolished) on South Main Street, its spot marked by a plaque. They were a common sight in the American West and were exported to Mexico, South America, South Africa, and Australia. Pulled by four or six horses, a Concord Coach could carry nine passengers inside, with a few more on the roof. Traveling around the clock, a coach could cover about 100 miles in a day.

The state's **Legislative Office Building** (North State Street), built by the federal government in 1889 to house the federal court and the post office, is an impressive and picturesque example of the Romanesque Revival style. One of Concord's oldest (ca. 1735) houses is the **Rev. Timothy Walker House** (276 North Main Street, private); Walker was Concord's first minister. Immediately north of it is the **Joseph B. Walker Cottage** (private), based on a pattern-book design by one of the prominent advocates of the Gothic

Revival, Andrew Jackson Downing.

Mary Baker Eddy, founder of Christian Science, lived for a time on Concord's Pleasant Street. She was born just south of Concord, in **Bow,** in 1821. The **First Church of Christ, Scientist** (North State and School streets) was her 1903 gift to Concord.

Franklin Pierce bought the 1838 **Pierce Manse** (14 Pennacook Street) when he came to Concord to practice law in 1842. He and his family lived there for six years. The two-story clapboard house has been restored to that period and contains many Pierce family furnishings, including Pierce's writing table, his wife's sofa, and a parlor table, all of which the family brought to the White House after Pierce was elected president in 1852. Many of the family's personal effects are also on display, including Pierce's top hat and shaving set and a Bible that belonged to his son, Benny. The house has been moved from its original location on nearby Montgomery Street; it now sits on the site where the town's Reverend Timothy Walker built his first log cabin.

ROCHESTER

From the late 1760s, apple orchards, dairies, and milling villages began to fill the valleys east toward Rochester. The discovery of iron deposits created the neighboring towns of **Gilmanton Ironworks, Loudon, Pittsfield, Barnstead,** and **Strafford.** Rochester was granted in 1623 but not incorporated for another century, in 1722. The town on the Cocheco River grew, with tanneries and factories that produced shoes, wooden boxes, woolen blankets, bricks, and other goods in great demand by a developing nation. Four railroads conveyed Rochester's and Dover's products to market. Rochester's commercial prominence is evident in the **McDuffee Block** (South Main Street), built for retail and office space by businessman John McDuffee in 1868. A mansard roof completes the largely Second Empire design. The **Parson Main Monument** in Central Square honors Reverend Amos Main, who was parson here from 1731 to 1774 and was beloved by both the townspeople and the local Indians.

DOVER

Almost coastal, Dover is on the Cocheco River, which flows into the Piscataqua. The water distance from Dover to the sea is but ten miles. Captain John Smith visited the site in 1614, and it was settled in 1623 by William and Edward Hilton at Dover Point. By 1630 a church was established. In the 1650s and 1660s Quaker missionaries visited the town, to their peril. In 1662 the Puritan authorities had three Quaker women tied to a cart, stripped to the waist, and whipped as the cart was pulled through Dover and Hampton. The women returned the following year; by then a third of the townspeople had become Quakers. Dover's Quaker Society, once one of the largest in northern New England, built two meetinghouses before the current **Society of Friends Meeting House** (141 Central Avenue), which dates from 1768. The parents of the poet John Greenleaf Whittier were married here.

In the eighteenth century Dover's main enterprises were fishing, shipbuilding, and harvesting timber for masts. As the region's inland seaport, Dover handled the commerce of Strafford, Belknap, and Coos counties. Cotton mills, first erected on the river in 1815, were the town's mainstay until the Pacific Mills (formerly the Cocheco Manufacturing Company) closed its doors in 1944. The crenelated tower of the company stands on Washington Street. At their peak, Dover's downtown cotton mills employed thousands of workers and produced some 60 million yards of cotton cloth each year. Woolens—including flannels and worsteds—were the specialty of **Sawyer's Mills** (Route 108 and Spaulding Turnpike), founded in 1824 and held in the Sawyer family until 1899. Most of the nineteenth-century mill buildings have been renovated and converted to offices and small factories. The flatiron **Hosea Sawyer's Block** (Portland and Main streets) was built in 1825, with stores on the ground floor and apartments above. **St. Thomas' Episcopal Church** (Locust and Hale streets) was built of local stone in 1891.

Established by the 1915 bequest of Annie E. Woodman, the **Woodman Institute** (182–190 Central Avenue, 603–742–1038) is devoted to the study of the natural history, art, and history of this region. There are three properties on the site: two substantial brick houses of the early nineteenth century and the relatively ancient **Damme Garrison,** a fortified house constructed of square oak logs in 1675. The institute displays collections of Indian artifacts, minerals, local furniture, and military items.

DURHAM

Linked to the sea by the Piscataqua and Great Bay, Durham drew settlers from England and Boston in the 1630s. The French commanded a series of Indian raids against Durham, from 1675 to the early 1700s, with great loss of life and homes—the Durham raids were among the most punishing of the French and Indian raids against the British. The town persevered, and peacetime brought a spurt of shipbuilding and trading as merchants took advantage of their link to the Atlantic and proximity to Boston. Durham's John Sullivan led one of the early acts of rebellion against the Crown when he commanded a party that seized a load of arms and ammunition from Fort William and Mary in December 1774. Sullivan, who went on to become a general and three-time governor, lived in a house built in 1740 at 23 Newmarket Road (private). Town history exhibits by the local historical association are upstairs in the old **Durham Town Hall** (Main Street and Newmarket Road).

South of Durham, in **Newington**, is the **Old Meeting House** (Nimble Hill Road), the oldest meetinghouse in the state. Built in 1712, it is still used for services by the Congregational church. Further down the road is the **Old Parsonage,** a ca. 1725 saltbox house now operated as a museum by the Newington Historic Society (603–436–7640). The museum displays a variety of seventeenth and eighteenth century furniture.

Newington's ca. 1725 Old Parsonage, now a museum.

WESTERN
AND
NORTHERN NEW
HAMPSHIRE

OPPOSITE: *In December 1776, Washington, New Hampshire, became the second town in the newly formed United States to rename itself in honor of General George Washington.*

In the 1730s, about a century after settlement had begun on New Hampshire's coast, large numbers of other pioneers began to arrive in western New Hampshire. Most of the newcomers were from Massachusetts and Connecticut, where farmland was becoming insufficient to support the burgeoning population. They farmed the fertile Connecticut River Valley, the richest agricultural land in a colony of thin, rocky soils. At Charlestown—founded about 1740 by Massachusetts families under the authority of that colony—the reconstructed Fort at No. 4 provides a good glimpse of the frontier life of the early Connecticut Valley settlers.

The French and Indian War slowed the settlement of the region somewhat. Although there was no major fighting here, the Valley was constantly on the alert for raids—one historian estimates that about fifty people were either killed or kidnapped during the war. Because the French instituted a policy of paying Indians for English captives—who could be held for a profitable ransom—men, women, and children from the valley were kidnapped and carried off through the wilderness, often at great hardship, to French posts.

The conclusion of the French and Indian War in 1765 brought on an explosion of growth in the region. Its budding sophistication was symbolized by the establishment in 1769 of the first college in New Hampshire, Dartmouth College, in Hanover, on the river. Its founder, like many of the new college's neighbors, was from Connecticut.

The western settlers remained linked by the river to their old colonies, to which they had closer ties than to their capital at Portsmouth. In addition, the Connecticut River settlers were Puritan farmers, with an independent outlook, whereas Portsmouth was dominated by an Anglican elite, whose close religious ties to the Church of England were mirrored by equally close commercial ties to English merchants. Tensions between the new settlements and the old colony increased in the two decades before the Revolution. When the Portsmouth government dispatched officials to oversee the rural courts, the outsiders were denounced as "a swarm of pettifoggers." Even common devotion to the cause of independence could not unite the old and new sections. When the revolutionary government at Exeter issued a state constitution in 1776 the westerners howled in protest, demanding that the document be put to a popular vote, which eventually it was. From 1776 to 1782 a portion of the valley regarded itself as entirely independent. In

The great natural beauty of New Hampshire, as depicted in Albert Bierstadt's ca. 1862 Moat Mountain, Intervale, New Hampshire *(detail).*

1781 33 Connecticut Valley towns (along with 17 from the Merrimack Valley) opted to join the newly formed republic of Vermont, and made preparations to resist New Hampshire's claims by force, until the matter was settled by the intervention of Congress.

Northern New Hampshire was sparsely settled at the time of the Revolution. Development was hindered by the harsh terrain and climate of the White Mountains, the northern extremity of the Appalachian chain, consisting of three principal ranges, the Franconia, Carter-Moriah, and the Presidential, which is the tallest. Overlooking Franconia Notch, one of several deep passes through the mountains, is the well-known geological formation, the Old Man of the Mountain.

In the mid and late nineteenth century the great natural beauty of the White Mountains led to the development of popular resorts in such towns as Bethlehem, Fabyan, and Bretton Woods. While some visitors came to New Hampshire to hunt (for black bear, beaver, rabbit, racoon, fox) and to fish in lakes and rivers, others came to write, paint, and sculpt—among the state's seasonal

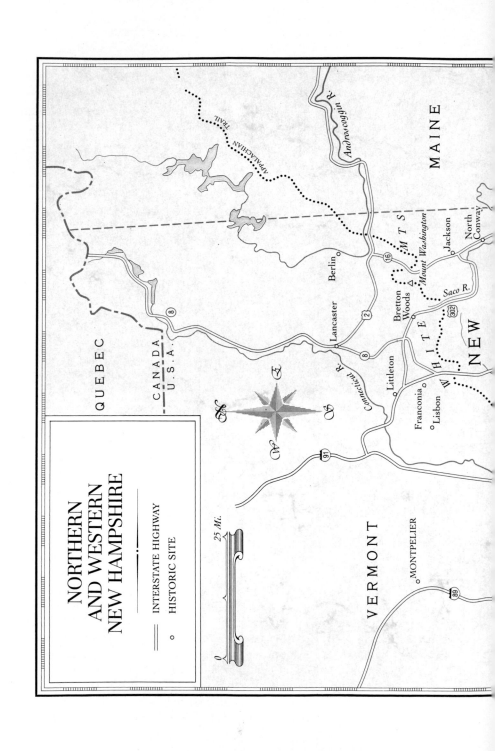

NORTHERN
AND WESTERN
NEW HAMPSHIRE

——— INTERSTATE HIGHWAY
o   HISTORIC SITE

25 Mi.

QUEBEC

CANADA
U. S. A.

VERMONT

MONTPELIER

MAINE

NEW

Androscoggin R.

APPALACHIAN TRAIL

Berlin

Lancaster

Littleton

Franconia

Lisbon

Connecticut R.

Mount Washington

Jackson

North
Conway

Bretton
Woods

Saco R.

WHITE

MTS

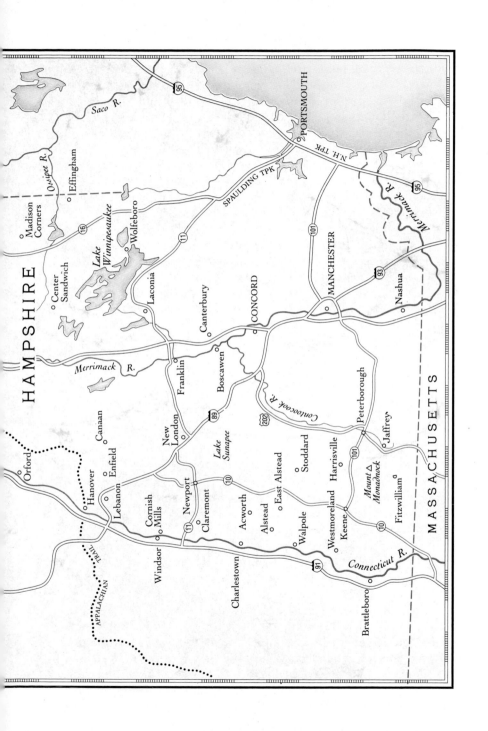

residents were the landscape painters Thomas Cole, Albert Bierstadt, and George Inness—all of whom worked in the North Conway area. The region remains one of the most popular, and rugged, recreational areas in the country. Looping through the
Whites, the Appalachian Trail takes hikers through some of the
most challenging terrain on the trail—freezing winds above the
timberline on Mount Washington, New Hampshire's tallest peak at
over 6,000 feet, have been clocked at 200 miles per hour.

Rich forests of the farthest frontier, the North Country and
Coos County, attracted lumbermen in the early nineteenth century. Small mills gave way to large-scale operations in the second
half of the century. One northern lumber mill processed seven and
a half miles of lumber a day. Since that time, the commercial capital
of the northern lumber region has been Berlin.

This chapter begins in southwestern New Hampshire at
Keene, proceeds up the Connecticut River Valley to the North
Country, and then heads south through the White Mountains to
the area around Canterbury and its Shaker community.

KEENE

Founded in the 1730s, Keene developed into a string of cabins
along Main Street before being abandoned a decade later, in the
face of Indian attacks. The town was resettled in the 1750s. Surviving from the eighteenth century is the **Wyman Tavern** (339 Main
Street, 603–357–3855), site of the 1770 founding meeting of Dartmouth College. Isaac Wyman, who built the tavern in 1762, led a
band of Patriots south to Boston, Massachusetts, in April 1775 after
the battles of Lexington and Concord. The New Hampshire men
participated in the Battle of Bunker Hill.

From a log-cabin settlement, Keene grew into a renowned arts
and crafts center: Pottery was made here beginning in the 1790s
and glass in the early 1800s. The site of **Hampshire Pottery Works**
is marked on Main Street.

Glassmaking began in New Hampshire in the town of Temple,
where a factory was founded in 1780, employing Europeans
schooled in the art of glassmaking. Others followed in **Stoddard,
Suncook, South Lyndeborough,** and the largest of them, in Keene.
The site of the **Keene Glass Factory** is marked on Washington
Street. The Historical Society of Cheshire County's **Colony House
Museum** (104 West Street, 603–357–0889) occupies the 1819

In 1770 Keene's Wyman Tavern was the site of the first meeting of the Dartmouth College trustees.

house of Keene's first mayor, Horatio Colony. Among its displays of native glass and pottery are green and amber Keene Glass bottles and flasks and examples of Hampshire pottery, developed in 1871 and prized by collectors. The home and many possessions of Mayor Colony's grandson, also named Horatio, are on display at the **Horatio Colony House Museum** (199 Main Street, 603–352–0460). The 1806 Federal style building displays Colony's collections of walking sticks, Buddhas, Oriental carpets, paperweights, and cribbage boards.

Textile manufacturing was also part of the local industrial scene—Keene flannels were regarded as particularly fine—as well as shoemaking and woodworking. By the turn of the century, five furniture factories were in operation, and Keene chairs were famous along the Eastern Seaboard. Products were conveyed to major markets on the Boston and Maine Railroad.

The industrial past is responsible for some of the handsomest buildings in Keene—the Second Empire **Colony's Block,** on the town's Central Square; the **Faulkner and Colony Mill** (now converted to stores), on West Street; the **Cheshire Railroad Maintenance Shops and Roundhouse,** on Gilbo Avenue.

Among the earliest industries of nearby **Fitzwilliam** were yarn-making and woodworking; granite quarrying became important in the late nineteenth century. The chief site, on the green, is the 1817 **Fitzwilliam Meeting House.**

JAFFREY

In the valley below Mount Monadnock, Jaffrey attracted many summer visitors in the nineteenth century, including Ralph Waldo Emerson, who wrote the poem "Monadnock" after climbing the mountain in 1845. The sturdy, foursquare **Old Meeting House** in Jaffrey Center was built between 1775 and 1799. Behind the meetinghouse is the 1801 grave of Amos Fortune, a slave who bought his freedom, set up a tannery, and endowed the local church and school. Also buried there are author Willa Cather and Hannah Davis, who patented wooden band boxes; she died in 1863. The **Stone Brothers and Curtis Mill** (Main Street) was built in 1872 as a textile factory; an addition dates to 1897.

East of Keene is **Harrisville,** a nineteenth-century industrial community that survives virtually intact from its milling heyday. It is one of the few towns of this type in the nation that imparts so complete a sense of that time. **The Harris Mill,** built over its source of power, Goose Creek, in 1830, is at the village center. The stone **Cheshire Mills** are recognized by the square-towered central building. A sorting house, storehouse, tenements, and other worker housing complete the factory district; beyond are private residences, churches, and public buildings also incorporated in Harrisville's historic district.

WALPOLE

The town of Walpole was granted as "No. 3" in 1736. It was the site of the first bridge across the Connecticut River, built in 1785. The bridge was replaced in 1840 and again in 1904. There are several fine Greek Revival houses (private) along Main Street, as well as the Walpole Academy building, built in 1830. It now houses the **Walpole Historical Society** (Main Street, 603–756–3602).

STODDARD

Settled in 1769, Stoddard developed into a glass-manufacturing center in the nineteenth century. The first of three glass factories opened in 1842, producing bottles for the popular Saratoga Springs mineral water, medicines and elixirs, and flasks. Stoddard glassmaking figured among New Hampshire's major early industries until 1873, when competitors' cost-efficient technologies forced the factories to close. The town's **Congregational Church** (Route 123), crowned by a crenelated belfry, was built in 1835.

Northeast of Walpole in the village of **Drewsville,** the Gothic Revival **St. Peter's Episcopal Church,** built in 1836, faces the village green.

ALSTEAD

The first paper mills in New Hampshire operated here on the Cold River in the early 1790s. Alstead was established in 1772 as a New Hampshire town but switched allegiance to Vermont a decade later; within a few months it rejoined New Hampshire. Nineteenth-century milling brought a measure of prosperity. North of the river is the **Universalist Church** (Route 123), built in 1844. South of the river, across from Milot Green, the town erected the domed, granite **Shedd-Porter Memorial Library** in 1910.

CHARLESTOWN

In Charlestown itself, Richard Upjohn designed **St. Luke's Episcopal Church,** on Main Street. Constructed in 1863, it is notable for its wooden construction and slate roof.

Fort at No. 4

Granted in 1735 by the Massachusetts Bay Colony as "No. 4," Charlestown was New England's northwesternmost settlement during the long period of the French and Indian wars. In 1744 the settlers built a stockade, enclosing log houses and lean-tos, a watch-tower, barn, smithy, and other buildings. The French and their

Indian allies attacked in 1747, but the fort held. During the Revolution, John Stark used the town as a military base for his 1,500-man expedition to Bennington.

The Fort at No. 4 has been reproduced on a twenty-acre site north of Charlestown. Fortifications and living quarters appear as they originally did; within the museum are furnished houses and exhibits of colonial and Indian artifacts. Costumed staff visit with the public and demonstrate skills of the early eighteenth century.

LOCATION: Route 11. HOURS: June through August: 10–4 Wednesday–Monday; first two weeks of September: 10–4 Saturday–Sunday; mid-September through mid-October: 10–4 Wednesday–Monday. FEE: Yes. TELEPHONE: 603–826–5700.

ACWORTH

Up the Cold River is the 1821 **United Church of Acworth,** one of the most beautiful churches in the state, looking out over the town from a rise on the common. Built by Elias Carter, the church has a superb bell tower with a Palladian window. Renovations made in 1886 harmonize with the original structure.

CLAREMONT

When settlers arrived here from Connecticut in the 1760s, they dammed the Sugar River and built a saw- and gristmill. The town soon had an iron foundry, a shoe factory, and a woolen mill. Sheep raising spread throughout the nearby valleys, and in 1846 the big Sugar River Manufacturing Company merged with another firm to become the **Monadnock Mills** (Water Street). For the next century they produced high-quality textiles, particularly quilts. Paper milling grew in the 1860s, at the same time that machine manufacturing came to Claremont, attracting workers from Poland, Canada, and Russia. Original factories and mill housing still line the riverbanks.

The oldest Episcopal church in New Hampshire is the 1773 **Union Church** (Old Church Road), the work of master carpenter Ichabod Hitchcock. The box pews within the church are original,

OPPOSITE: *The United Church of Acworth, built in 1821 by Elias Carter.*

as are the stables behind it. Also in Claremont is the state's oldest Roman Catholic Church, **St. Mary's** (Old Church Road), built of brick in 1823.

East of Claremont is the former fur-trading post of **Newport,** quickly industrialized due to its proximity to the Sugar River. The **Dexter Richards and Sons Mill** (Sunapee Street), built in 1905 on the river, is among the most handsome of New England's industrial buildings, with patterned brick walls and a campanile-like tower. On South Main and Church streets is the 1822 Federal-style **South Congregational Church.**

Newport was the hometown of Sarah Josepha Buell Hale, author of the verse "Mary Had a Little Lamb." Born in Newport in 1788, Hale, a schoolteacher, edited *Godey's Lady's Book* and became a champion of women's rights.

On the high land across Lake Sunapee and the mountains of the same name is **New London,** home of **Colby-Sawyer College** (Main Street, 603–526–2010). Among its founders was New Hampshire's governor Anthony Colby; his daughter Susan was the school's first principal. Chartered in 1837 as the New London Academy for young women, the academy was actually coeducational when its doors opened in 1838 and remained so until it became a junior college for women in 1928. In 1975, the school's name was changed to Colby-Sawyer College and it began granting baccalaureate degrees. Today the college occupies a number of fine buildings on Main Street. New London's **Historical Society** (Little Sunapee Road, 603–526–6564) has restored several buildings from 1800 to 1830—a house, barn, carriage house, schoolhouse, general store, meetinghouse, and smithy.

Spanning New Hampshire and Vermont near Cornish on the Connecticut River is the **Cornish–Windsor Bridge,** at 460 feet the longest covered bridge in the United States. Just south of the bridge is the **birthplace of Salmon Portland Chase** (private), a two-story frame house on Route 12A. Born into a large family of lawyers in 1808, Chase studied at Dartmouth and in Washington. As a young lawyer, he often defended the rights to freedom of runaway slaves. After practicing in Ohio, Chase went on to become senator and governor of that state and to help found the Republican Party. He was a presidential possibility in 1860. Abraham Lincoln named Chase secretary of the treasury and in 1864 appointed him chief justice of the Supreme Court.

THE SAINT-GAUDENS NATIONAL HISTORIC SITE

When artists took to the hills of Cornish around 1900, they were following the lead of one of the country's foremost sculptors, Augustus Saint-Gaudens. Brought to America from Ireland in 1848 at the age of 6 months by his French father and Irish mother, Saint-Gaudens grew up in New York, attending public schools and working as a cameo cutter. He later studied sculpture at Cooper Union and the National Academy of Design. In 1867 he traveled to France, where he studied at the Ecole des Beaux-Arts. He won commissions in Rome and returned to New York, where others came his way, including a monument to Civil War hero Admiral David Farragut for New York's Madison Square. Critics noted Saint-Gaudens's ability to invest heroic sculpture with individual character. Stanford White, the most celebrated architect of the day, created a pedestal for the Farragut statue, and the two men embarked on an exciting collaboration that helped redefine public sculpture. Other notable Saint-Gaudens works include the Diana

The sculptor Augustus Saint-Gaudens executed many of his major works while living in this house near Cornish.

for the roof of the original Madison Square Garden (the sculpture is now in the Philadelphia Museum of Art) and memorial statues of Mrs. Henry Adams (in Rock Creek Cemetery, Washington, DC) and Robert Louis Stevenson (in Edinburgh, Scotland).

In 1885 Saint-Gaudens rented a former inn (called Huggin's Folly) on the Connecticut River; a few years later, he bought the 1805 Federal-style structure and began renovation, making a studio in the hay barn and landscaping the grounds. He named the property Aspet, after his father's French birthplace, and lived and worked there—summers at first, then year-round—until his death in 1907. Some of his finest reliefs and statues were executed here, including standing and seated portraits of Abraham Lincoln. Saint-Gaudens attracted many colleagues in the arts to his studio, and they too were moved by the countryside. The Saint-Gaudens house, appointed with family possessions, is open to the public, along with the studio, stable, gallery, and gardens. Much of the artist's work is on view.

LOCATION: Off Route 12A, two miles north of the Cornish–Windsor Bridge. HOURS: June through October: 8:30–4:30 Daily. FEE: Yes. TELEPHONE: 603–675–2175.

LEBANON

The prolific architect Ammi Burnham Young was born here in 1798. Thirty years later he designed the town's **First Congregational Church,** overlooking the green. For much of the nineteenth and early twentieth centuries Lebanon was a busy mill town—mills along the Mascoma River processed wool until the 1940s.

LOWER SHAKER VILLAGE

This remarkable village was an active Shaker community from 1793 to 1923. Thirteen Shaker buildings are preserved in the village itself, and there are seven others in the area. At its peak in the 1850s the community had 350 adults and 100 children in residence. In the nineteenth century Shaker communities were a haven for homeless children and adults wandering the countryside. The village supported itself by selling seeds, medicinal herbs, brooms, buckets, tubs, and woolen goods (it kept a herd of 3,000 merino sheep).

OPPOSITE: *The Great Stone Dwelling in the Shaker Village at Enfield, designed in 1837 by Ammi B. Young, is the largest structure ever built by Shakers.*

The most important building in the village is the **Great Stone Dwelling,** designed by Ammi Burnham Young and built between 1837 and 1841. The largest building ever constructed by the Shakers, it was the dwelling for the Church Family, the 150 adults who formed the core of the community.

The **cow barn,** built in 1854, is the only wooden Shaker cattle barn still standing. The upper two floors remain unchanged. The 1820 **West Brethren Shop** and the 1819 **East Brethren Shop** were workshops. Other structures in the village include barns; laundries; dairies; the ministry shop, where the elders lived and worked; and a stone machine shop. The **Sacred Feasting Grounds,** a large field surrounded by trees, is where the Shakers held outdoor ceremonies. A **museum** displays Shaker artifacts, including early sulfur matches (a Shaker invention), furniture made in the village, and seed-sorting boxes. The village offers many demonstrations of weaving, box-making, dying, and basketmaking and maintains large herb and vegetable gardens.

In 1923 the last residents of the village, seven sisters and one brother, moved to the community at Canterbury, which is still active today. The village was sold to a Roman Catholic teaching order. In 1985 the order sold the village to the private group that currently manages it as a museum of Shaker life. Some buildings in the village have been converted to modern shops and inns and are not part of the restoration proper.

LOCATION: Route 4A, Enfield. HOURS: Mid-May through mid-October: 10–5 Monday–Saturday, 12–5 Sunday; mid-October through mid-May: 10–4 Saturday, 12–4 Sunday. FEE: Yes. TELEPHONE: 603–632–5533.

CANAAN

Incorporated in 1761, Canaan was settled by people from Norwich, Connecticut. Although a great fire in the 1820s leveled most of the downtown area, mile-long Canaan Street, bordering the west side of Canaan Street Lake, looks much as it did in the early nineteenth century. The first historic district formed in New Hampshire, this road, once called Broad Street, is lined with handsome Federal and Greek Revival buildings—the 1791 **Old Meeting House,** with its original bell clock; the 1828 Gothic Revival **Old North Church;** and the ca. 1840 **Canaan Historical Museum** (603–523–4202), with exhibits of Shaker artifacts, tools, old scientific and medical equipment, and other items of local history. The museum building was formerly an academy and site of one of the first integrated schools in the country. (Canaan was one of the stops along the underground railroad.) The town was a popular summer resort in the late nineteenth and early twentieth centuries.

DARTMOUTH COLLEGE

The farming village of **Hanover,** granted in 1761, and Dartmouth College, founded eight years later, grew together. Hanover continues to be a college town—education, medical facilities, and research fuel the local economy, and the college enlivens the cultural life of the entire area.

A classroom in Dartmouth College's 1829 Wentworth Hall.

The college was founded when Eleazar Wheelock, a minister who operated Moor's Indian Charity School in Connecticut, decided to move the school to New Hampshire and start a companion institution for English youth. He sent two of his pupils, Samson Occom and Nathaniel Whittaker, to England to raise funds for his educational endeavors. The Earl of Dartmouth made a generous donation for the education of Native American youth, but some of the money was used to found the college for English boys, which Wheelock named after the Earl. Wheelock chose Hanover for the site when the town offered him 3,000 acres, labor, and cash. Governor John Wentworth bestowed a royal charter to officially establish the school. Wheelock called the first meeting of the college trustees at the Wyman Tavern in Keene. Classes commenced in 1770.

Confusion over the precise legal status of the college and the powers of its president and trustees culminated in the famous Dartmouth College case, argued before the Supreme Court in 1818 by Daniel Webster, a Dartmouth graduate. (In his arguments Webster uttered one of his memorable phrases: "It is . . . a small college, and yet there are those who love it.") The case had wide, but temporary, ramifications for the course of American business, because the Court decided that the royal charter was a contract and that the state of New Hampshire could not interfere with its terms. For a brief time American corporations enjoyed total immunity from state regulations in the writing of contracts. The Supreme Court later gave the states certain regulatory powers.

On the campus, **Dartmouth Row** is an array of four impressive buildings: the 1829 **Wentworth Hall; Dartmouth Hall,** a 1904 replica of the 1791 original destroyed by fire; the 1829 **Thornton Hall;** and Ammi Burnham Young's 1839 **Reed Hall.** The architect also designed the college's **Shattuck Observatory.** Dartmouth claims one of the state's finest examples of the Romanesque style, **Rollins Chapel,** built in 1886. It's contemporary, **Wilson Hall,** on Wheelock Street, mirrors the style. A newer building, the 1928 **Baker Memorial Library,** imitates Philadelphia's Independence Hall. While teaching at Dartmouth, the noted Mexican artist Jose Clemente Orozco painted a series of frescoes in the library. Near it, at 30-B Main Street, is one of Hanover's oldest houses, the **Webster Cottage,** built in 1780 and named for Daniel Webster.

LOCATION: Main and Wheelock streets. TELEPHONE: 603–646–1110.

OPPOSITE: *Dartmouth's Webster Hall is named for its famous alumnus, Daniel Webster.*

North of Hanover are fertile meadowlands and farming villages that define the rural New England ideal—**Lyme, North Dorchester, Piermont,** and **Haverhill.** In **Orford,** the **Orford Street Historic District** consists of a tree-lined roadway with houses built between 1773 and 1839. Architectural styles range from Adamesque to Greek Revival. The town architecture took an exuberant Victorian turn in its 1854 **Congregational Church.**

Route 302 passes through **Lisbon,** where charcoal was made for the area's iron industry. The **Old Coal Kiln,** one of many that burned pine scrap from nearby lumber mills, stands on Route 302, about two miles north of the Route 117 junction.

FRANCONIA

The New Hampshire Iron Factory Company began operations here in 1790; its production peaked during the Civil War years. Cast-iron Franconia Stoves were famous, as were locally made farm tools. A **stone iron furnace** stands south of the junction of routes 18-116 and 117. Summer visitors to Franconia included some of the nineteenth century's best-known writers.

The Robert Frost Place

The poet Robert Frost came to Franconia in 1915, at the age of 40, and bought a simple white clapboard farmhouse set on a ridge overlooking the Franconia Valley. He spent five years here, writing poetry and farming the land, then sold the house, returning every summer as a renter. The years he lived here were productive ones: in 1915, Frost had yet to be published in this country; by 1920, he had published three books and won a Pulitzer Prize. The house, built in 1859, is now a cultural center, featuring poetry readings, workshops, a poet-in-residence, and exchange programs. Two rooms are given over to a museum of Frost memorabilia, including his writing desk and signed first editions, and an audio-visual presentation describes the poet's life and work. On the grounds, a trail winds for half a mile through woods and fields; fifteen of Frost's poems are engraved on plaques along the way.

LOCATION: Ridge Road. HOURS: June: 1–5 Saturday–Sunday; July through August: 1–5 Wednesday–Monday; September through mid-October: 1–5 Saturday–Sunday. FEE: Yes. TELEPHONE: 603–823–5510.

OPPOSITE: *The porch of Robert Frost's farm, with its view of the Franconia Valley.*

The Old Man of the Mountain, a series of granite ledges in the White Mountains, juts into the

The **Old Man of the Mountain** (Route 93, Franconia Notch State Park), a famed New England landmark far to the northeast, is a series of five granite ledges that resembles a craggy human face in profile. The "face" measures forty feet from chin to forehead and protrudes from cliffs 1,200 feet above Profile Lake. Nathaniel Hawthorne, who set some stories in the White Mountains, immortalized the Old Man in "The Great Stone Face." Among other well-known visitors to the area was Daniel Webster, who is said to have remarked about this monument: "Men hang out their signs indicative of their respective trades: shoemakers hang out a gigantic shoe; jewelers, a monster watch . . . but up in the mountains of New Hampshire, God Almighty has hung out a sign to show that there He makes men."

landscape at Franconia Notch State Park.

BRETTON WOODS

The town of Bretton Woods lies in a glacial plain at the base of
Mount Washington. The White Mountains cut off the valley from
easy contact with Portsmouth until the 1790s, when a rough and
winding road was cut through Crawford Notch, a cleft in the
mountains. The Notch had been discovered by accident in 1771 by
Timothy Nash while tracking a moose. A year later (with the help
of a block and tackle), he and a companion brought a horse
through the Notch, proving that, with difficulty, it could be tra-
versed. According to local lore a young woman lost her life here in
1778 when her lover abandoned her and left for Portsmouth. She
followed him and froze to death before she could catch up.

Inns operating as early as 1800 received sportsmen, tourists, artists, and writers—Nathaniel Hawthorne came, as did Ralph Waldo Emerson and Henry David Thoreau. In the late nineteenth and early twentieth centuries Bretton Woods took its place with Newport, Bar Harbor, and Saratoga as a fashionable resort. One of the great attractions of the area was the **Mount Washington Cog Railway,** which opened in 1869. It was an audacious task to lay such steeply graded track, but the engineers succeeded—cog-wheeled, steam-powered cars have chugged up and down the mountain for over a century. Railroad magnate Joseph Stickney opened the lavish **Mount Washington Hotel** (Route 302, 603–278–1000) in 1902. It was an immediate sensation. Billed as the largest wooden building in New England, the hotel remains in business. In 1944 it was the site of the Bretton Woods Conference, which established international monetary policies for the post–World War II period, including the use of the U.S. dollar as the basis of international currency exchange.

Started in 1869, the Mount Washington Cog Railway still carries passengers up and down the mountain.

Mount Washington, New Hampshire, *by Alexander Wust, ca. 1869 (detail).*
OVERLEAF: *The Mount Washington Hotel, opened in 1902, still welcomes visitors to its spectacular setting at the foot of the Presidential range.*

LITTLETON

One of New Hampshire's oldest inns, its three-story Doric columns towering above Littleton's Main Street since 1848, is **Thayer's Hotel.** Across the street is the late-nineteenth century **Community House.** The 1894 **Town Building** contains the local opera house as well as the town hall; in addition, it has served as the courthouse, jail, and fire station.

   In the Victorian age, every proper parlor was filled with various games and amusements, including stereoscopes. In the United States, most of these double-picture viewers were manufactured here at the **Kilburn Brothers Factory** (43 Cottage Street). The factory, which operated from 1867 to 1909, is now apartments.

LANCASTER

Settled in the 1760s, Lancaster grew into a manufacturing center in the 1800s, with mills and factories along the Israel River. It also

became an important transportation link in New Hampshire's northern reaches, as a major railroad junction in Coos County. At **89 Bunker Hill Street** (1885) is one of northern New England's rare Eastlake houses, trimmed with ornate brackets, braces, and openwork friezes that carpenters achieved with special saws and lathes. Also of architectural interest are the **Coos County Courthouse** (Main Street), with its mansard tower, and the Gothic Revival **St. Paul's Episcopal Church** (Main Street), built in 1875 of board and batten. In 1835, Lancaster lawyer John Sullivan Wells built a Greek Revival house (140 Main Street, private) of local granite; the result is a striking juxtaposition of classical columns and rough stone. The 1780 **Wilder-Holton House** (226 Main Street, 603–788–3004), the first two-story house in Coos County, may have been a rendezvous point on the underground railroad. Its rooms and collections of pewter, stoneware, and local antiques are on view.

Above Lancaster and **Stark,** known for its **Union Church** and **covered bridge,** both built in the 1850s, Coos County is sparsely populated, much as it was two centuries ago when it was known chiefly to hunters and fishermen, Indian, French, and English. Such towns as **Colebrook, Pittsburg,** and **Clarksville** were part of the frontier claimed by both the United States and Canada in territorial disputes that did not stop with the Revolution. In 1832 these most independent of settlers formed their own Republic of Indian Stream. The state of New Hampshire formally annexed the territory in 1840.

BERLIN

Coos County's anchor city is Berlin, on the edge of the White Mountain forests and straddling the mighty Androscoggin River. It was the last town settled in Coos County. In 1825 two farmers began a logging operation here as winter work. This was the beginning of a logging and milling industry that would make Berlin into "The City that Trees Built." By midcentury Berlin had a small sawmill that was later greatly expanded to become one of the largest in the East. About twenty-five years later came a shift to pulp and paper production. A small pulp mill was started in 1877 and a large mill was built later, but the process was not profitable and had to be abandoned. About 1881 the sawmill company and a competitor both put up newsprint mills, using wood pulp with rags added for strength. Paper towels were also manufactured. With the start of the pulp and paper mills, the demand for labor brought a flood of immigrants—French-Canadians mainly, along with some Scandinavians, Russians, Irish, Germans—and Yankees.

In 1881 the Berlin Mills Company gave land on Main Street for the Stick-style **Congregational Church of Christ.** Russian immigrants built their own Eastern Orthodox church, the **Orthodox Church of the Holy Resurrection,** complete with onion domes (20 Petrograd Street). **St. Anne's Catholic Church,** at 58 Church Street, was built by a French-Canadian congregation.

The **Berlin Public Library** (Main Street, 603–752–5210) has an exhibit of stone implements made by the region's Indians as long as 7,000 years ago. The Indians hollowed out a cave on Mount Jasper to obtain the stone for their tools.

Due south through the White Mountains is the village of **Jackson,** a lonesome wilderness settlement until it emerged in the late nineteenth century as a resort. Below Jackson in **North Conway** is the eclectic Victorian **North Conway Depot** (603–356–5251). Built in 1874 by the Portsmouth Great Falls & Conway Railroad, the twin-towered station saw regular passenger-train service until 1961. Its nineteenth-century layout is intact, with Ticket and Telegraph Office, women's and men's waiting rooms, Baggage Room, and upstairs offices. The station's telegraph and telephone equipment, baggage wagons, benches, and other furnishings are original, as is the brass-and-iron clock, still wound weekly. Out on the tracks are forty-five railroad cars, including Pullman sleepers, and six nineteenth- and twentieth-century locomotives. Equipment on the grounds includes the water spout used to fill steam locomotives, hand-operated gates, and early electric crossing signals. There is a specially designed stand from which fast-moving trains snatched mailbags. Also on the grounds are the century-old **Roundhouse,** a **garage** for locomotive repair, and an 1870s **Freight House.** The Conway Scenic Railroad operates out of the station, taking passengers on an eleven-mile tour of Mount Washington Valley.

North of the village of **Madison Corner** is a survivor of the Ice Age, a large erratic boulder measuring eighty-three by thirty-seven by twenty-three feet and weighing an estimated 7,650 tons. One of the largest known erratic boulders, it was deposited here by a glacier (Route 113).

EFFINGHAM

One of the state's finest early-nineteenth-century houses is here, **Squire Lord's Great House** (Route 153, 603–539–4803), built in 1822 by the successful merchant Isaac Lord. The twenty-room house features a ballroom, hand-carved woodwork, imported wall-papers, and an elliptical stairway that rises to the cupola. It is part of a cluster of historic houses (private) on **Lord's Hill.**

CENTER SANDWICH

The 1869 **Durgin Covered Bridge,** named for the miller who built it, is the fourth to span the banks of the aptly named Swift River—floods washed away the earlier bridges. The 1850 **Elisha Marston House,** typical of this farming country, is a simple Cape Cod structure with subtle Greek Revival decoration. The Sandwich Historical Society, which owns and administers the house, displays rooms of period furniture and rotating exhibits (Maple Street, 603–284–6269). The **Brick Store** (Route 109) served as Sandwich's general store and post office from its construction in 1845 until it closed in 1985; the building now houses a silversmith's shop.

Throughout the lake region are towns that established themselves in the mid-1700s with farming, often only on a subsistence level. Those located near fast water could put in mills and start up industry on a modest scale: within the fertile triangle formed by Conway, Center Sandwich, and Wolfeboro are **Ossipee, Moultonborough,** and **Madison,** handsome survivors of New Hampshire's colonial days. In Moultonborough is **Castle in the Clouds** (Route 171, 603–476–2352), the lavish 6,000-acre estate of millionaire shoe manufacturer Thomas G. Plant. Designed by Plant himself, and built primarily of stone, the buildings reflect an eclectic set of influences: Norman, English, Japanese, Norwegian, and Swiss Chalet. The interiors display Plant's desire for a house that was both luxurious and supremely modern and efficient, featuring conveniences highly uncommon for the time (1913).

WOLFEBORO

Located at the southern end of Lake Winnipesaukee, Wolfeboro benefited from a philanthropist, John Brewster, who in 1886 endowed the **Brewster Free Academy** (52 South Main Street, 603–569–1604) for any student—regardless of age, race, or sex—"of

Located on a hilltop 750 feet above Lake Winnipesaukee, the eclectic Castle in the Clouds was designed by millionaire shoe manufacturer Thomas G. Plant.

good moral character." Brewster also built the **Municipal Building** (South Main Street), a sprawling Romanesque structure noted for its clock and bell tower. In 1768, John Wentworth, New Hampshire's last royal governor, built a lakeside estate here. The Wolfeboro Historical Society maintains the 1778 **Clark House,** the 1826 Pleasant Valley **Schoolhouse,** and a **Fire Museum,** all on South Main Street (603–569–4997).

The natural history of the region is explored in the **Libby Museum** (Route 109 North, 603–569–1035). Specimens of a variety of flora and fauna are on display; other exhibits include Abenaki Indian tools; artifacts from the site of Governor John Wentworth's summer home, which is currently being excavated; nineteenth-century farm and home implements; and a 350-year-old dugout canoe that was raised from nearby Rust Pond. The museum was built in 1912 by Henry Forest Libby, a retired Boston dentist, to house his collection of mounted specimens. The stuccoed frame building features a Greek-style portico, handsome mahogany doors, and a view of Winter Harbor on Lake Winnipesaukee.

LACONIA

Laconia was once part of nearby Gilmanton (chartered in 1727) and Meredith. Mills operated on a canal built in 1800, and railroad lines linked the town to Concord and Boston by 1848. The Laconia Car Shops opened in 1859 for the manufacture of railroad cars; other factories produced nails, hosiery, knitting machinery, and starch. The **Belknap-Sulloway Mill** (Beacon Street East, Mill Plaza), distinguished by the weathervane atop its cupola, went up on the Winnipesaukee in 1823; it now houses a cultural center. Across from it is the larger **Busiel-Seeburg Mill,** a hosiery factory constructed in two stages, in 1853 and 1878. On Court Street is Laconia's **South Baptist Church,** its doorway dwarfed by a central gabled tower. The **Boston and Maine Railroad Station** (Church and Pleasant streets), with its splendid porte-cochere, opened in 1892. The **Gale Memorial Library** (North Main Street, 603–524–4775), built in Romanesque Revival style in 1901, contains a museum.

Daniel Webster, perhaps New Hampshire's best-known public figure, was born in 1780 on a farm outside **Franklin.** The two-room farmhouse known as the **Daniel Webster Birthplace** (off Route 127, 603–934–5057), is a replica of the original, containing books and furniture from the days of Webster's youth.

Daniel Webster was born in this farmhouse near Franklin in 1782, while his father was serving in Washington's army.

CANTERBURY SHAKER VILLAGE

A few years after she arrived in the Hudson River Valley from England to found the Shaker religion in 1774, Mother Ann Lee dispatched two followers to New Hampshire's Canterbury Hills. Here they established a thriving community, one of two still in operation in the United States. In Canterbury, 22 buildings remain of the 100 that graced the original 4,000-acre community, including houses, barns, workshops, mills, and a schoolhouse.

By the early 1800s the Canterbury Shakers numbered about 300, and the community was augmented by converts throughout the nineteenth century. The men and women worked together, farming (herbs and seeds were their specialties) and making textiles and a variety of farm and household implements—all of them for sale. The Shakers were inventors, dedicated to improving the condition and quality of their labor. Self-sufficient to a degree, the group relied on its own tinsmiths, cooks, cabinetmakers, weavers, and broommakers. Many ailments were treated by the community's own nurses, using medicinal herbs, but the Shakers did not forbid the use of outside doctors.

The first building in the Canterbury village was the **Meeting House,** raised in 1792. Like all Shaker architecture, it shows the sect's concern for order and simplicity. Next came the **Dwelling House,** with an impressive row of dormers beneath its chimneys and cupola. The last surviving brick structure is the 1838 **Trustee's Building.**

LOCATION: Route 93, Canterbury. HOURS: May through October: 10–5 Tuesday–Saturday. FEE: Yes. TELEPHONE: 603–783–9511.

A small island in the Merrimack River, in what is now the town of **Boscawen,** was the scene of an early episode of frontier violence. Hannah Dustin was brought here after being kidnapped by Indians from her home in Haverhill, Massachusetts; two others were taken captive with her, and her baby was killed before her eyes. When night fell, the three slew and scalped their captors and escaped down the river in a canoe. The incident is commemorated in a marker on the bypass of routes 3 and 4 in Boscawen; a nearby footbridge leads to the island (now known as Dustin's Island), where a statue of Dustin stands.

SOUTHERN
MAINE

OPPOSITE: *The Portland Head Light, which George Washington ordered constructed in 1790.*

The northeasternmost corner of the United States gave chilly reception to its first transatlantic visitors. The Vikings probably were the first to sail into Maine's waters, about AD 1000. Sixteenth-century explorers scouted the coast, seeking Norumbega, a mythical land of riches much like the El Dorado sought by Hernando Cortes in Mexico at about the same time. Though the explorers never found the Norumbegan paradise and pots of gold, they did discover a more beautiful and—winters excepted—a more hospitable country than they might have expected from the Algonquin name for the place, Land of the Frozen Ground.

No one knows when European fishermen first began making semipermanent camps on the Maine coast to dry their fish, repair their boats, and trade for furs with the Indians. The kings of France and England both granted patents for Maine (the French in 1603 and the English in 1606). The first English settlement in Maine of which there is any record was established in 1607 at the mouth of the Kennebec River. Led by Sir George Popham, these colonists, many of them parolees from English jails, built the first English vessel constructed in America but disbanded after their first winter, the likes of which they had never felt in England.

Exploring the Maine coastline in 1614, Captain John Smith exulted over the natural abundance of "Lobsters . . . Fruits, Birds, Crabs," and "such excellent fish as many as their Net can hold." In 1622 two Englishmen eager to harvest Maine's abundance, John Mason and Sir Ferdinando Gorges, obtained a charter to the sixty-mile strip of coast between the Merrimack and Kennebec rivers and to all of the interior land between them. A 1629 division gave Gorges the land between the Piscataqua and the Kennebec. He planned to create large estates, along feudal lines, but a set of misfortunes, including the wreck of a new ship that was to carry him to America, prevented him from re-creating on this rugged coast a little England of colonial nobles and sturdy peasants. Maine continued as the domain of a tough lot of fishermen and traders.

Massachusetts assumed judicial control over Maine in 1652, and in 1677 Gorges's grandson sold the patent to Massachusetts. (Maine would remain part of Massachusetts until 1820.) The origin of the name of the province is obscure—it may have been so called to distinguish it, the mainland, from the offshore islands. In 1641, the English crown chartered its first city in America at the site of present-day York, Maine. That did not mean, however, that Maine belonged to England alone: The French, allied with Indians,

The Old Fishing Docks, Portland.

fought for their claims, and the Dutch came to fleetingly stake out
some territory of their own.

From the 1670s to the end of "Queen Anne's War" in 1713,
southern Maine was wracked by a series of wars with the Indians,
marked by brutality on both sides. In those decades, the Indians
succeeded in reclaiming much of their old land from the English.
Entire settlements were abandoned, and streams of impoverished
refugees descended on the towns of eastern Massachusetts, where
they subsisted on official and private charity. The settlement at
Wells survived only by transforming itself into a virtual fortress. In

the thirty years of peace after Queen Anne's War, the coast and portions of the interior were rapidly resettled. French territory east of the Penobscot River came into English possession at the end of the French and Indian War in 1759, and the French formally surrendered their interest in the Treaty of Paris, signed in 1763. Except in the far northern borderlands (where the French language still can be heard), Maine became indisputably English.

At the end of the French and Indian War, Maine was still the least developed part of New England, with just fifteen incorporated towns and a population of roughly 20,000, about half that of New Hampshire, and a third of the population of Rhode Island. Fishing and farming settlements dotted the coast between Kittery and the Kennebec River. A primitive road ran parallel to the coast up to the Kennebec. (John Adams, travelling along it in 1771, called the trip "vastly disagreeable.") The interior was settled only to a distance of about twenty miles from the shore, with some deeper settlements along the rivers.

Southern Maine saw no fighting during the Revolution, with the notable exception of the British raid on Falmouth in 1775, in which the town was virtually destroyed. Most of the fighting in the state took place farther north. After the Revolution, Falmouth was rebuilt and renamed Portland. Despite a burgeoning population and some discontent with the policies of the state government in distant Boston, Maine would not become a separate state until 1820. It was admitted to the Union as part of the Missouri Compromise—Maine entered as a free state, Missouri as a slave state. Abolitionist groups formed in Portland and other cities as early as 1830, and Maine sent about 70,000 men to fight for the Union. Hannibal Hamlin, Abraham Lincoln's vice president during the war, was a former Maine governor and U.S. senator.

Industry developed rapidly after the war, when the railroads joined overseas shippers in getting Maine's huge timber harvests to market. The lumber, paper, and pulp industries, granite quarrying, iron and copper mining, and ice harvesting all contributed to the state's economy in the nineteenth century, as did its maritime pursuits—lobstering, cod fishing, sardine canning, and whaling.

This chapter covers the southern corner of Maine, beginning at Kittery and then following a route north along the coast, describing along the way the industrial cities of Berwick; Saco and Biddeford; Portland, Maine's most important urban center; and Brunswick (the site of Bowdoin College).

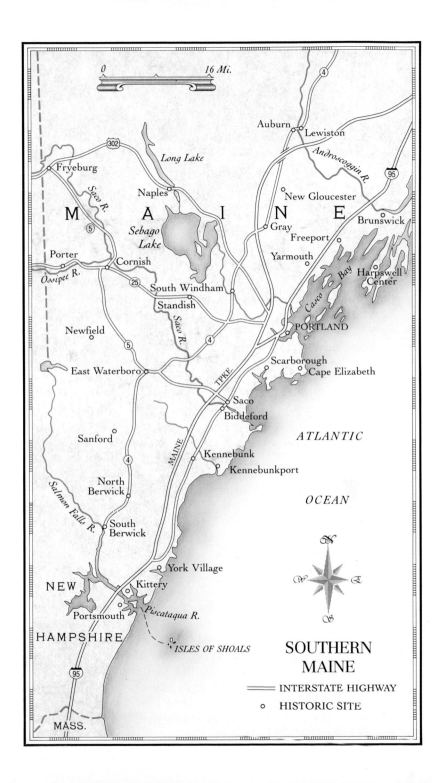

0   16 Mi.

302
Fryeburg

Long Lake

4

Auburn   Lewiston

Androscoggin R.

95

Naples
New Gloucester

M   A   I   N   E

Saco R.

5
Sebago
Lake

Gray
Freeport

Brunswick

Porter

Cornish

Ossipee R.

25
South Windham

Yarmouth

Harpswell
Center

Casco Bay

Standish

Newfield

Saco R.

4

PORTLAND

5
East Waterboro

TPKE.

Scarborough
Cape Elizabeth

ATLANTIC

Sanford

MAINE

Saco
Biddeford

4
Kennebunk
Kennebunkport

OCEAN

Salmon Falls R.

North
Berwick

South
Berwick

York Village

N

NEW
Kittery

W   E

Portsmouth

Piscataqua R.

S

HAMPSHIRE

ISLES OF SHOALS

SOUTHERN
MAINE

95

═══ INTERSTATE HIGHWAY

○   HISTORIC SITE

MASS.

KITTERY

Shortly after Kittery's founding in 1647, the British began building ships in this port city on the Piscataqua River. English warships were constructed here until 1776, when a Continental Navy ship, the *Raleigh,* was launched. In 1777, the *Ranger* sailed out of a Kittery shipyard under the command of John Paul Jones. (A monument to the Revolutionary War hero stands on Route 1, in the center of town.) The *Ranger* proceeded to France to bring news of Burgoyne's surrender, where she received the first official salute given the American flag by a foreign warship. Then, disguised under various flags, the *Ranger* confounded and waylaid British shipping vessels, adding to the war effort at home. She was captured by the British in 1780 and added to their navy.

Kittery remained active in shipbuilding after the Revolutionary War. In 1800 the U.S. Navy established the Portsmouth Naval Shipyard, which today continues to service ships and submarines on a number of Kittery's islands. Submarine construction began at the shipyard with the 1917 *L8.* Seavey Island, the original shipyard site (not open to the public), is almost entirely an historic district with eighteenth-century warehouses and other industrial structures and the Greek Revival residence quarters of naval officers. The **Kittery Historical and Naval Museum** (Rodgers Road, near routes 1 and 236, 207–439–3080) interprets Kittery's and the country's naval shipbuilding history, as well as the history of the community and the lives of the townspeople, through models of ships from the eighteenth century to the present, dioramas, photographs, and paintings. Special exhibits display the museum's assorted artifacts, including early examples of lighting, physicians' instruments, and other trade tools.

Fort McClary

The rise in the land at Kittery's Point, the oldest section of town, was officially ordered fortified in the early eighteenth century against the French, Indians, pirates—and to protect boats from the taxes and duties imposed by the government of New Hampshire. The initial breastwork that made up the fortification was named Fort William in honor of Sir William Pepperrell, a distinguished Maine colonist, justice of the peace, and loyalist. Fort William was garrisoned at the time of the Revolution and renamed Fort McClary in honor of Major Andrew McClary, a casualty of Bunker

The hexagonal blockhouse of Fort McClary, perched on a granite point that has been fortified for nearly three centuries.

Hill. The fort was considered too well fortified for British attack during the Revolution; it was garrisoned during the War of 1812, Civil War, Spanish-American War, and World War I, when it was equipped as an observation post.

Fortification was improved in three major efforts, the first ca. 1808, next in 1844, and again in 1864, during the Civil War. The hexagonal blockhouse, probably built during the middle construction, is composed of a cut-granite first story on a mortared fieldstone foundation, topped with the traditional overhanging second story of squared logs. Maine's Bureau of Parks and Recreation administers the fort's surviving structures: the brick magazine, barracks' foundation, and granite wall from the first phase of improvements ca. 1808; the blockhouse and rifleman's house from the 1844 additions; and the granite powder magazine, unfinished perimeter walls, and two caponiers from the final modifications.

LOCATION: Kittery Point Road, off Route 103. HOURS: June through September: 9–5 Daily. FEE: None. TELEPHONE: 207–439–2845.

The **First Congregational Church** and **Old Parsonage** (Pepperrell Road) are survivors from the early eighteenth century. The church was incorporated in 1714, and the present building—the oldest church building in the state—dates from 1730. The Old Parsonage, now a parish house, was built in 1729.

Nearby is the **William Pepperrell House** (Pepperrell Road, private), built in 1720 as the residence of a Welsh lumber magnate and shipper who first settled on the Isles of Shoals before building this house. His son was named a baronet for leading the attack on the French fort at Louisbourg in King George's War in 1745. The house was remodeled by successive generations of Pepperrells into the structure seen today. Pepperrell died in 1759; in 1760, Lady Pepperrell took advantage of her wealth and built herself a stately and fashionable Georgian mansion. The **Lady Pepperrell House** (Pepperrell Road, private) overlooks the Piscataqua River and Portsmouth Harbor. A hipped roof covers the projecting center pavilion, which is flanked by two-story Ionic pilasters surmounted by a closed pediment. Dentil molding beneath the roof line encircles the house. The porch, fence, and grape arbor are additions from the 1920s. Nearby is a picturesque graveyard with a number of nineteenth-century headstones.

Also on Pepperrell Road is the 1870 **summer home of William Dean Howells** (private), author and editor of *Atlantic* magazine. Howells bought the house in 1902 and spent his summers here, writing and gardening, until 1912. He wrote from his "barnbry," stables he had moved from a corner of the lot and converted to a library, which his son later turned and attached to the house. Howells was publisher and friend to such literati as Henry James and Samuel Clemens, both of whom were guests here. In 1979, Howells's heirs donated the house to Harvard University.

ISLES OF SHOALS

Maine and New Hampshire share the Isles of Shoals. Lying nine miles off the coast, the handful of islands (Duck, Appledore, Smuttynose, Malaga, and Cedar belong to Maine) have a richer history than their barrenness suggests. Credited to Captain John Smith for discovery, they were originally called Smith's Islands and were home to all-male settlements of fishermen until 1647, when a man

OPPOSITE: *The stylish Georgian Lady Pepperrell House, above, and the gambrel-roofed Sir William Pepperrell House, below.*

Stone houses and churches, Isles of Shoals.

named Reynolds battled the General Court of Massachusetts for the right to live with his wife and livestock on the island. It was decided that the woman could stay but the livestock had to go, for fear of disrupting the open-air fish drying and curing. That decision brought families to the Isles of Shoals, primarily to Appledore and Star islands. The islands gained a reputation for decent government, righteous churches, and outstanding education; mainlanders were known to send over their children for schooling. In 1715 the village of Gosport was settled on Star Island, and the islands thrived on whaling and fishing plus a healthy trading business with Spain.

The islands' vulnerability to British attack precipitated the settlers' relocation to the coast at the time of the Revolution. Afterwards, the islands were repopulated, but this time gained a reputation for rum, shipwrecking, and pirating.

Tales of ghosts, pirate treasure, and shipwrecked Spaniards proliferated, but by the 1820s the coast had exerted a proper civilizing influence over the islands. In 1847 Thomas Laighton of Portsmouth, New Hampshire, established the first summer hotel on Appledore Island and then another on Star Island. Through the early twentieth century the islands attracted intellectuals and artists, counting among their visitors Nathaniel Hawthorne, John Greenleaf Whittier, James Russell Lowell, and Frances Hodgson Burnett. An 1873 double murder on Smuttynose Island, which led to one of the last penal executions in Maine, revived images of the islands' post-revolutionary reputation and most likely aided their decline.

The islands are open to the public for day trips; ferries run regularly from Portsmouth, New Hampshire (603–431–5500).

YORK

Originally settled in the 1630s, the coastal village of York (incorporating York Corner and York Harbor) has a beautifully maintained historic district along both sides of the York River. The town was known earlier as Gorgeana, after its founder, Sir Ferdinando Gorges, before it was renamed in honor of the county in England.

The townspeople defended themselves against a series of Indian raids by raising a series of garrison houses at strategic points. A garrison house is often characterized by its bulky overhanging second story, but other configurations were used as well. The function of the house, providing a stronghold for both defense and offense, overshadowed any strict adherence to one specific form. The **MacIntire Garrison** (Route 91, private) was constructed ca. 1707 but architecturally recalls the seventeenth century. Its sawn log walls, nearly eight inches thick, are covered in dark clapboard siding, giving the structure a dark, seemingly impregnable mass. This garrison house has a second-story overhang and a large central chimney, which was rebuilt in 1909.

In the 1760s, York merchant and civic leader Jonathan Sayward bought a 1718 Georgian house, enlarged it, and filled the rooms with Queen Anne and Chippendale furniture, paintings, and porcelain. (The story goes that Sayward furnished his house with spoils from an expedition he led against the French in 1745.) Later Sayward generations and subsequent owners kept the house and its furnishings intact. The **Sayward-Wheeler House** (79 Barrell Lane Extension, York Harbor, 207–363–2709) now belongs to the Society for the Preservation of New England Antiquities.

During the Revolution, patriotic local citizens staged their own version of the Boston Tea Party, seizing a shipment of tea from an English sloop rather than pay taxes on it. Residents were also early industrialists—the town's 1811 cotton mill is among the oldest in the state. After the Civil War, York was a popular summer resort.

The **Old York Historical Society** (York Street and Lindsay Road, 207–363–4974) administers a complex of seven historic buildings dating from the mid-eighteenth century. The society's offices and library are housed in the George Marshall Store, a mid-nineteenth-century general store overlooking Hancock Wharf. Some of the society's collections of furniture, textiles, and books belonged to York's earliest families. Tours of the society's properties, listed below, begin from **Jefferds Tavern** (Lindsay Road). Built in 1750 by Captain Samuel Jefferds, the tavern serves as a visitor center with exhibits and crafts demonstrations.

The 1719 **Old York Gaol** (Jail), one of the oldest public buildings in the country, was originally the King's Prison for the District of Maine. With fieldstone walls nearly three feet thick, it was used as a jail until 1860. In addition to the dungeons and cells used for

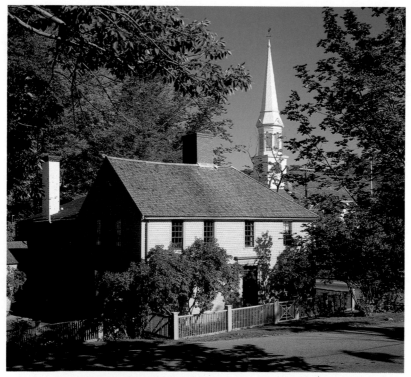

A pre-Revolutionary York landmark, the putty-colored Emerson-Wilcox House.

felons and debtors, the gaoler's quarters may also be viewed, furnished according to the household inventory of 1790.

The 1742 **Emerson-Wilcox House** has been many things—post office, tavern, tailor's shop, and private house several times over. It is now a museum of local history and crafts, displaying the country's most comprehensive collection of crewelwork bedhangings; twelve period rooms showcase furniture made in the region.

York's 1745 **Old Schoolhouse,** one of the oldest one-room schoolhouses in Maine, is furnished with original desks, benches, and books as well as exhibits on early schooling in the area. The **John Hancock Warehouse,** named for the Patriot who owned it, is the earliest commercial building in York, built in the mid-1700s. Interpretive materials illustrate river commerce and maritime trade of the region. The Society also administers the 1732 **Elizabeth Perkins House** (South Side Road at Sewall's Bridge). The former home of York's pioneer preservationist reflects the eclectic tastes of a family of collectors of the Colonial Revival period.

SOUTH BERWICK

The town of South Berwick, settled in 1623 on the Salmon Falls River near the Maine–New Hampshire border, figures prominently in Maine's agricultural and industrial history. In 1634 a shipload of the first cows in the state was unloaded on the banks of the Salmon Falls River, thus beginning dairy farming in the area. The first sawmill in Maine was established in 1634 on the falls, downriver from South Berwick village. The town is perhaps best known in New England for the **Berwick Academy,** a highly regarded secondary school dating to 1791.

The **Sarah Orne Jewett House** (5 Portland Street, 207–384–5269) is named for the noted New England author. Built in 1774, the house, which belonged to Jewett's grandfather, brought elegance to South Berwick—its hipped roof, dormer windows, and pediment doorway separated it from its simpler colonial neighbors. The house's interior is elaborate; local legend has it that three ships' carpenters spent 100 days carving the wainscotting, cornices, and door moldings. Jewett's sea captain grandfather and physician father lavishly appointed the house with imported furniture, tapestries, porcelains, and silver.

OVERLEAF: *Hamilton House, which was the setting for one of Sarah Orne Jewett's novels. It faces the Piscataqua River.*

The master bedchamber of Hamilton House contains such fashionable turn-of-the-century appointments as Currier & Ives prints, bird-and-vine wallpaper and a fishnet bed canopy. The chest to the left of the doorway was made by a Piscataqua-area craftsman in the late eighteenth century.

Jewett set her Revolutionary War romance, *The Tory Lover,* in **Hamilton House** (Vaughan's Lane, off Route 236, 207–384–5269), which is dramatically sited on the Piscataqua River just outside the town of South Berwick. Colonel Jonathan Hamilton built the house on the river bluff in 1785. It passed to other owners and survived changes in the local economy from timber to shipping, farming, and manufacturing. In the 1840s the Hamilton estate was a sheep farm. Emily Tyson, a friend of Sarah Orne Jewett's, bought the house at the turn of the century and became one of the country's first patrons of historic house restoration. Tours of the property include the main house, the gardens, and the summer house.

The Old Berwick Historical Society is located in the **Counting House** (Route 4, 207–384–8041), an 1830 brick cotton mill. Local collections include a Jewett family library, Gundalow models, and historic papers.

NORTH BERWICK

The English settlers of North Berwick were fur traders in the 1630s and held on to their town when other settlements were abandoned during the upheavals of the French and Indian Wars. A veteran of those wars, Thomas Hobbs, Jr., built the **Hobb House,** a small inn on Wells Street, in 1763. Quaker Winthrop Morrell built his own two-story farmhouse in 1763, and his family has kept it for centuries. Known as the **Old Morell House,** it, like the Hobbs House, is privately owned.

In the nineteenth century, manufacturing dominated North Berwick's economy. Manufacturers specialized in plows and other farm tools, as well as sleds and toboggans. The **Hussey Plow Company** (Dyer Street, 207–676–2271), a family business since 1835, has turned its original store front and factory into a museum, displaying early agricultural equipment.

SANFORD

At the foothills of the White Mountains, Sanford was named for Peleg Sanford, a seventeenth-century governor of Rhode Island whose stepfather held the original deed to this verdant land. Sawmills and gristmills were operating on the Mousam River as early as 1740. After the Civil War Sanford became a major textile-manufacturing center. Woolen blankets and heavy cotton robes were local specialties. Later, Sanford mills became the automobile industry's major supplier of plush upholstery fabrics. One of the town's industrialists, Thomas Goodall, provided his workers with housing and recreational facilities and built the public library, the town hall, hospital, and baseball stadium. Goodall's **1871 Victorian house** is at 232 Main Street (private).

The **Emery Homestead** (Lebanon Street, private) dates from the 1830s and is an excellent example of "continuous architecture," with main house, barns, sheds, and other structures attached.

KENNEBUNK

Kennebunk's history as an important shipbuilding center is evident in its great variety of nineteenth-century houses. Ranging in style from Colonial to Queen Anne, from somber Federal to exuberant Gothic Revival, the houses were home to the shippers, shipbuilders, and sea captains who populated the town. Among the residences are the **James Smith Homestead** (Route 35, private), a mid-eighteenth-century Georgian farmhouse; the **Bourne Mansion** (8 Bourne Street, private), perhaps the finest Federal house in Maine; and the **Wedding Cake House** (Summer Street, private), a Victorian steamboat fantasy, supposed to have been a sea captain's extravagant gift to his new bride.

The **Brick Store Museum** (117 Main Street, 207–985–4802) began in an 1825 brick dry-goods store built by local merchant and shipowner William Lord and has expanded to fill three connected nineteenth-century buildings. Rotating exhibits pertaining to local social and maritime history are held in the first-floor galleries; on the second floor is a formal gallery of Federal-period furniture, portraits, and paintings of ships. Books, manuscripts, and personal effects of the Maine writer Kenneth Roberts and the novelist and playwright Booth Tarkington are also on display.

The museum also operates the 1803 **Taylor-Barry House** (24 Summer Street), built by the architect and builder Thomas Eaton for a prominent local family of shipmasters and shipowners. The Federal style house features a hipped roof, and the interior retains its original woodwork, moldings, and in the hallway, stencilling attributed to the itinerant stenciller Moses Eaton. Rooms are furnished with original pieces and are decorated in the Federal and mid-Victorian styles. The studio of Edith Barry, a twentieth-century painter, is at the rear of the house. Exhibits on local artists and authors are occasionally held in the house.

KENNEBUNKPORT

Nestled between Cape Porpoise Harbor and the Kennebunk River, this village began as a fishing and shipbuilding center. The historic district (along North and Maine streets and Ocean Avenue) is rich with houses from the eighteenth and nineteenth centuries, showing a stylistic progression from Colonial to Federal, Greek Revival, Gothic Revival, Italianate, and Second Empire. At the close of the nineteenth century, when shipbuilding was on the wane, Kennebunkport emerged as a summer resort. The most conspicuous evidence of the town's resort life is the 1889 **Kennebunk River Club,** a rambling Shingle-style clubhouse on Ocean Avenue, beside the river as it approaches the sea.

OPPOSITE: *A collection of Oriental export Rose Medallion porcelain is kept in the dining room of the Taylor-Barry House, just off the stencilled entrance hall.*

Among the notable houses are **White Columns** (Maine Street. 207–967–2751), an outstanding Greek Revival house with a monumental Doric colonnade topped by a bold pediment. The house was built in 1853 by Charles Perkins, a merchant who sold supplies to the big clipper ships as well as investing in their cargoes. He and his wife, Celia Nott Perkins, moved into the house as newlyweds; an interpretive tour of the house draws heavily from the detailed diaries Celia kept throughout her life there. The house retains all the original wallpaper, carpets, and furnishings, including a painting of the Perkins's daughter, Lela, by Kennebunkport artist Hannah Skeele and two magnificent embroidered crazy quilts made by Celia Perkins.

The three-and-a-half story Federal-period **Captain Lord Mansion** (corner of Green and Pleasant streets) was built from 1812 to 1815 by Captain Nathaniel Lord, a wealthy shipbuilder. The house features an octagonal cupola and a widow's walk. Charles P. Clark, president of the New York–New Haven Railroad and a grandson of Lord, used the house as a summer residence in the late nineteenth century; it is now being operated as an inn.

One of the country's best preserved gristmills is the **Perkins Tide Mill** (Mill Lane). Built in 1749, the mill, powered by tidal waters, remained in operation for nearly two centuries, finally shutting down in 1939. It is currently occupied by a restaurant.

The **Clark Building** (North Street, 207–967–2751) contains a small marine museum displaying artifacts of the shipbuilding era, such as ship models, paintings, tools, and anchors. The building formerly housed the offices for the Clark shipyards.

BIDDEFORD

Divided by the Saco River, the twin towns of Biddeford and Saco became Maine's first major industrial area. The first sawmill was constructed in 1653, and the nineteenth century brought vast brick mills, which still dominate the downtown area. The products of these mills—textiles, textile machinery, lumber, and flour—supplied a large domestic and foreign market.

A **monument** at Leighton's Point in Biddeford commemorates the explorer Richard Vines, who spent the winter in this area in 1616. Permanent settlement was established on June 25, 1630. The **Biddeford Historical Society** (270 Main Street, 207–282–9165), which resides at the McArthur Library, holds the town's records from 1653 to 1855. The library houses local genealogies, mill histories, and historic memorabilia—including photographs and architectural records of the region. The Society also administers the **First Parish Meeting House** (3 Meeting House Road), erected in 1759 and renovated in 1840, which may be seen by appointment.

SACO

Sharing Biddeford's industrial history, Saco is also home to the **York Institute Museum** (371 Main Street, 207–282–3031). Established in 1867, the museum houses a superb collection of Maine fine and decorative arts. The adjacent 1881 **Dyer Library** has a large collection of Biddeford and Saco records, including early newspapers, city records, and personal papers.

Nearby on Elm, North, and Upper Main streets are accomplished examples of Federal-period architecture interspersed with the later dwellings of textile-mill owners and workers. Several fine Greek Revival houses (all private) line the side streets.

SCARBOROUGH

On a peninsula just south of Portland is the small town of Scarborough. Its oldest structure, built in 1684, is the **Richard Hunniwell House** (Black Point Road, 207–883–8427), named for its owner, a captain during the Indian wars of the late seventeenth century. The modest shingled house and herb garden are typical of the period.

Winslow Homer, a longtime resident of Scarborough, painted many scenes of Northern New England such as the 1873 Boy in a Boatyard *(detail).*

In 1884, the artist Winslow Homer moved to a carriage house in Prout's Neck, an area of Scarborough, making it both home and studio until his death in 1910. The house, a modest structure built about 1870, offers vast views of the Atlantic that recall the artist's well-known paintings of the sea. The house has changed little since Homer's tenure and remains in his family.

In the Dunstan area of Scarborough is the **Scarborough Historical Society Museum** (Route 1, 207–883–6159). Housed in a 1911 brick building used as a generator house for trolley cars, the museum's collections include records of the town's early families, as well as their household items and tools, and fifteen murals by Roger Deering representing Scarborough's early history beginning in 1630.

On the Dunstan Landing Road a **millstone marker** identifies the birthplace of Rufus King, a signer of the U.S. Constitution, and his brother William, Maine's first governor.

Rising above Maine's rocky shore: the Portland Head Light.

CAPE ELIZABETH

Jutting out into the Atlantic, Cape Elizabeth is the site of two of Maine's lighthouses—the **Portland Head Light,** built in 1790, and **Two Lights,** made of cast iron in 1874. Probably the best-known lighthouse on the eastern seaboard, the Portland Head Light is practically unchanged since George Washington ordered its construction. Off the cape is Richmond's Island, where an early-seventeenth-century trading post and fishing station has been preserved as an archaeological site.

PORTLAND

Beginning in 1623, the Casco Bay Peninsula attracted a series of French and English settlers who fought with one another, with Indian tribes and pirates—and with the brutal winters. The fragile European settlements hung on for nearly a century, occupied in fur trading, fishing, and lumbering. A hardy Massachusetts contingent arrived in 1715 and fortified the site with stone garrisons. By 1770, the place had gained a name—Falmouth—and some prosperity, from shipbuilding, as well as stepped-up exports of fish, furs, and lumber. White pines from the nearby forests became sturdy masts for the British Navy. From the West Indies came molasses to be distilled into rum.

During the Revolution, in October 1775, British ships dropped anchor in Casco Bay and opened fire, nearly leveling the town. Even in ruins, Falmouth was too important to abandon, and a few hundred colonists stayed on through the Revolution.

The town was gradually rebuilt after the war, and as Portland—so named on July 4, 1786—it grew into one of the Atlantic seaboard's major commercial centers. The nineteenth century saw fortunes made from the shipyard, railroad, textile, and lumber industries. By the 1850s, a dozen shipyards were launching trade vessels bound for Russia, India, and Europe. One of the first sugar refineries in the United States was the Portland Sugar Company, opened in 1855. A heavy manufacturer, the Portland Company, made train locomotives and other large industrial equipment for an international market. By the late 1860s, Portland ranked among the top U.S. ports—fourth in imports, fifth in exports. There was also the business of government: Between 1820 (when Maine joined the Union) and 1831, Portland was the state capital. Immigrants arrived from Scandinavia, Ireland, Italy, and Great Britain.

During the Civil War, strongly abolitionist Portland sent 5,000 troops and a fleet of gunboats to the Union. Shortly after the war the city experienced the disaster that has visited so many others: On July 4, 1866, a fire swept out of a tiny boat-house to engulf entire blocks of buildings. One third of Portland was destroyed, altering the development of many of the city's districts. Fore, Middle, and Exchange streets were the hardest hit by the fire. Whereas many of the buildings on the waterfront side of Fore Street survived, leaving architectural examples of Colonial, Federal, and Greek Revival buildings intact, the rebuilding of the devastated Exchange Street provided an array of later architectural styles. The fire accelerated Congress Street's transformation from residential to commercial development, which in turn opened the Eastern and Western promenades to residential building. The Western Promenade became Portland's affluent residential neighborhood, exhibiting the popular Victorian style of the day.

Along the historic waterfront and Portland's older residential streets are houses, churches, and commercial buildings that survived the fire. The **Tate House** (1270 Westbrook Street, 207–774–9781), a handsome Georgian residence built in 1755, belonged to George Tate, "mast agent" for the Royal Navy. Tate's job was to oversee the selection of trees, primarily white pine, used for masts on the king's ships. Mast production and trade helped establish Portland as a center of commerce after suitable timber from Portsmouth, New Hampshire, grew scarce. Tate lived in the house from 1755 to 1794. His son has the distinction of being the only American to become a first admiral in the Russian navy.

The building is unusual for its clerestory, an indented, windowed exterior wall rising above the second story. Inside, the first floor contains fine wood panelling, wide stairways, and tall chimney breasts: The central chimney serves eight fireplaces. The interior is furnished to exhibit the style customary to a wealthy eighteenth-century official. Letters and artifacts relating to Tate's son and collections of pewter and iron kitchen utensils are also displayed.

The Wadsworth-Longfellow House

Boyhood home of American poet Henry Wadsworth Longfellow, this house was the first brick house built in Portland. In 1785 General Peleg Wadsworth, the poet's grandfather, ordered the

OPPOSITE: *A quiet street in Portland. State Street Church rises to the right.*

bricks from Philadelphia and succeeded in having the first story built before running out of them. Perhaps the shortage was due to inexperience with the new building material—the first story has sixteen-inch-thick walls, twice as thick as usual. The second story was built in 1786 with the second shipment of bricks. The top story and Federal style roof of this primarily late Georgian three-story house were completed in 1815 after a fire destroyed the original roof. The changes in the brick patterns from story to story provide evidence of the building's history.

Henry Wadsworth Longfellow's family moved to the house in 1807, when he was an infant. There he grew up with his seven brothers and sisters, his parents, and his aunt. Both the Wadsworths and the Longfellows were descended from *Mayflower* Pilgrims, and his upbringing reflected the family's emphasis on education and moral purpose. Longfellow moved away to attend Bowdoin College in 1821 but returned frequently for lengthy visits. The house was given to the Maine Historical Society in 1901 by Anne Longfellow Pierce, the poet's sister. Wadsworth and Longfellow family furnishings, mementoes, and portraits, as well as an eighteenth-century kitchen are on display.

LOCATION: 487 Congress Street. HOURS: June through mid-October: 10–4 Tuesday–Saturday. FEE: Yes. TELEPHONE: 207–772–1807.

Founded in 1822, the **Maine Historical Society** (485 Congress Street, 207–774–1822) is the fourth oldest such organization in the United States, ranking behind those of Massachusetts (1791), New York (1804), and Rhode Island (1822). Located behind the Longfellow House, its galleries and extensive collections cover genealogy and local and regional history.

At the turn of the nineteenth century, the Federal style of architecture gained in popularity, as evidenced by the buildings of Portland. The **Joseph Holt Ingraham House** (51 State Street, private) was built in 1801 for the prominent businessman and silversmith who is credited with the development of State Street; he later lost his wealth in the War of 1812. The house, which was designed by famed New England architect Alexander Parris, has undergone major changes, leaving the fanlight and cornice the only remaining

OPPOSITE: *A genealogy in sampler form, made by Elizabeth Mountfort of Portland in 1820, from the collection of the Maine Historical Society.*

the GENEALOGY of

Daniel and Elizabeth Mountfort

Daniel Mountfort born at Portland February 9 1762

Elizabeth Isley born at Portland April 2 1768

Married September 30 1787

Isaac Mountfort born July 21 1788

Died at Havanna October 5 1809

Joseph Mountfort born December 11 1789

Died at Portland September 14 1809

James Mountfort born September 13 1791

Daniel Mountfort born July 25 1794

John Mountfort born September 3 1796

William Mountfort born October 18 1799

Mary Ann Mountfort born July 23 1801

Jane Mountfort born April 16 1804

Elizabeth I Mountfort born Febuary 24 1806

Harriet Mountfort born March 11 1808

Sarah I Mountfort born April 23 1810

Joseph Mountfort born June 10 1812

O RESIGNATION heavenly power   Teach us the hand of love divine
Our warmest thoughts engage   In evils to discern   need
Thou art the safest guide of youth   'tis the first lesson which we
The sole support of age   The latest which we learn.

WHEN blooming youth is
snatched away
By deaths resistless hand
Our hearts the mournful
tribute pay
Which pity doth demand

Elizabeth I Mountfort
Æ 14 years Portland July
27 1820

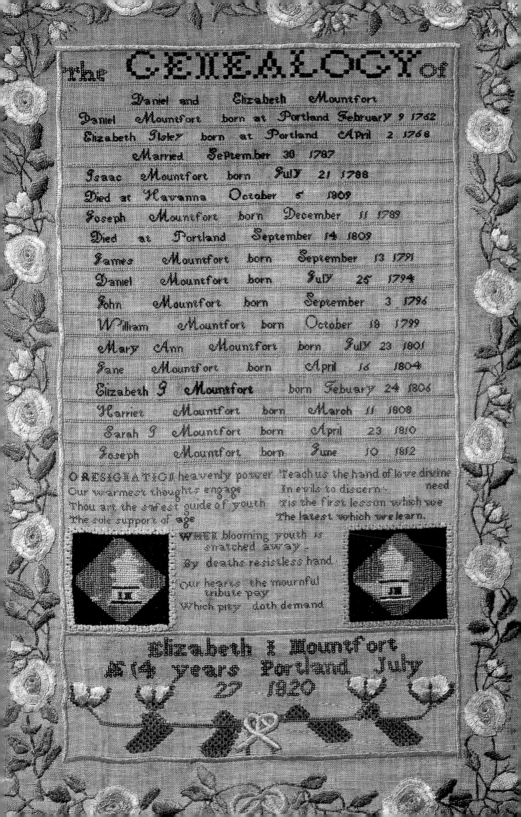

Federal details. Parris also designed the **Richard Hunnewell House** (156 State Street, private). Built in 1805 for Colonel Hunnewell, a participant in the Boston Tea Party, this Federal mansion was remodeled in the 1920s by John Calvin Stevens, who enlarged it and added the front portico and Palladian window.

McLellan-Sweat House

This house remains an outstanding example of Federal architecture and a tribute to the expectations of a growing city and young country. The three-story brick mansion was built from 1800 to 1801 by John Kimball, Sr., for Major Hugh McLellan, a mariner and founding businessman of Portland. However, the Embargo of 1807 so set back the McLellan fortune that in 1815 the house was sold to Asa Clapp for about a quarter of the cost of its construction. The house was again sold in 1880 to Colonel Lorenzo de Medici Sweat, whose wife bequeathed it to the Portland Society of Art on her death in 1908.

The exterior of the McLellan-Sweat House now boasts its original ochre color, complementing a Palladian window and porticoed doorway with fanlight and sidelights in Federal style. Inside, the optimism of the times is depicted in the dining room mantel ornamentation: A goddess of plenty rides a chariot accompanied by a cupid and cornucopia. Both the interior and exterior of the mansion highlight the attention to detail and scale inherent in Federal styling. The Portland Museum of Art arranges tours through the unfurnished house, focusing on its architectural elements and plan.

LOCATION: 103 Spring Street. HOURS: By appointment. FEE: Yes. TELEPHONE: 207–775–6148.

The **Park Street Row** (88–114 Park Street), the largest rowhouse structure to be erected in Portland, was originally built in 1835 as twenty townhouses forming a U-shape around a park. The remaining fourteen attached brick houses gracefully carry Greek Revival details such as the cast-iron railings that unite the second-floor balconies. Begun as a real estate venture, the complex was sold by the stockholders before completion. Although the project was finished by the individual buyers, it remains a tribute to the forward thinking of its originators.

Morse-Libby House

A dramatic departure from the elegant Federal and restrained Greek Revival houses in Portland is the 1860 Morse-Libby House, better known as the **Victoria Mansion**—the style of the mansion a tribute to the Victorian age of opulent decoration and to the Queen herself. Ruggles Sylvester Morse, a Maine native, earned his fortune in the hotel business in New York, Boston, and New Orleans. He hired the architect Henry Austin to design this mansion in the grand manner of the South. The house was intended to be a summer home, away from the heat of New Orleans, where Morse lived at the time, but with the onset of the Civil War, he and his wife moved to Portland permanently.

A stone villa, complete with Tuscan tower: Portland's Victoria Mansion, also known as the Morse-Libby House.

Extravagant window treatments, ceiling and wall decoration, and suites of furniture in the Morse-Libby House display the fashionable excess of the Rococo Revival.

A fine example of the Italian Villa style, the Victoria Mansion dominates the corner of Park and Danforth streets. A central square tower rises above two stories, a prominent cornice on one side, a classic pediment on the other. The pediment is echoed above the second-story windows on the one side while heavy hood-molds trim those on the other.

Within, the house displays a panoply of ornamentation: extravagant carvings, etched and stained glass, vibrant paintings and frescoes, medallions, cherubim, and richly appointed light fixtures. The painted and carved walls and ceilings, thought to be designed by Gustave Herter of New York, were executed by numerous artisans. A mahogany staircase ascends from a base flanked by bronze torch bearers; hand-carved chestnut panelling adorns the dining room walls; gilt, damask, satin, rosewood, mother of pearl, and marble accent the craftsmanship throughout. Most of the furnishings are original to the Morse household and reflect the taste and wealth of a Victorian entrepreneur.

Morse died in 1893; the house and furnishings were purchased from his estate in 1894 by Joseph Ralph Libby, a Portland merchant. In 1940, after more than a decade of abandonment, the house was bought by Dr. William Holmes and his sister, Clara, who subsequently donated it to the Victoria Society in 1943.

LOCATION: 109 Danforth Street. HOURS: June through August: 10–4 Tuesday–Saturday, 1–4 Sunday. September: 10–1 Tuesday–Saturday, 1–4 Sunday. FEE: Yes. TELEPHONE: 207–772–4841.

Neal Dow Memorial

Built in 1829, this mansion was home of reformer Neal Dow and a center of political activity focusing on temperance, abolition, prison reform, and women's rights. A brigadier general in the Civil War, twice the mayor of Portland, a state legislator, and presidential candidate on the Prohibition ticket, Dow was internationally known for his temperance work. Portland's prosperous rum trade was an affront to Dow, and his response was the Maine Law, which in 1851 prohibited the making and selling of alcohol in the state. He spent much of his life touring the U.S. and abroad to promote his reforms. Dow's son bequeathed the home and furnishings to the Maine Woman's Christian Temperance Union, which maintains it as a memorial to Dow and as their headquarters. Rooms display furnishings original to the house from various periods, as well as paintings, portraits, silver, ornamental ironwork, and family memorabilia—including a set of china emblazoned with Dow's picture, a gift to his wife.

LOCATION: 714 Congress Street. HOURS: 11–4 Daily. FEE: None. TELEPHONE: 207–773–7773.

At 387 Spring Street stands a fine example of mid-nineteenth-century Gothic Revival architecture, a style made popular by American architect Andrew Jackson Downing and reflecting the prevailing romanticism of the day. Designed by Henry Rowe, the John J. Brown House, also known as the **Gothic House** (private), has a central gable with bargeboards and a porch with a Tudor arch, above which sits a simple tracery window. In 1971 the house was moved a half-mile to this location to preserve it from destruction.

The 1866 **Leonard Bond Chapman House** (90 Capisic Street, private) is notable for its mansard roof and concave tower. Chapman was a local historian whose collection of documents forms the foundation of the Maine Historical Society's library holdings on Portland's history.

Portland's oldest church is **First Parish Church** (425 Congress Street), also the city's first stone public building. This Colonial-Federal style structure was built in 1825–1826 on the site of "Old Jerusalem," the parish's wooden meeting house where Maine's constitution was drafted by the Constitutional Convention in 1819. The parish itself dates back to 1674 and its current members work to keep the church as it was when it was built; the pulpit, minister's chair, lighting fixtures, communion table, and even the pulpit Bibles date to the 1820s.

The **Portland Observatory** (138 Congress Street, 207–774–5561) sits on Munjoy Hill, where George Munjoy settled as early as 1659 and where victims of the 1866 fire dwelt in tent cities. The observatory was built in 1807 as a signal tower; a system of signal flags alerted citizens to approaching ships, and ships in distress could be spotted. The tower was closed at the turn of the century and reopened in 1939 as a historic site. The octagonal tower rises 221 feet above sea level, affording panoramic views of the harbor and the White Mountains; visitors climb 102 steps to reach the top.

Also on Munjoy Hill lies the oldest cemetery in Portland, the **Eastern Cemetery** (Congress at Mountfort streets). Chartered in 1688, it dates from the time when Portland was called Falmouth. Many of Portland's prominent citizens were buried here from 1670 to the late 1800s.

The 1828 **Mariner's Church** (368 Fore Street) brought Greek Revival architecture to Portland, though embellished with Federal style cornice and fanlight. The church was part of an unusual scheme: The large, columned structure housed shops on the ground floor—their rent financed the church and its missions—while the church maintained its chapel on the third floor. Built in the dock area of this rum-trading town where temperance was on the rise, the church meant to serve and educate the seamen. The building stands mostly unchanged, with shops operating on the ground floor, but the church is no longer used for worship services.

Another Portland church noted for its architecture is the **Chestnut Street United Methodist Church** (17 Chestnut Street). Designed by Portland architect Charles A. Alexander and built in 1856, it is an early example of Gothic Revival architecture.

At 32 Thomas Street, the 1878 **Williston-West United Church of Christ** stands in its high Victorian Gothic splendor, designed by Francis Fassett and later altered by his onetime partner John Calvin Stevens. Stevens also built the parish house, in 1904. This church is noteworthy not only for its outstanding ecclesiastical architecture but also as the home of the Young People's Society of Christian Endeavor, begun here in 1881. The society sparked the Sunday school movement, providing religious education tailored for children.

The **U.S. Customhouse** (312 Fore Street), a grand edifice in the Second Empire style, is a reminder of Portland's nineteenth-century prosperity. The massive building occupies a complete block on the waterfront, its mansard-roofed towers rising above two stories of New Hampshire granite, topped by an encircling balustrade. The interior chandeliers, woodwork, painted and gilded ceilings, and marble floors remain as elegant as when they were new; both within and without, little has been altered since the building was completed in 1871.

Eighteen hundred buildings were lost in the Great Fire of 1866 and for months many of the 10,000 homeless victims lived in emergency shelters and tent camps, eating in soup kitchens. The **Portland Fire Museum** (157 Spring Street, 207–775–6361, ext. 201), housed in the 1837 granite Greek Revival Fire Station No. 4, documents the history of firefighting in Portland and the Great Fire of 1866, using photos and artifacts.

Portland Museum of Art

As the oldest public art museum in the state, founded in 1882, the institution's original facilities include the 1800 McLellan-Sweat House and the 1911 L.D.M. Sweat Memorial. In 1983, the opening of the Charles Shipman Payson Building, designed in the Postmodern style by Henry Nichols Cobb of I. M. Pei & Partners, increased the museum's space tenfold and provided its current home. Five levels of galleries hold the museum's collections of American and English silver, Chinese art, Federal-period furnishings, American primitives, glass, maritime art, and paintings from the eighteenth century to the present. The core State of Maine Collection includes works by artists such as Charles Codman, Andrew Wyeth, Benjamin Paul Akers, Marsden Hartley, and Peggy Bacon, all of whom lived or worked in the state. The Charles Shipman Payson Collection of Winslow Homer paintings is also part of this core collection. Gallery space is provided for traveling exhibitions of fine and decorative arts.

LOCATION: 7 Congress Square. HOURS: 10–5 Tuesday–Saturday, 12–5 Sunday. FEE: Yes. TELEPHONE: 207–775–6148.

The 1941 Broad Cove Farm, *and other Andrew Wyeth paintings of the Cushing area, are in the Portland Museum of Art (detail).*

Fort Gorges was begun in 1858 on Hog Island, at the entrance to the city's harbor, and served as Portland's principal Civil War fortification. The fort is a massive hexagonal granite pile, typical of defensive military architecture of the time. Ironically, even before its completion in the 1860s, Fort Gorges's architecture was already obsolete. During both world wars, the U.S. Navy stored equipment and ammunition here.

Local architect George M. Harding, practicing in Portland from the 1850s to the 1870s, designed three prominent buildings on Middle Street, known as the Woodman, Rackleff, and Thompson blocks. The buildings were some of the earliest commercial structures built in Portland after the devastating fire of 1866, which explains their homogeneous character. The **Woodman block** (133–141 Middle Street) was the first of the three, built in 1867. Its rounded mansard roof, the most prominent Second Empire feature, tops an Italianate arrangement of windows and ground floor arcade. The cast-iron storefronts on the ground floor were made locally by the Portland Company. Harding put his name at the base of one of the pilasters. The first floor arcade and window arches of the **Rackleff block** (129–131 Middle Street) echo those of the Woodman; the facade, however, sits one foot lower. The flat roof and vertical groupings of windows give this structure a distinctive Italianate expression. Beyond its rounded corner and across the street, the **Thompson block** (117–125 Middle Street) imitates the Woodman block even more closely. Here a flat mansard roof tops a set of windows. A repetitive oak-leaf-and-acorn detail ornaments the building. Together, the blocks exemplify the grand commercial architecture of the late nineteenth century while concretely asserting Portland's viability after the Great Fire.

Another of Portland's outstanding commercial buildings commemorates the life of John Bundy Brown, the city's embodiment of the American Dream. Brown started work as a grocery clerk and died in 1881 the city's leading capitalist, having founded the Portland Sugar Company and the Falmouth Hotel, a favorite society spot. John Calvin Stevens designed the Queen Anne style **John Bundy Brown Memorial Block** (529–543 Congress Street) in Brown's memory. Its richly textured surface, asymmetrical facade, and variegated roofline are typical elements of this style, more often reserved for domestic structures. The **Greater Portland Landmark Association** (207–774–5561) offers walking tours of these areas.

SOUTH WINDHAM

The little town of South Windham is home to one of the finest Georgian residences in New England, the **Parson Smith House** (87 River Road, 617–227–3956), built in 1764 by the settlement's second pastor. The clapboard house has a handsome, if simple interior, with hand-planed panelling and spacious rooms, a showcase for the decorative styles of the day. The Smith family, among South Windham's original settlers, kept the house for almost 200 years, and many of its furnishings belonged to them. The eighteenth-century kitchen is primarily original, with a ten-foot hearth incorporating a later beehive oven. The house is owned and administered by the Society for the Preservation of New England Antiquities.

Babb's Covered Bridge, originally built in 1864 and reconstructed after a fire in 1973, crosses the Presumscot River off River Road, about two miles north of town.

STANDISH

The fine Georgian **Marrett House** (Route 25, 617–227–3956) went up for sale the same year it was built—when the Reverend Daniel

Marrett bought it in 1789, the house was only a few months old. It remained in the Marrett family for over 150 years, and each generation made changes outside and in. As a result, its architecture and furnishings reflect many decades of evolving styles. Among its many fine pieces are a Victorian parlor set, an eighteenth-century Newport card table, and Parson Marrett's standing desk, where he wrote his sermons. Marrett's descendants gave the house to the Society for the Preservation of New England Antiquities.

Reverend Marrett's church was Standish's first parish meeting-house, the **Old Red Church** (Oak Hill Road). The large but graceful frame structure, topped with an impressive cupola, went up in 1804 on land donated by the minister himself. Marrett served as pastor until 1829. Currently owned by the town of Standish, the church holds services in summer. The **museum** of the Standish Historical Society is located on the second floor.

Garden of the Marrett House, Standish.

In nearby **Newfield** is the museum village **Willowbrook** (207–793–2784), an early nineteenth-century compound that includes a schoolhouse, two farmhouses, barns, and sheds.

PORTER

Porter profited from its position downstream from **Kezar Falls,** which powered many woolen mills near the New Hampshire border. Porter also attracted the Bullockites, followers of Jeremiah Bullock, a fundamentalist Baptist. In 1819 the Bullockites built their own church, stark and boxy, now known as the **Porter Old Meeting House** (Colcord Pond Road, 207–625–4667). Until 1900, town meetings were also held here. The historical society has administered the property since 1947.

FRYEBURG

Situated on the fertile Saco River plain, the land called Pequawket by the Indians became one of Maine's first English farming communities. It was later named in honor of Colonel Joseph Frye, who laid out the town lots in 1762.

Two of Fryeburg's earliest residences were incorporated into later structures. The **Squire Chase House** (151 Main Street, private) incorporates the ca. 1767 home of one of the first settlers, Nathaniel Marrill, moved from its original site in 1824. The current structure has been modified by Italianate detailing. The Federal-style **Benjamin Wiley House** (Fish Street, private) also contains an earlier structure, dating from 1772.

NAPLES

Arriving from Massachusetts in 1776, the Perley family acquired farmland around Naples and joined the ranks of the state's most prominent and politically active citizens. Their homestead, originally consisting of 2,000 acres of timberland, includes the 1809 **Perley Farmhouse.**

The **Songo Lock** is a relic of Naples's economic past. Built in 1830, the lock operated for years on the Cumberland–Oxford Canal (off the Songo River), an important trade artery between Portland and points north and west. From the Civil War to the turn of the century, the lock—a massive piece of machinery consisting of a stone frame and wooden gates—conveyed logs to sawmills. It is now used for private boat travel.

YARMOUTH

Sharing Casco Bay with Portland, Yarmouth is now a commuter town, lying just north of the city. A fishing village in the late 1600s, Yarmouth grew into a shipping and shipbuilding center in the nineteenth century. One of its oldest surviving buildings is the **Old Ledge School** (West Main Street, 207–846–6259), a 1738 one-room schoolhouse administered by the Yarmouth Historical Society. The Society also operates a **Museum of Yarmouth History** housed in the town's Merrill Memorial Library, designed in 1905 by A. W. Longfellow of Boston. Exhibits illustrate the region's heritage.

On the campus of **North Yarmouth Academy** (123 Main Street, 207–846–9051) are the Greek Revival **Russell** and **Academy** halls. Russell Hall was built in 1841; Academy Hall went up five years later. The town's **Baptist Meeting House** sits on an elevation above Hillside Street. Renovated twice since it was built in 1796, the church now blends Federal, Greek Revival, and Gothic Revival styles. A twentieth-century treasure is the **Grand Trunk Railroad Station** (57 Main Street). The small, ornate station was built in 1906, when Yarmouth was a stop on the Boston-to-Bangor rail line. It is now a shop.

FREEPORT

An eighteenth-century farming and fishing village, Freeport grew industrially in the 1800s. The **Freeport Historical Society** (45 Main Street, 207–865–3170) is housed in an 1830 brick house furnished with reproductions of nineteenth-century furniture and crafts. The Society also administers the **Pettengill House and Farm,** an eighteenth-century saltbox house on a 140-acre saltwater farm. Characterized by their proximity to the sea, saltwater farms combined agricultural and marine activities—their farmers used salt marshes as pasture land and supplemented their income with shipping and fishing. The farm also includes three outbuildings.

NEW GLOUCESTER

In the early 1700s sixty citizens from Gloucester, Massachusetts, established themselves in Maine in a settlement they named after their old home. Rebuilt after attacks during the French and Indian Wars, New Gloucester grew rapidly on a primarily agricultural basis after the Revolutionary War. Many of its white farmhouses and gray barns are over 200 years old.

ABOVE *and* OVERLEAF: *Shaker Meetinghouse, near Sabbathday Lake and New Gloucester. The blue paint on the interior beams is almost 200 years old.*

The **Shaker Village** (Route 26, 207–926–4597), near Sabbathday Lake, is the remnant of the Shaker community founded there in 1783. The village consists of thirteen buildings, all of them exemplifying the Shaker ideal of uncluttered, functional beauty; some of them—the boys' shop, Shaker store, meetinghouse, ministry's shop—and the herb gardens are open to the public. Within the meetinghouse, the **Shaker Museum** displays many examples of the elegantly simple and functional designs for which the Shakers are known. Collections include furniture, textiles, farm tools.

LEWISTON/AUBURN

Known as Maine's twin cities, Lewiston and Auburn are divided by Lewiston Falls on the Androscoggin River. In its village days of the early nineteenth-century, the west bank of the river—the Auburn side—was known as Goff's Corner, for developer James Goff, Jr., whose store became a popular meeting place. The falls were harnessed to power both cities' textile mills and shoe factories. Shoemaking was a particularly big business in Auburn, with the first of the city's twenty-five shoe factories established in 1835.

Most of the people employed by the factories after the Civil War were French Canadians, who created a rich bicultural society. The French influence is still felt and heard today, particularly in Lewiston where many family names are French. The neighborhood within Oxford, Lincoln, Cedar, and River streets is known as "Little Canada." Lewiston, on the east side of the river, was settled in the 1770s by Paul Hildreth, from Massachusetts. He built a log cabin on the Androscoggin, and operated the first ferry. Lewiston and Auburn grew steadily, as more arrivals from New England, Europe, and Canada came to work in the mills.

Lewiston and Auburn's historic sites date from the cities' late-nineteenth century industrial heyday and include handsome commercial rows, mills built of granite and red brick, and some grand Victorian houses and churches.

In Lewiston's Little Canada, the brick tenements of **Continental Mill Housing** originally spanned many blocks of Oxford Street. Two of the 1865 buildings survive, at numbers 66 to 82. The site of settler Hildreth's log cabin is now occupied by the **Continental Mill** (Oxford Street), a massive structure combining French Empire and Italian Renaissance styles. No longer an active mill, it is still readily identified by its high towers and long mansard roof. Across the street is the Norman Gothic style **St. Mary's Church,** built of Maine granite in 1907. The 1882 **Dominican Block** (141 Lincoln Street, private), a five-story Queen Anne-style building of brick and granite, housed the first school for French Canadians. It was designed by Lewiston's George M. Coombs, one of Maine's busiest architects at the turn of the century.

Coombs also designed the Second Empire **residence of U.S. Senator William P. Frye** (453 Main, private), one of Lewiston's grandest houses. One of Coombs's notable public commissions was the Romanesque **Oak Street School,** featuring elaborate interior woodwork. In 1902, Coombs designed another Romanesque edifice for the city, the public **library** on Park Street. Coombs also left Lewiston its most exotic building, the Shriners' **Kora Temple,** a Moorish, copper-domed structure on Sabattus Street.

The **Grand Trunk Railroad Station** (Lincoln Street) is another important landmark in the city's French-Canadian history—thousands of immigrants arrived in Lewiston at the small, Shingle-style terminal, opened in 1874 on a new branch of the Montreal-to-Portland line. Also of interest are the 1870 **Savings Bank Block**

(215 Libson Street), unified beneath a long mansard roof, and Lewiston's baroque **City Hall** (Pine and Park streets), ornate and spired, which was completed in 1892.

In the 1850s Irish immigrants populated the area south of Oxford and Lincoln streets, where some of their modest houses may still be seen. The area was also the site of the city's **1854 gasworks,** although a small brick Greek Revival office building and decorative iron framework that once contained a huge gas tank are all that remain.

On the quiet southern edge of Lewiston is **Bates College.** Founded in 1855 as a Baptist seminary, it was named for Boston benefactor Benjamin E. Bates in 1864, the same year that it became one of the first coeducational colleges in New England. The school's oldest buildings are **Hathorn Hall** and **Parker Hall,** both designed by Gridley J.F. Bryant and both dating to the mid 1850s.

One of the oldest structures in Auburn is the 1827 **Edward Little Mansion** (Main and Vine, private), the Federal-style home of the man known as the city's founding father. Little inherited an enormous tract of land and did much to develop Auburn, establishing the local academy and Auburn's first church.

Auburn's commercial development during the 1870s and 1880s is evident along Main Street. The **Roak Block,** once known as "the cradle of the shoe industry," was named for Jacob Roak, shoe manufacturer, banker, and developer. The industrial rowhouse is composed of nine distinct sections, designed to house nine separate manufacturing operations. Built in 1871, it extends nearly 300 feet in length. Auburn's major textile mill, the 1873 **Barker Mill** (Mill Street), is a decorative industrial facility, with mansard roof, brick relief, and pedimented windows.

The city's high Victorian Gothic style is seen in the **First Universalist Church** (Elm and Pleasant streets). Built in 1876, the brick structure has a high steeple rising from a white, windowed tower. Two of Auburn's notable houses, both private, are the **Charles A. Jordan House** (63 Academy Street), an 1880 Second Empire mansion built by architect Jordan for himself, and the 1889 **Charles L. Cushman House** (8 Cushman Place), designed by George M. Coombs.

The oldest frame building in Auburn is the **Knight House,** built on the west bank of the Androscoggin in 1796 by a settler named Caleb Lincoln. Bought in 1861 by Nathaniel Knight, a butcher, the house stayed in the Knight family until 1918. Knight's brother, John Adams, published a pro-Union newspaper in England during the Civil War called *The London American*. Agricultural implements, household utensils, clothing, documents, and photographs are displayed at the **Androscoggin Historical Society** (207–784–0586) in the County Courthouse, built 1855–1857, at the corner of Court and Turner streets. An 1882 **monument** to Union soldiers of the Civil War stands on the courthouse grounds.

BRUNSWICK

In 1714 a group of Bostonians bought Brunswick in the Pejepscot Purchase (named for the Indians who inhabited the area). Previous settlements had disappeared, partially due to Indian raids, and in Lovewell's War of 1722 another raid depleted the new settlement. By 1727, however, settlement at Brunswick was stabilized, and the town was incorporated in 1739. Its location at falls on the Androscoggin River, with easy access to the Atlantic Ocean, promised industry and prosperity. The first dam across the river was built in 1753; Maine's first cotton mill was erected at Androscoggin Falls in 1809. The falls provided more than power—the waters were full of salmon to be caught, cured, and shipped throughout New England and overseas. Shipping, lumbering, and related industries also flourished, and in 1802 Bowdoin College opened.

The structures in the **Federal Street Historic District** (including Bowdoin College campus and Park Row), built in the early 1800s in a variety of architectural styles, were restricted by a twenty-foot setback and a two-story limit on buildings. The graciously proportioned lots and wide streets further display the town planner's concern with appropriately exhibiting prosperity.

The **Lincoln Street Historic District** is an early example of lot subdivisions. True to his orderly sense of urban growth, Dr. Isaac Lincoln made the lots an even four rods (66 feet) along the street; a few corner lots were six rods and twenty links (112 feet), with setbacks of sixteen links (10.5 feet). The lots were sold within fifteen months and the majority of dwellings built within two years, giving the district an architectural homogeneity indicative of the mid-nineteenth century.

Harriet Beecher Stowe lived at 63 Federal Street from 1850 to about 1852. While her husband, Calvin Stowe, taught Natural and

Harriet Beecher Stowe wrote Uncle Tom's Cabin *by candlelight in the kitchen of this rambling Federal house.*

Revealed Religions at Bowdoin College, she wrote her famous work, *Uncle Tom's Cabin.* The 1807 structure where the Stowes lived is now an inn.

St. Paul's Episcopal Church, at 27 Pleasant Street, is a modest 1845 work of Richard Upjohn. The same year, Upjohn designed the **First Parish Church** (Main Street and Bath Road), a more characteristic example of the architect's Gothic Revival style.

The century-old **Pejepscot Historical Society** (159 Park Row, 207–729–6606) owns two Victorian houses notable for their architecture and their residents. The **General Joshua L. Chamberlain Civil War Museum** (226 Maine Street), a simple single-story structure when it was built in 1820, was home to Henry Wadsworth Longfellow when he taught at Bowdoin College in the 1830s. Chamberlain—a Civil War hero at the Battle of Gettysburg, governor of Maine, and president of Bowdoin—moved the house to its present location and enlarged it. Among Chamberlain's guests was Ulysses S. Grant. Restored by the historical society, the house contains period furniture and Civil War mementoes.

The **Skolfield-Whittier House** (161 Park Row), also administered by the Society, is an Italianate double mansion topped by an eight-sided cupola. It was built in 1858 by George Skolfield, grandson of Irish immigrants who came to Brunswick in 1739, and founder of Brunswick's Skolfield Shipyard in 1801, for his two sons and daughter. The two sides of the house mirror each other, presenting a unified facade, but are split in the rear by an alleyway. Skolfield descendants lived on the south side of the mansion for over 100 years, and in 1982 they donated the house to the Pejepscot Historical Society as a house museum, virtually unchanged since the last half of the nineteenth century. The north side of the mansion, altered extensively in the interior by its successive owners, was purchased by the Society in 1983 and now houses the **Pejepscot Historical Museum.** It contains exhibits on local history, furniture, clothing, household items, and other collections illustrating life in Brunswick from the eighteenth century to the present.

In its seventeen rooms, the south side of the Skolfield-Whittier House Museum reflects three generations of life in Brunswick while remaining true to its Victorian origins. The large drawing room windows are hung with drapes of twill and velvet; also remaining are the twenty-four-candle Belgian chandeliers, an English rosewood piano, delicately needlepointed footstools, and a porcelain French clock with matching vases. The seafaring nature of the Skolfield and Whittier families is documented in paintings of master shipbuilder George Skolfield and the Skolfield ship, *Roger Stewart,* and the display of a ship's barometer used on many Atlantic crossings by Captain Alfred Skolfield. The accumulations of generations of this Yankee trading family add up to a rare trove of nineteenth-century history: Mechanical toys, china-head dolls, pots, pans, books, and ship's logs fill the shelves.

Bowdoin College

Chartered in 1794 and opened in 1802, Maine's oldest college is named for James Bowdoin II, a Massachusetts governor whose son generously endowed the liberal arts institution. Bowdoin College has graduated a number of the country's foremost citizens, among them Franklin Pierce, fourteenth president of the United States; William Pitt Fessenden, secretary of the treasury under Lincoln;

OPPOSITE: *The pantry in the Skolfield-Whittier House contains bowls, tin cups, and other utensils owned by the family.*

A ca. 1840 print of the Bowdoin campus, viewed from the west, with Massachusetts Hall at left. Newer buildings—and pine trees—have filled in the grounds.

Admiral Robert E. Peary; Nathaniel Hawthorne; Henry Wadsworth Longfellow; and the noted abolitionist and Maine governor John Albion Andrews.

The public is welcome on the handsome 110-acre campus, which is part of the Federal Street Historic District. The representative architecture of the campus includes the work of Samuel Melcher; Richard Upjohn; McKim, Mead & White; Hugh Stebbins; and Edward Larabee Barnes. Guided tours of the campus begin at the Moulton Union (207–725–3000).

Massachusetts Hall, the oldest building on campus, was designed by Aaron and Samuel Melcher and has a cornerstone dating from 1799, when construction began. As a result of financial distress suffered by the college in its early years, the building wasn't completed until 1802. At that time it housed the entire college: eight students, one teacher, and the president. Remodeled in the early 1870s and restored and altered in 1936, the building is currently used for dormitory facilities but maintains its original Federal style exterior.

The **Hawthorne-Longfellow Library,** which contains 725,000 volumes plus a fine collection of rare books and manuscripts, is named for Nathaniel Hawthorne and Henry Wadsworth Longfellow, both members of the class of 1825. On the third floor the library regularly mounts displays from its special collections of Hawthorne and Longfellow manuscripts, books, pamphlets, and memorabilia as well as examples from novelists Kenneth Roberts, Kate Douglas Wiggins, Marguerite Yourcenar, and others.

Peary-Macmillan Arctic Museum

Administered by Bowdoin College, the Peary-Macmillan Arctic Museum commemorates the explorations of Admirals Robert E. Peary and Donald B. Macmillan, another pair of famous alumni, classes of 1877 and 1898, respectively. Peary is best known for his trip to the North Pole; some credit him with being the first man to reach that point. He and his crew sailed from New York in July of 1908 on board the *Roosevelt,* harboring at Cape Sheridan in September and then continuing on sledges in February 1909. Macmillan was his chief assistant on that trip, but his feet froze and he could not complete the journey. When Peary, by his account, reached the Pole on April 6, 1909, his camp consisted of himself, Matthew Henson, and four Eskimos; the others had been sent back as supplies dwindled.

The museum is divided into three sections. The first covers Peary's early career in the tropics and the Arctic with documents, photographs, navigational instruments, and other artifacts from his expeditions. Stuffed musk oxen, polar bears, seals, and a walrus are exhibited on a platform above the gallery.

Peary's famous trek to the North Pole in 1908 to 1909 is covered in the second section of the museum, with in-depth exhibits depicting the methods and equipment he used. Highlighted artifacts include Macmillan's North Pole log and one of five sledges Peary took to the Pole. The box in which Peary carried his navigational equipment, Macmillan's snowshoes, and their pickaxes, guns, and fur garments are also on display. The fur outerwear was Peary's adaptation of Inuit fur clothing worn in North Greenland.

The recent release of Peary's North Pole journal has again cast controversy around his claim to be the first person to reach the North Pole: His navigational errors and extraordinary speed records, in addition to information on Arctic weather patterns, currents, and ice drifts, raise the possibility that Peary missed his goal by as much as sixty miles. However, Peary's Arctic explorations are deservedly commemorated here.

The third part of the museum focuses on Macmillan, whose career included twenty-seven Arctic expeditions, and on the Arctic in the first half of the twentieth century. Inuit soapstone and ivory carvings, bone and antler tools, embroidered and beaded skin clothing, paintings, a full-size kayak, and an egg and bird collection help describe the area and the time. The cameras Macmillan used to capture the Arctic people and landscape are also on display.

Bowdoin alumni have had a strong tie with exploration: In 1869 a Bowdoin professor crewed his ship with students while sailing the coast of Labrador and Greenland. The museum is housed in Hubbard Hall, named for another Bowdoin alumnus and benefactor of both the college and Peary's Arctic adventures. The designer of the museum, Ian M. White, accompanied Macmillan on a trip to the Arctic in 1950.

LOCATION: Hubbard Hall, Bowdoin College. HOURS: 10–4 Tuesday–Friday, 10–5 Saturday, 2–5 Sunday. FEE: None. TELEPHONE: 207–725–3416.

The **Bowdoin College Museum of Art** (207–725–3275), once housed in various campus buildings—including the Chapel, designed by Richard Upjohn—now occupies the Walker Art Building, an 1894 Beaux Arts edifice designed by Charles Follen McKim of McKim, Mead & White. McKim commissioned artwork for the four murals gracing the impressive rotunda to represent the "Four Cities of Art," Athens, by John LaFarge; Florence, by Abbott Thayer; Rome, by Elihu Vedder; and Venice, by Kenyon Cox.

In 1811 James Bowdoin III, first patron of the college and Thomas Jefferson's foreign minister to France and Spain from 1805 to 1808, bequeathed his collection of old master drawings to the school. Today the collection has been expanded to include the Boyd Gallery of American Federal and Colonial portraits, silver, and furniture; the Sophia Walker Gallery, housing American painting and sculpture by John Sloan, Mary Cassatt, Marsden Hartley, Daniel Chester French, and others; the large Winslow Homer Gallery, with memorabilia, graphics, and paintings; a gallery of European painting, sculpture, and decorative arts; and a collection of Mediterranean objects and Oriental ceramics.

The 1849 **Henry Boody House,** now the dean's residence, is named for the college's first professor of rhetoric and oratory. The house, at 256 Maine Street, is conspicuous for its exuberant Carpenter Gothic exterior.

HARPSWELL

On a peninsula just east of Brunswick is Harpswell, a picturesque sea village. **Orr's and Bailey's islands** are off its shores. The **Harpswell Meeting House,** a simple clapboard structure built in 1757, is the oldest surviving meetinghouse in Maine.

After graduating from Bowdoin College in 1877, Robert E. Peary took a job in Washington with the Coast Survey. He took the opportunity to purchase an island in Casco Bay, off the mainland at Harpswell, that he had explored as a youngster. He renamed the island **Eagle Island,** perhaps in token of the first ship that took him to the Arctic, the *Eagle,* and began to build a summer home in 1904. The family spent much time here until Peary's death in 1920, and in 1966 the island was donated to the State of Maine by Peary's daughter. The small, dramatic, rocky island, crossed by nature trails, is accessible from a public landing pier, and the house (207–725–3416) contains Peary family furnishings, photographs from explorations, and mounted animal specimens.

Janquish and Bailey's islands, Casco Bay.

THE
MAINE COAST

OPPOSITE: *Relics of the shipbuilding era, the 1918* Hesper *and the 1917* Luther Little, *in Wiscasset's harbor.*

The Maine coast has long been known as one of the most beautiful landscapes in America. In 1734 a Massachusetts visitor wrote that "All that Coast appears to be full of commodious Rivers, Bays, Harbours, Coves, and delightful Islands; the most agreeable part of the *Massachusetts Province,* both for Scituation, Fishery, Lumber-Trade, and Culture; and highly worthy of the Publick Care." More than a century earlier, the explorer Samuel de Champlain called the mouth of the Penobscot River "marvelous to behold," with its "numerous islands, rocks, shoals, banks, and breakers on all sides." Marvelous it was, but dangerous as well: Champlain had several mishaps on this coastline.

The first attempt to put down a permanent European colony in the New World took place in far northern Maine—one of the least hospitable places for such an endeavor. The French established a colony on the St. Croix River in 1604, but the pioneers had to give up after just a year. In the international tangle of royal land grants, the territory from Pemaquid to the St. Croix River was part of the colony of New York, granted to the Duke of York in 1664. However, a 1667 treaty ceded the land between the Penobscot and the St. Croix to France. It was soon occupied by the colorful Baron Castin, who lived as a local potentate among the Indians, marrying an Indian woman and carrying on a profitable trade in furs. Castin led Indian raids against the English during King Philip's War but was burned out of his house by an English attack in 1688. The land between the Penobscot and the St. Croix became England's after the French and Indian War.

During the Revolution, the coast of Maine was the site of the war's first naval battle—a small affray in which the people of Machias seized an English boat, the *Margaretta*—and an American naval disaster on a much larger scale. A fleet of forty-four Massachusetts ships attempted to take Fort George at Castine, and all of them were destroyed. One of the participants in the debacle was Paul Revere. In the finger-pointing that followed, Revere was accused of insubordination, unsoldierly conduct, and cowardice, but he was acquitted in a court martial. During the War of 1812 the British captured Castine, rebuilt Fort George, and made it their coastal strongpoint—they controlled the coast from Penobscot to the east throughout the war.

The spectacular scenery along the coast is actually a drowned mountain range, the creation of an ice age 13,000 to 15,000 years ago, when the ocean level was 300 to 500 feet lower. An ice sheet

TRAVERSE SAILING,
EXAMPLE I,

A Ship from the Island of Teguean and bound to Nantu with a head wind sails the following Courses Viz, S.E. 50 miles W.b.S. 30 miles S.E.b.E. 60 miles — Demand her Latt Come In too and Longitude In. with the Bering and distance of Nantuckit Lite house

Detail from an 1805 navigation book, hand-written and illustrated by Captain Francis Rittal of Dresden, Maine.

scraped across a bed of volcanic granite, carving and gouging ridges and U-shaped valleys and depositing large "erratic" boulders. As the ice melted, the earth—freed of the great weight of ice—rose, as did the level of the ocean. The granite valleys were flooded, but the peaks remained above water. Somes Sound, 168 feet deep, is the only fjord on the east coast. In the nineteenth century, the beauty of this area attracted some of the country's foremost landscape painters as well as thousands of wealthy summer visitors, who flocked to the fashionable resort at Bar Harbor. Acadia National Park preserves the rugged landscape of Mount Desert Island, which was visited and named by Champlain.

This chapter begins at Bath and makes its way up the coast to Calais on the St. Croix River.

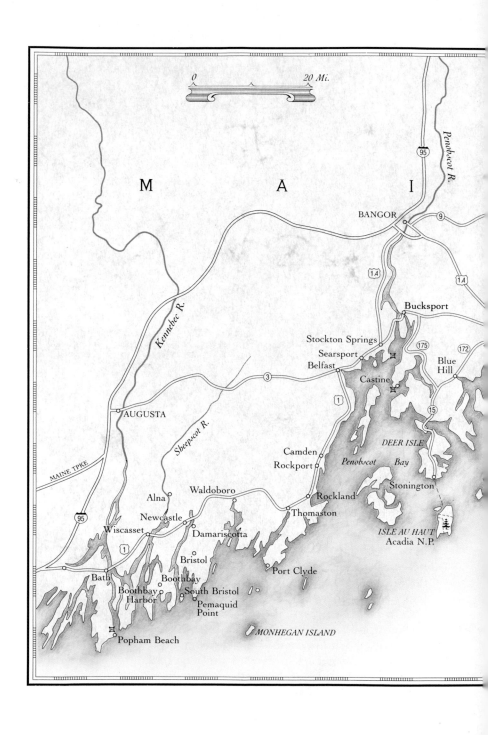

0   20 Mi.

M   A   I

Penobscot R.

95

BANGOR

9

1A

1A

Kennebec R.

Bucksport

Stockton Springs

175

172

Searsport

Belfast

Blue Hill

3

Castine

1

15

AUGUSTA

Sheepscot R.

DEER ISLE

Camden

Penobscot Bay

Rockport

MAINE TPKE

Stonington

Waldoboro

Rockland

95

Alna

Newcastle

Thomaston

ISLE AU HAUT

Wiscasset

Acadia N.P.

Damariscotta

1

Bristol

Port Clyde

Bath

Boothbay

Boothbay Harbor

South Bristol

Pemaquid Point

Popham Beach

MONHEGAN ISLAND

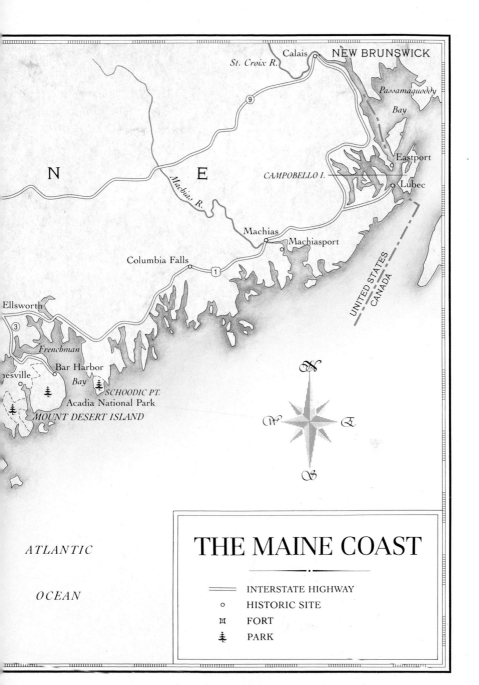

St. Croix R.

Calais

NEW BRUNSWICK

Passamaquoddy

Bay

9

N   E

Machias R.

Eastport

CAMPOBELLO I.

Lubec

Machias

Machiasport

Columbia Falls

1

UNITED STATES
CANADA

Ellsworth

3

Frenchman

Bar Harbor

Bay

SCHOODIC PT.

Acadia National Park

MOUNT DESERT ISLAND

esville

ATLANTIC

OCEAN

N

W   E

S

THE MAINE COAST

===== INTERSTATE HIGHWAY

o HISTORIC SITE

⊞ FORT

🌲 PARK

MID-COAST: BATH TO CAMDEN

The road from Bath to Camden passes historic ports and islands, shipbuilding centers, towns built up around sawmills and gristmills, and fishing villages. The path is anything but direct, winding through gently rolling hills and skirting seaside cliffs. Some agriculture is evident, from roadside stands selling squash and corn to blueberries raked up in nearby fields.

BATH

Shipbuilding began early in the Bath area when English settlers christened the thirty-ton *Virginia* near here in 1607. Along the banks of the Kennebec River, Bath became a center for masting, shipbuilding, and trade, accompanying the progress of many Maine coastal towns. Various factors, however, lent the town the strength to survive the Embargo of 1807 and the War of 1812. Bath withstood the impact of the Embargo by building a healthy trade relationship with New Orleans and the east coast of America. Industrial diversification increased Bath's resources as iron founding grew in the early 1800s, and the combination of iron and ships gave the town a very prosperous nineteenth century. Italianate, Greek, and Gothic Revival architectures testify to Bath's heyday, especially in the North End, where prosperous shipbuilders made their homes and the commercial district thrived.

Maine Maritime Museum

In 1762, Bath's first commercial shipyard opened. After the Civil War, trade with foreign countries dropped off and, with it, the building of ocean-crossing vessels. Coastal trading demanded a different type of transport, and two Bath shipwrights, Samuel R. Percy and Frank A. Small, knew how to build fine, wooden schooners, perfect for the new trade routes. From 1896 to the 1920s the Percy and Small Shipyard produced over forty schooners and gained a reputation for building some of the largest and finest wooden ships on the coast.

Today, the history and craftsmanship of Maine shipping and shipbuilding are explored and re-created at the **Museum Shipyard,** on the site of the Percy and Small Shipyard. The *Wyoming*,

OPPOSITE: *A replica of an 1830s double masted pinky schooner, the* Maine *was launched by Bath's Maine Maritime Museum Shipyard in 1985.*

the largest wooden sailing vessel in America, was built here in 1909. The tradition of fine boatbuilding craftsmanship continues through the museum's apprenticeship program, and visitors can view the apprentices at work on small boats, both specially commissioned and for sale through the museum. Other exhibits at the shipyard include models of classic boats, tools and instruments, dioramas, trade goods, and seamen's possessions. Restored shipyard buildings such as an 1897 paint and trenail shop, an 1899 mill and joiner shop, and a 1905 pitch oven portray the shipbuilding industry, while lobstering and cod fishing are explored at a replica lobster cannery and on board the schooner *Sherman Zwicker* when she is in port.

The museum also operates the 1844 Georgian Revival **Sewall House,** named for the prominent shipping family that bought it in 1898. On view here is a trove of maritime art, scrimshaw, ship models and half models, navigational instruments, and sailors' mementoes, as well as displays on shipbuilding, seafaring families, and famous vessels of the Bath Iron Works.

LOCATION: *Percy and Small Shipyard,* 263 Washington Street; *Sewall House,* 963 Washington Street. HOURS: *Shipyard and House:* Mid-May through mid-October: 10–5 Daily; *House (off season):* 10–3 Monday–Saturday, 1–4 Sunday. FEE: Yes. TELEPHONE: 207–443–1316.

Looming over Route 1, the **Bath Iron Works** (207–443–3311) grew out of an 1826 foundry and remains active in shipbuilding. It is open to the public for launching and commissioning ceremonies.

The 1843 **Winter Street Church** (Washington at Winter Street), merging Gothic and Greek Revival styles, dominates the town green. Its striking design was the work of local builder Anthony C. Raymond. The soaring central steeple and solid temple facade effectively unite the two styles of architecture, presenting one of the finest examples of American Gothic in New England.

The unusual church at 804 Washington Street is the Gothic Revival **Chocolate Church,** named for its brown color. Built in 1846, it has recently been rededicated as an arts center, with performance space and an art gallery.

The **Old Bath Custom House and Post Office** (1 Front Street, 207–443–4282) was designed by Ammi Burnham Young in 1858 while he was supervising architect of the Treasury Department. In the lobby is a model of the Bath waterfront as it appeared in the 1800s. The stone Italianate building stands on the site of the estate of William King, a Bath shipbuilder who became first governor of

Maine. King also owned an **1809 stone cottage,** one of the earliest Gothic Revival structures in America. On Whiskeag Road, it is now privately owned.

POPHAM

South from Bath, Route 209 winds through grassy marshland to the sea. The terminus of the road is **Popham Beach,** named for Sir George Popham, who in 1607 led a band of his fellow Englishmen to this protected harbor. Popham did not survive his first winter in Maine, and his colony disbanded within a year—though not before they had launched the *Virginia,* the first European ship built in the colonies and the vessel that inaugurated Bath's fame.

In 1775, Benedict Arnold set off from Popham on his daring but ill-fated march against the British in Quebec. His expedition, which had a good chance of conquering Canada, came to grief when a message from Arnold to another American officer fell into British hands, spoiling Arnold's element of surprise. Markers chart the 194-mile **Arnold Trail** to Coburn Gore on the Canadian border. From Popham the trail passes through Hallowell, Skowhegan, Solon, Moscow, Stratton, and Sarampus.

Fort Popham, named for the nearby 1607 English settlement, was built to fortify the mouth of the Kennebec River against Con-

Built in 1861, the granite-walled Fort Popham stands on a strategic site—where the Kennebec River meets the sea—first fortified during the American Revolution.

federate and pro-Confederate European intervention at the beginning of the Civil War. The semicircular granite structure faces the river with thirty-foot walls, broken by two stories of vaulted casemates built to contain thirty-six cannon.

WISCASSET

North from Bath, Route 1 leads straight through picturesque Wiscasset. First settled as a section of the larger town of Pownalborough in the early 1700s, Wiscasset was abandoned during the Indian wars of that time, and resettled around 1730. By 1795 Wiscasset was a town of wealth and prosperity. Its riches came from the post–Revolutionary War lumbering and shipping that aided many of Maine's coastal towns. Along with these towns, Wiscasset was badly hurt by the 1807 Embargo Act and the War of 1812. But during the years of lucrative commerce the citizens of Wiscasset built many large homes and mansions reflecting the wealth and prestige of shipping merchants and lumber barons. Many of these are to be found within Wiscasset's **historic district,** encompassing the village and waterfront.

The 1807 Old Academy Building, Wiscasset, above the Sheepscot River.

Nickels-Sortwell House

One of New England's finest Federal houses, this grand three-story house was built in 1807 by Captain William Nickels, a shipmaster and local politician who made his fortune in lumber and shipping. Two-story pilasters frame the porticoed entry and its elliptical fanlight. The interior is notable for the curved three-floor stairway, lit from a skylight, and handsomely carved woodwork throughout.

After Nickels' death in 1815 the house became Wiscasset's best inn, variously known as Turner's Tavern, Mansion House, Belle Haven, and Wiscasset House. It fell into disrepair and was bought in 1900 by Alvin F. Sortwell, then mayor of Cambridge, Massachusetts, and made into his summer home. The Sortwells restored the house and refurnished it to reflect its Federal origins. The house now belongs to the Society for the Preservation of New England Antiquities, which maintains the property as a museum.

LOCATION: Main and Federal streets. HOURS: June through September: 12–5 Wednesday–Sunday. FEE: Yes. TELEPHONE: 617–227–3956.

Down Federal Street from the Nickels-Sortwell House is the unusual octagonal **Captain George Scott House** (private), built in 1855 by the nineteenth-century shipmaster to plans of Orson Squire Fowler, a phrenologist and proponent of octagonal dwellings. The brick house is in the gracious Italianate style with sandstone and granite window sills and lintels.

The 1807 **Red Brick Schoolhouse** (Warren Street) is also part of Wiscasset's historic district. Used as a school until 1923, it has since functioned in various capacities. The one-time **Customs House and Post Office** (Water Street), now a private residence, has retained its 1870 brick-and-granite Italianate exterior. The **Lincoln County Museum and Old Jail** (207–882–6817) on Federal Street features exhibits on local history that highlight textiles and samplers, photographs of the area, scrimshaw, and Indian artifacts. Two structures make up this site. The jail was built between 1809 and 1811 to accommodate the rowdy seamen and woodsmen attracted to the boom port town. Its walls are built of granite up to forty-one inches thick. The brick jailer's house (1839) was built to replace a previous wooden one that burned down. The kitchen has been restored to its 1840s appearance, and antique farming and carpentering tools are on display in the tool shed. The jail was in use until 1953.

Probably designed to recall a Scottish castle, the Lee-Tucker House is celebrated for its mid-nineteenth-century sea captain's furnishings and freestanding spiral staircase.

Overlooking Wiscasset Harbor, the **Lee-Tucker House,** locally known as **Castle Tucker** (Lee and High streets, 207–882–7364), was built by Judge Silas Lee in 1807. Heavily mortgaged to three neighbors, the house had a variety of occupants until 1858 when it passed to Captain Richard H. Tucker, Jr., third generation of Wiscasset ship captains and owners. He added the portico in 1860 and purchased most of the furnishings now on view. It is still in the possession of his descendants.

Slowly deteriorating in the river harbor are the hulls of two schooners. Side by side, the 1918 *Hesper* and the 1917 *Luther Little* are believed to be the last four-masted schooners built in New England.

FORT EDGECOMB

Just east of Wiscasset, across the Sheepscot River on the tip of Davis Island, is Fort Edgecomb. In the early nineteenth century, Wiscasset's prosperity lay in shipping to and from England and France.

As hostilities between these two countries escalated and England threatened to impound U.S. ships entering French ports, Congress passed the Embargo Act of 1807, which closed all American ports. Built in 1808, Fort Edgecomb was one of many defenses authorized by Congress in response to feared English reprisals. When news of war reached Fort Edgecomb in 1812, the U.S. colors were raised and guns fired, but never in battle. One soldier stationed at Fort Edgecomb in 1814 noted in his diary, "The enemy . . . it is reported are coming with an intent to destroy this fort and Wiscasset," and the British ship *Bulwark* spent that summer harassing the Maine coast. With news of peace in 1815, the guns fired again. The fort was quickly garrisoned in 1864 when the Confederate ship *Tallahassee* sailed into northern waters, but once again, no action was needed.

Today the two-story octagonal blockhouse of massive timber and the semicircular earthworks remain within the stockade, which was reconstructed in 1961. Two stone bastions along the river are connected by a curved stone wall. Harbor seals are often seen here in the Sheepscot River.

LOCATION: Davis Island. HOURS: Memorial Day through Labor Day: 9–sunset. FEE: Yes. TELEPHONE: 207–882–7777.

BOOTHBAY

English settlements sprang up in and around this harbor after Captain John Smith sailed up from Jamestown in 1614 and pronounced it an "ideal" fishing station. The town grew first as a seaport, then as a shipbuilding center. Fishing and shipbuilding are still active in Boothbay, and since the nineteenth century it has been a popular resort.

In 1937 a theater was started to entertain the summer residents, an offshoot of which became the country's first museum exclusively devoted to theater, established in 1957. The **Boothbay Theatre Museum** (Corey Lane, 207–633–4536) occupies the 1784 Federal house of Nicholas Knight, one of the town's first settlers. The museum collections date from the eighteenth century to the present, encompassing American theater scale models, portraits, photographs, playbills, set models, costumes, stage jewelry, and holograph material. South of the village proper is **Boothbay Harbor,** known for its lighthouse, the 1822 **Burnt Island Light Station.**

Though the English are credited with its discovery in the late fifteenth century, Monhegan Island was probably visited by Vikings 500 years earlier.

MONHEGAN ISLAND

Situated to the northeast of Boothbay Harbor in the Atlantic Ocean, this island was recorded by John Cabot in 1498. In 1614 Captain John Smith landed here, and his favorable accounts probably hastened settlement, which came in 1625. Abundant fishing has maintained a permanent community here since 1674.

In 1822 Congress appropriated $3,000 to build the **Monhegan lighthouse and keeper's quarters.** First illuminated on July 2, 1824, the light was supervised by a keeper until it was automated in 1959. The lighthouse and its outbuildings are now part of a museum with exhibits on the historical, natural, and economic features of the island. Monhegan Island may be reached from the mainland by ferry from Boothbay Harbor and Port Clyde.

BRISTOL

A center of archaeological activity, Bristol is the location of the **Nahanda Village Site,** a prehistoric coastal Indian encampment. It is believed that the camp was occupied as much as 2,000 years ago, although the majority of the material uncovered dates to ca. 1600. It is probable that this is the Indian village visited by members of the Popham colony in 1607, at which time they recorded the name of the area as Pemaquid. At **Colonial Pemaquid** (Route 130, 207–677–2423), the site of an early-seventeenth-century English settlement, archaeologists have excavated household items, farming implements, stone foundations, and walls.

The settlement is part of a state historic site along with **Fort William Henry,** also on Pemaquid Point. The foundations of the original fort, built by English settlers in 1692 to ward off Indians, pirates, and their French rivals, are here along with a modern replica of the circular, crenelated fort, resembling the stout tower of a medieval castle. Historical artifacts are also on display.

The **Pemaquid Lighthouse** was erected in 1827; its tower was rebuilt eight years later. In 1857 the original stone **keeper's house** was replaced by the present wooden structure, now occupied by the **Fishermen's Museum** (207–677–2494). Maine's 400-year-old fishing industry is illuminated by old charts, photographs, ship models, harpoons, anchors, and nets.

Representative of the eighteenth century is the **Harrington Meeting House** (Old Harrington Road, 207–529–5578). It has

American artist Edward Hopper painted this view of the Pemaquid Lighthouse in the 1920s (detail).

been restored to its 1772 condition, complete with original box pews. That same year, the citizens of Bristol built the **Walpole meeting house** (Route 129) for its sister settlement, **South Bristol.** First a Presbyterian, then a Congregational, church, it reflects superior colonial workmanship inside and out: Even the hand-shaved roof shingles are intact (and still watertight). The pulpit and box pews are original, handcrafted by Bristol cabinetmakers.

Slightly farther out Route 129 is the **Thompson Ice House,** facing a South Bristol pond where ice was harvested for over 150 years, from 1826 to 1986. Ice from this spot was shipped as far as South America. Nine inches of sawdust insulate the double walls. Modern refrigeration has all but ended this Maine industry, which once supplied the nation with 3 million tons of ice each year. The structure is undergoing restoration (1988) and will reopen as a museum.

DAMARISCOTTA

Farther up the Bristol peninsula is Damariscotta, settled on the eastern shore of the Damariscotta River in 1625. Its location at the head of navigable waters encouraged shipbuilding, which brought prosperity to the town in the nineteenth century. A fire in 1845 destroyed most of the town's early buildings, but their replacements, built during the shipbuilding boom, remain intact as the **Main Street Historic District.** Also on Main Street is the one-and-a-half-story **Chapman-Hall House,** built in 1754 by Nathaniel Chapman. Constructed of wood, with a cedar-shingle rooftop and small-paned windows, the house has a central entrance and a central brick chimney. The interior consists of pine panelling and wide-board spruce and pine floors. The house, Damariscotta's oldest surviving building, is open to the public; exhibits include photographs of ships built on Damariscotta River during the period 1754–1820 and small models of ships.

Also in the historic district is the 1802 Federal style **Matthew Cottrill House** (private). Cottrill, an Irish immigrant, became one of Damariscotta's premier merchants. The architect, Nicholas Codd, an Irishman himself, also designed the oldest Catholic church in New England, **St. Patrick's,** on Academy Road in nearby **Newcastle.** Irish immigrants founded the parish in 1796. The steeple houses a Paul Revere bell cast in 1818, the year he died.

WALDOBORO

A German settlement dating from 1748, Waldoboro lies just inland on the Medomak River, protected from the sea while having immediate access to it. Shipbuilding was a major industry here, and five-masted schooners sailed out of local shipyards. Waldoboro's early German heritage resonates in the **Old German Church** (Route 32, off Route 1), built on the Medomak River in 1772. For many years its services were conducted in German.

The **Waldoborough Historical Society Museum** (Route 220, near Route 1) administers a complex of three buildings, including the **Town Pound,** a rough stone corral put up to contain wandering livestock. Such pounds were common throughout Maine in the early nineteenth century; this one, an 1819 renovation of a 1785 original, is a well-preserved example. The museum also maintains a restored country school, farm kitchen, and a collection of shipping memorabilia, tools, documents, and photographs.

THOMASTON

East of Waldoboro the coastal lands open up, rolling gently to the sea. Thomaston, a trading post in 1630, withstood Indian attacks to grow into a town with a lively economy based on shipping, lime

After serving as George Washington's first secretary of war, Henry Knox retired to Thomaston and built Montpelier.

Montpelier's eighteen rooms are furnished with the Knox family's belongings, including a ca. 1785 mirror-fronted bookcase and ca. 1795 Windsor chairs, made in Philadelphia.

processing, and cask making. The town got a champion with the arrival of Major General Henry Knox, honored veteran of Bunker Hill and the nation's first secretary of war.

A replica of Knox's elegant home, **Montpelier** (Route 131, 207–354–8062), is one of Thomaston's best-visited sites. The making of the Federal house was apparently a 1793 collaboration between famed Boston architect Charles Bulfinch and Knox, who specified such details as an oval parlor, flying staircase, and clerestory windows. The original house, completed in 1795, was badly neglected after it was abandoned by Knox descendants in the 1850s, and it was finally razed later that century. The reproduction, exact in countless details, contains many Knox family treasures, including Colonial and Federal furniture.

The houses in Thomaston's **historic district** date from the nineteenth century, when the town was a bustling port. Fine examples of the Federal, Greek Revival, Gothic Revival, Italianate, and Second Empire styles, built by prosperous seafaring families, line the quiet streets of the district.

ROCKLAND

Once part of Thomaston, Rockland was incorporated as its own town in 1854. Marine enterprise naturally figured here long before then—early-eighteenth-century English settlers recorded its local Indian name as "Great Landing Place." Through the 1800s, the town grew with shipbuilding and limestone quarrying; the twentieth century brought the resort business, which, unlike its predecessors, continues to thrive.

Farnsworth Homestead

One of Maine's great houses, this Greek Revival townhouse was built in 1854 by Rockland's most prominent businessman, William A. Farnsworth. It was inherited by his surviving child, the reclusive and eccentric Lucy Farnsworth, who lived to be 96. Although Miss Farnsworth neglected the house, she left behind directions for the family estate and the means to finance them. The result is a fine house, museum, and library complex. The museum's permanent collection is especially strong in American art and the decorative arts of the eighteenth and nineteenth centuries, in addition to holdings of European and Oriental art objects.

LOCATION: 19 Elm Street. HOURS: October through May: 10–5 Tuesday–Saturday, 1–5 Sunday. June through September: 10–5 Monday–Saturday, 1–5 Sunday. FEE: Yes. TELEPHONE: 207–596–6457.

The Farnsworth Homestead kitchen, equipped with a slate sink.

ROCKPORT

Once part of a single municipality with Camden, Rockport has been a separate town since 1891, linked by Route 1. The smaller of the two is Rockport, a longtime exporter of canned sardines, pickled herring, and frozen blueberries. The town also became known for sailmaking and the manufacture of lime used in mortar and plaster. The **Rockport Lime Kilns** produced 2 million casks of the powder in the 1880s and 1890s, when Maine led the country in lime production. A few of the old fieldstone-and-brick kilns still stand on the **Rockport Waterfront.** As the larger coastal towns took over lime production, Rockport turned to the development of its harbor, which remains a favorite among yachtsmen.

CAMDEN

To some, Camden marks the beginning of Maine's mountainous landscape—the local saying is that the town rests "where the mountains meet the sea." To Captain John Smith in 1614, it was the place "under the high mountains . . . against whose feet the sea doth beat." Camden was one of Maine's earliest resorts, attracting seasonal residents as early as the 1830s. By the turn of the century the town was a favorite among the very rich who wanted nothing simple when it came to summer "cottages." One of the grandest of Maine's late-nineteenth-century houses is **Norumbega** (61 High Street, private), built by rags-to-riches millionaire Joseph P. Stearns. His baronial villa and Queen Anne style carriage house are fine examples of the resort lifestyle. The gable-roofed 1904 **American Boathouse** (Atlantic Avenue, 207–236–8500) is another reminder of the country's Gilded Age, when wealthy and often eccentric sportsmen built elaborate shelters for their yachts. In 1926 a prominent seasonal resident, Cyrus H. K. Curtis, publisher of the *Saturday Evening Post,* gave the town the property on which the **Camden Yacht Club** is situated (Bay View Street, 207–236–3014).

The **Conway House** (Conway Road, 207–236–2257) affords a glimpse into Camden's more distant past. The ca. 1770 frame farmhouse still has its brick oven and original hand-hewn woodwork. The house is part of a complex, also including a barn, blacksmith shop, and a museum.

OPPOSITE: *Among Camden's opulent private houses is Norumbega, named for Maine's mythical land of riches.* OVERLEAF: *Seen from Mount Battie, white houses and white boats dot the town of Camden and Penobscot Bay.*

THE NORTHERN COAST

The landscape varies in the northern stretch of the Maine coast, from the green farmlands around Belfast to the rocky promontories of Lubec and Eastport to the flat river harbor of Calais. Historians have suggested that these are the coastlands first explored by the Vikings. Certainly they were known to such later adventurers as Samuel de Champlain, John Cabot, and Captain John Smith. East of the resort islands of Deer Isle and Mount Desert, the Maine landscape opens up—it is a rougher, scrubbier land than that which lies to the south. The ocean, too, seems more powerful this far out; the tides here are among the highest in the world.

BELFAST

Named by the Scotch-Irish who landed here in 1770, Belfast is sited on Penobscot Bay. Scattered during the Revolution, the Belfast settlers regrouped and were thriving by the end of the 1780s. Fishing was their mainstay, as well as agricultural enterprises; Belfast is still a major poultry producer. Tied to Bangor by waterways and later by the railroads, Belfast was an important market and port for inland potato growers and lumbermen throughout the nineteenth century. Its prime location on the bay and the Passagassawakeag River encouraged shipping and shipbuilding.

Many buildings survived from this prosperous period in Belfast's **Commercial Historic District** (Main Street). Chief among these are the elaborate 1879 **Belfast National Bank** and the 1878 Gothic **Masonic Temple** by George M. Harding; the 1856 **Post Office and Custom House** (120 Main Street) by architect Ammi B. Young; and the **Waldo County Courthouse** (73 Church Street) by Benjamin S. Dean.

The Federal-style **First Church in Belfast** (6 Court Street, 207–338–2282), built in 1818, is part of the **Church Street Historic District.** The homes of this residential area reflect the affluence of this port city during the 1800s. A fine example is the 1842 **James Petterson White House** (1 Church Street, private). The architect Calvin A. Ryder modified the temple form of the Greek Revival style to create a sophisticated mansion for one of Belfast's leading citizens. In the early 1800s most of the town's wealthy businessmen built their homes on **Primrose Hill,** where Church and High streets come together; from here they could overlook the prosperity they promoted. This grouping of residences is now a historic district. The **Belfast Museum** (66 Church Street) contains items of local history, including ship paintings, antique tools and a ca. 1850 drugstore counter.

SEARSPORT

A few miles up the coast from Belfast is Searsport, settled in the 1760s by soldiers from nearby Fort Pownal. The town took hold quickly, with shipbuilding an established industry by the early 1790s. Set on a rolling green landscape, Searsport seems less bucolic than a serious seaport town, with its heavy granite buildings expressing the confidence that they could match whatever the stormy seas might toss ashore.

Penobscot Marine Museum

Seven nineteenth-century structures form this reminder of Searsport's heritage in the heyday of Maine shipping. Some 250 sailing vessels and 286 sea captains came from this community. The museum complex includes the **Searsport Town Hall** and four sea captain's homes. Three other buildings display navigational and shipbuilding tools, whaling and fishing artifacts, and treasures from the Orient.

LOCATION: Church Street. HOURS: May through October: 9:30–5 Daily. FEE: Yes. TELEPHONE: 207–548–2529.

FORT KNOX

Named for Thomaston's Henry Knox, this fortification was meant to protect the vulnerable and vital Penobscot River Valley during the Maine–New Brunswick boundary disputes with Britain in the 1840s. The enormous structure, measuring 350 by 250 feet, with walls 40 feet thick, took twenty years to complete. Union soldiers trained here during the Civil War. The first of Maine's granite forts, the massive complex was strategically situated on the west bank of the Penobscot, the gateway to Bangor. Original equipment includes ten-inch and fifteen-inch Rodman cannons, and two hot-shot furnaces. The soldiers' quarters, batteries, parade ground, bakery, powder magazines, and storerooms may be toured.

LOCATION: Route 174, Prospect. HOURS: May through October: 9 AM–Dusk Daily. FEE: Yes. TELEPHONE: 207–469–7719.

This nineteenth-century view of Owl's Head, a resort village south of Rockport in

CASTINE

Facing Belfast across the Penobscot Bay, Castine is named for the
Baron Castin, who arrived from Quebec in the 1670s to take over
the trading post for France. He did so handily, winning it from the
English, whose first claim on the spot came in 1629, and the Dutch,
who briefly occupied it in the 1670s. Castin's life, as it has been
recounted over the years, was one legendary adventure after another. An impoverished nobleman, he arrived in New France,
determined to claim a royal land grant made to his family. He
befriended the Abenaki Indians, canoeing from Quebec to the
mouth of the Penobscot. Along the way the teenage baron took on
the Abenaki ways and eventually married into the tribe. Castin held
his claim for about twenty years until English colonists won it back
while the Frenchman was off on a fishing trip with his Indian
family and friends.

The British again took over the town of Castine in 1779,
building **Fort George** (Wadsworth Cove Road) to keep their hold
on the strategic Penobscot Bay. Revolutionaries sailed up from
Boston that year, two thousand strong in a fleet of forty-four ships.

Penobscot Bay, was painted by American artist Fitz Hugh Lane.

A delay in action allowed time for British reinforcements to arrive. None of the American vessels survived—they were either sunk, abandoned, or taken over by the better-prepared British in one of the worst defeats in American naval history. One of the shipwrecks, the *Defense,* is the subject of ongoing archaeological study, and the well-preserved earthwork foundations of Fort George may be toured. Castine is one of the prettiest of Maine's coastal towns, preserving many nineteenth-century buildings along Main and Perkins streets. By the docks on Water Street, at the foot of Main, are several late-eighteenth-century brick commercial buildings. At the end of Battle Street, **Dyces Head Lighthouse,** built in 1828, overlooks the Penobscot River.

The Wilson Museum

This complex on Perkins Street includes the one pre-Revolutionary War house to survive in the Castine area, the ca. 1763 **John Perkins House.** Framed by hand-hewn timbers and constructed with hand-forged nails, the house was occupied by the British during the Revolution and again during the War of 1812. It is now restored

Perkins House, now part of the Wilson Museum complex on Castine's harbor. The town's earliest house, it was designed with a Tuscan front doorway.

and furnished with late-eighteenth-century items. The museum, which is administered by the Castine Scientific Society, also includes permanent exhibitions of prehistoric artifacts from North and South America, Europe, and Africa. Displays follow the growth of the human ability to fashion and use tools. Ship models, farm and home equipment, Victorian-era memorabilia, and local historic items are also on display. Special emphasis is given to the North American Indian tribes native to northern New England. Also on the grounds is a working blacksmith shop.

LOCATION: Perkins Street. HOURS: Memorial Day through September: 2–5 Tuesday–Sunday. FEE: For Perkins House.

SEDGWICK–BROOKLIN

Sedgwick is named for Major Robert Sedgwick, who routed the French from Penobscot Bay in 1654. More than a century later the town was incorporated and grew with fishing and farming. A 1790 boat launching inaugurated shipbuilding. The town's cemetery dates from 1794; the First Baptist Church was built in 1823. Brooklin was chartered in 1859 on land that originally was part of Sedgwick. The Sedgwick-Brooklin Historical Society occupies the 1795 **Reverend Daniel Merrill House** (Route 172, 207–359–8930). The house contains various artifacts from the area's early settlement years, and horse-drawn hearses are on display. Recently moved to the grounds is an 1874 one-room schoolhouse.

At the end of the peninsula, at **Naskeag Point,** a granite marker commemorates a 1778 British raid, apparently provoked by a Patriot who fired upon a passing ship, killing a sailor.

DEER ISLE

Granite quarrying and sardine canning were the founding businesses of Deer Isle, which attracted a resort trade in the late nineteenth century. The high seas lap up to these jagged shores, and legend has it that Deer Isle drew more than its share of smugglers, pirates, and slave runners. Worn memorial stones in the island's cemeteries honor sea captains and sailors lost off the coasts of Africa, China, and Greenland.

One of Deer Isle's earliest houses is the 1775 **Reverend Peter Powers House** (Sunshine Road, private), a gift from the First Congregational Church to its new minister. The islanders found a staunch defender of American independence in Powers, who had been hounded out of New Hampshire by his Tory congregation.

The **Deer Isle–Stonington Historical Society** maintains the 1830 **Salome Sellers House,** which has been restored and furnished with original and period items. Antique farm, quarry, and carpenter's tools are on display in the toolroom. An exhibit building contains displays of ship models, compasses, telescopes, and other local and maritime items.

BLUE HILL

A group from Andover, Massachusetts, settled the undulating western shore of Blue Hill Bay in 1762 and went to work as lumbermen and fishermen. In the nineteenth century, shipbuilding and overseas trade brought some wealth to the town, and the discovery of copper in 1876 ushered in a mining boom. Starting about the same time, granite quarries were opened. Many eighteenth- and nineteenth-century houses, as well as public and commercial buildings, overlook the harbor, forming a historic district that includes the **Holt House** (Water Street), a restored Federal residence. Administered by the Blue Hill Historical Society, it is noteworthy for local memorabilia and its stenciled wall decorations. The carriage house holds examples of early local industries.

Blue Hill's first minister was Jonathan Fisher, who came here in 1796. Fisher was a linguist, printer, inventor, gifted artisan, and painter who built and furnished his 1815 house largely by himself. His house is now open as the **Jonathan Fisher Memorial** (Main Street, 207–374–2757).

ELLSWORTH

Since its founding in 1763, Ellsworth has made the most of the sixty-foot Union River Falls. Sawmills and shipbuilding flourished here. With its spire and colonnade, the **Ellsworth Congregational Church** (Cross Street) has been the focal point of the town since 1846, when the edifice went up on a hill above the Union River. Equally impressive are the pair of **Old Hancock County Buildings,** stout Greek Revival landmarks on Cross Street. Probably the most famous site in Ellsworth is the **Colonel Black Mansion** (West Main Street, 207–667–8671), built by John Black, who came from England at the age of 13 to be the clerk of the great Bingham Estate in

The Black Mansion introduced Georgian formality to the mill town of Ellsworth. OPPOSITE: *Portraits hang over the mansion's beautifully wrought staircase.*

Maine. He became agent in 1810 and later general agent, a position he held until his son was appointed in his place in 1850. Black spared no expense on his stately home, importing its distinctive red bricks from Philadelphia—the 1826 residence could be a Georgian townhouse on Rittenhouse Square. The rooms of period furniture, porcelain, and glass; the carriage house; and the gardens are open.

The Ellsworth **Public Library** occupies the 1817 **Seth Tisdale House,** named for its owner, celebrated locally for his service in the Revolutionary War. The Ellsworth Historical Society on State Street is headquartered in the brick-and-granite **Old Jail,** built as the county jail and sheriff's residence in 1886. The **Stanwood Wildlife Sanctuary** (Route 3, 207–667–8460) includes a Cape Cod–style house built in 1850 by Ellsworth sea captain Roswell Stanwood. It passed to his daughter, Cordelia, an ornithologist and photographer. A bird sanctuary was later established on the grounds. The homestead and sanctuary are open year-round.

MOUNT DESERT ISLAND

Maine has been called the land of a thousands islands, a claim upheld by Mt. Desert's abundance of satellites, many of them with charming names: Burnt Porcupine, Egg Rock, Ironbound, Turtle, Rum Key, Cranberry, Little Duck. Geological forces have formed Mt. Desert itself into perhaps the single most dramatic natural setting in the state, with its hills—one of them a 1500-foot "mountain"—craggy seaside cliffs, lakes, and heavily forested interior. The island, it seems, has always been known for its terrain: the Abenaki Indians who came over from the mainland to fish and gather shellfish on the island called it Pemetic, "the sloping land." When Samuel de Champlain landed here in 1604, he looked to the rugged mountaintops and named it "L'isle des monts deserts," the "Isle of bare mountains."

The first open clash between the French and the English over territory in the New World took place here in 1613, when the English explorer Samuel Argall burned a Jesuit mission and took the survivors captive, selling some into slavery and casting the rest adrift on the open sea. Disputes over the island continued until the English finally gained control of it in 1760, in the French and Indian War. After the Revolution, the settlers prospered on logging, fishing, farming, and shipbuilding.

The transformation of Mount Desert Island from an island of small towns to a popular resort began in the 1850s, with the advent of regular steamboat runs from the mainland. The painter Thomas Cole, founder of the Hudson River School, was one of the first to discover the spectacular scenery on the island; he came here to paint in the summer, and other artists and writers soon joined him. As word of this relatively unspoiled area spread, it became a popular place for wealthy families to escape the discomforts of summer in the city. By the end of the nineteenth century, many of the richest families in the country—the Astors, the Vanderbilts, the Rockefellers—had built summer homes on the island. Referred to somewhat disingenuously as "cottages," many of these houses were more on the order of mansions.

Efforts to preserve the natural beauty of the island began in the early 1900s, when a group of summer residents, led by Boston millionaire George Dorr, began acquiring land. By 1913, they had accumulated about 6,000 acres, which they donated to the federal government. In 1919, this land was made a national park, which has continued to grow as a result of additional donations. Known today as **Acadia National Park,** it now covers some 38,000 acres, encompassing a large area of Mount Desert Island, portions of several smaller islands, and part of Schoodic Peninsula.

The first permanent settlement on Mt. Desert was **Somesville,** a nine-family hamlet established in 1759 by the Massachusetts governor. Somesville's white-painted Victorian houses range in style from the simple to the exuberant, meshing with the scenery as if they had grown from the ground. It is a beautiful spot, probably the first place on the island to be discovered by artists and "rusticators," as the city folk who sought seasonal country comforts and Atlantic air were known. Thomas Cole and Frederic Church, another Hudson River School painter, were among Somesville's visitors in the 1850s.

The **Mount Desert Island Historical Society Museum** (opposite the mill pond, 207–244–3898) is in Somesville, and its collection of maps, deeds, and various artifacts sets forth a colorful local history. The Society maintains a list of landmarks in the island's communities, including **Northeast Harbor, Bernard,** and **Tremont.** In addition, information is available on **Islesford, Southwest Harbor,** and the **Cranberry Isles.**

BAR HARBOR

In its heyday, this scenic town rivaled even fashionable Newport as a mecca for the rich and socially prominent; it remains popular today, and many extravagant and stately houses still stand as reminders of the Gilded Age. Artists and other visitors began coming here in the 1850s, boarding with the villagers. In 1855, the Agamont House was opened as an inn for summer residents, and the local economy began to shift from fishing and shipbuilding to the care and feeding of city folk.

The first summer residence, **Petunia Cottage** (West Street), was built in 1877 for the express purpose of renting to vacationers but was soon bought by physician and author S. Weir Mitchell. Soon, the off-islanders began building their own homes, usually on a grand scale. Many of the houses were designed by prominent Boston and New York architects, and a variety of styles are represented. **Redwood** (Bayberry Lane), built in 1879, is one of the earliest Shingle-style houses in the United States. Other notable houses include the magnificent Colonial Revival **Reverie Cove** (Harbor Lane), built in 1895; **The Turrets** (Eden Street), an 1895 granite cottage done in the Chateauesque style; the 1910 **Eogonos** (Eden Street), designed by Guy Lowell, architect of the Boston Museum of Fine Arts; and **La Rochelle** (West Street), a 1903 French Renaissance mansion. The 1932 **Criterion Theatre,** an art deco movie palace, is one of the finest examples of this style in the country. The history of Bar Harbor is documented in photographs, hotel registers, and other memorabilia in the **Bar Harbor Historical Society Museum** (34 Mt. Desert Street, 207–288–4245).

Abbe Museum

Overlooking the wild gardens of Acadia is the Abbe Museum. A New York surgeon, Robert Abbe amassed great collections of prehistoric artifacts during his summers in Bar Harbor, and in 1926 he built a museum to house them. Most of the exhibits represent Northeast American Indians, including the Passamaquoddy and Penobscot tribes: arrowheads and stone implements, baskets of birchbark and sweet grass, tools and ornaments of bone.

LOCATION: Route 3. HOURS: Mid-May through June: 10–4 Daily. July through August: 9–5 Daily. September through mid-December: 10–4 Daily. FEE: Yes. TELEPHONE: 207–288–3519.

OPPOSITE: *Basketry from the Abbe Museum collection.*

COLUMBIA FALLS

The early nineteenth-century prosperity of Columbia Falls is evident in one of Maine's most beautiful residences, the **Thomas Ruggles House** (Route 1, 207–483–4637), named for the local jack-of-all-trades—Ruggles was a judge, lumber magnate, owner of a general store, and postmaster. His house, built in 1818, is one of understated elegance. Its celebrated flying staircase and detailed interior woodwork, often said to be the work of an English craftsman using a single penknife, are more likely the work of New England woodcarver Alvah Peterson. The delicate woodwork of the 1820 **Samuel Bucknam House** (Route 1, private) is also attributed to Peterson. Bucknam's grandfather, Revolutionary officer John Bucknam, was one of Columbia Falls's first settlers; the **Captain John Bucknam House** (Route 1, private), built in 1792, is one of the oldest in Columbia Falls.

MACHIAS

The small coastal town of Machias was the scene of the first naval battle of the Revolution, in June 1775. The townspeople, stirred by the recent events at Lexington and Concord, refused to supply a British schooner, the *Margaretta*, with lumber intended for British barracks in Boston. The ship's captain, a Captain Moore, threatened to fire on the town if they did not comply. In response, a band of forty townspeople led by Jeremiah O'Brien boarded a British sloop, the *Unity*, and, "armed with guns, swords, axes and pitchforks" (in O'Brien's words), engaged and defeated the *Margaretta*. Captain Moore died the next day of wounds sustained in battle. O'Brien was given command of the *Unity*, which was rechristened the *Machias Liberty* and armed with the *Margaretta*'s guns; a few weeks later, he captured another British schooner.

The townspeople gathered to plan the attacks in the 1770 **Burnham Tavern** (Free and Main streets, 207–255–4432), and the wounded were brought there after the battle. Now a museum, the tavern is furnished with pieces dating from the 1600s to the Revolution; muskets used in the battle are on display, along with other artifacts of local history.

OPPOSITE: *Ruggles House, a treasure box of craftsmanship, is celebrated for its flying staircase and detailed woodcarving.*

Machias was an important railroad center for lumbering communities up north, and a relic of that trade, the oak and iron **Steam Locomotive *Lion*,** is on permanent display at the University of Maine's Machias campus. In service for half a century, the locomotive was retired in 1896.

Nearby is **Machiasport,** first settled by English colonists in 1763 and later a prosperous lumber and shipbuilding center. The Federal style **Gates House** (Route 92, 207–255–8461) has been restored to its 1807 construction and interior decoration. Home to the Machiasport Historical Society, the house includes a museum as well as period rooms and a marine and genealogical library.

EASTPORT

At the tip of Passamaquoddy Bay on Moose Island is Eastport, the easternmost city in the U.S. Settled in 1772, Eastport grew with fishing and sardine canning. The Border Historical Society operates the **Barracks Museum,** which was part of the original officers' quarters and barracks of Fort Sullivan, built in 1808 as tensions rose between England and the U.S. The British invaded Eastport in 1814 and held the town four years—long after the War of 1812 was over. Among the museum's collections are war artifacts, ships' tools, geneological records, and costumes. Remains of the fort's **Powder House** may be seen on Fort Hill, on McKinley Street. (The hill also affords a view of Campobello, site of Franklin Delano Roosevelt's summer home in Canada.) Since before 1794 British soldiers, smugglers, sea captains, and shipwreck victims have been buried in Eastport's **Hillside Cemetery,** on High Street. The town's Federal-style **Central Congregational Church** on Middle Street was built in 1829.

In 1891 a new customs house and post office was built to replace an 1850 structure that burned in an 1886 fire. Much of Eastport's downtown historic district, built after the fire, reflects the Italianate styling popular at the time. Back on the mainland is **Pleasant Point** (207-853-4045), a Passamaquoddy reservation (population about 700), and the **Waponahki Museum.** The museum's exhibits present a pictorial history of the Indians, as well as displaying artifacts, a 100-year-old birchbark canoe, and mannequins in traditional Passamaquoddy dress.

Nineteenth-century houses in Calais.

CALAIS

Calais was established on the St. Croix River in 1809 and steadily grew as word spread among the French and English colonies of its fine forests, fishing, and arable soil. The **Calais Historic District** faces the river from Main Street, with few of its significant buildings predating a devastating 1870 fire. Among those survivors are the Gothic Revival **Gilmore** (316 Main Street, private) and **Washburn** (318 Main Street, private) houses, and a Victorian mansion so outrageously ornate it is known as **Hamilton's Folly** (78 South Street, private), after the man, Thomas Hamilton, who built it and went bankrupt.

In July 1604, Samuel de Champlain and the Sieur de Monts landed on the island of **St. Croix** with a group of eighty Frenchmen, intending to set up a trading post. Had the venture been successful, it would have been the first permanent settlement north of South Carolina, but it was doomed to failure by the harsh winter, lack of drinking water, and an outbreak of scurvy that wiped out half the colonists. The village was abandoned the following year. Foundations and graves have been unearthed by archaeological excavations, but no structures remain standing. St. Croix is not open to the public, but it may be viewed from a small red-granite **enclosure** atop a hill overlooking the island (off Route 1). Brass plaques detail the history of the short-lived settlement.

THE
MAINE INTERIOR

OPPOSITE: *Mount Katahdin, from the rivers of Baxter State Park.*

Maine is large—half the size of all of New England—and about 80 percent of it is covered with forests of white pine, balsam fir, basswood, birch, oak, maple, hemlock, beech, and spruce. Mile-high Mount Katahdin, in the center of Maine, is the state's tallest peak. More than 5,000 rivers and streams pour through Maine; lakes and large ponds number 2,500. For thousands of years these waters were fished for salmon, brook trout, and bass by the Indians and in more recent times by sport fishermen. Men of means built great lodges in the woods or stayed at fashionable resort hotels.

The interior was sparsely settled by Europeans, but Indians occupied these lands almost as soon as the glaciers receded, 10,000 to 12,000 years ago. Evidence of human occupation in that era has been found in the vicinity of Chase and Munsungun lakes, which are believed to have been formed by glaciers. Stone tools and animal bones dating from 6,000 to 8,000 years ago have been found near Cobbosseecontee Lake. Of more recent date, from 3,000 to 6,000 years ago, was the culture of the Red Paint people, so called because their burials all contained deposits of a red ochre paint. Little is known of them, despite the many Red Paint graves that have been discovered, beyond the fact that they were skilled artisans. The Indians of the historical period were the Abenaki, of the large Algonquin linguistic group.

French traders generally coexisted peacefully with the Abenaki, trading furs, while the land-hungry English settlers clashed repeatedly with the Indians. The Abenaki, particularly along the coast, suffered tremendously in an epidemic in 1616—estimates of mortality run as high as 75 percent. The series of wars that began with King Philip's War in the 1670s went well for the Indians at first, but their defeat in the French and Indian War in the 1750s broke their power.

In 1786 the state of Massachusetts sold huge tracts of unsettled land in northern Maine to wealthy speculators, notably William Bingham of Philadelphia, who bought 1 million acres and acquired another million from General Henry Knox. At the same time, the surviving Indians of Maine were made wards of the state and lost title to all their lands. Few Mainers regretted any discomfiture of the Indians, but many resented the land policies of Massachusetts and the absentee landowners.

OPPOSITE: *Detail from Frederic E. Church's* Mt. Ktaadin *(Katahdin), painted in 1853.*

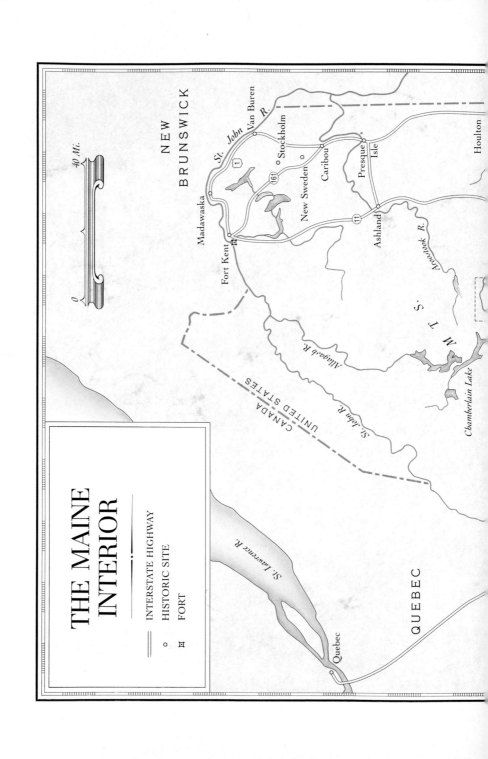

THE MAINE INTERIOR

—— INTERSTATE HIGHWAY
∘ HISTORIC SITE
⌂ FORT

40 Mi.
0

NEW BRUNSWICK

St. John R.
Van Buren
Stockholm
1
161
New Sweden
Caribou
Presque Isle
Ashland
11
Aroostook R.
Houlton
Madawaska
Fort Kent

Allagash R.
St. John R.
CANADA
UNITED STATES

Chamberlain Lake

M T S.

St. Lawrence R.

Quebec

QUEBEC

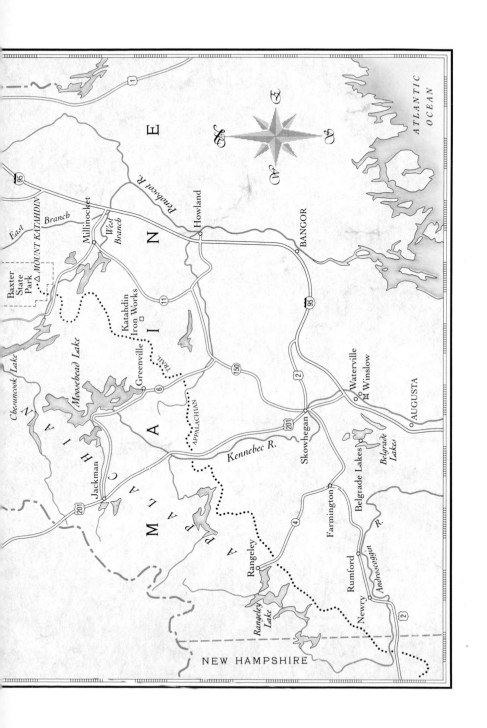

The far northern county of Aroostook is the largest and lone-liest county in Maine. Towns of any size are the exception on these wide-open flat acres. Potato farming is a major industry in this region, and enormous trucks carry the crops southward to markets in Maine, New England, and other parts of the country. Along the green St. John River valley are small farming communities, many of them founded by Acadians, the French Canadians driven from their homes by the English in the late 1700s.

After the Revolution, the United States and Britain anxiously shared the northern border region, competing for its wealth of timber, game, and minerals. Each country trespassed against the other in disputes that lasted over fifty years. Between February and May 1839 there was a confrontation, called the "Aroostook War," which threatened to erupt into violence. Some 10,000 Maine troops massed along the Aroostook River, and the federal govern-ment agreed to send 50,000 more. But before any shooting started, a border was agreed upon by negotiation and formalized in the Webster-Ashburton Treaty.

Maine's great lumber boom began after the Revolution and gathered force through the nineteenth century. Augusta and Ban-gor both prospered as centers of milling and trade in lumber. The Penobscot River carried the harvest of the interior forests to Ban-gor, which, in the middle of the nineteenth century, was one of the world's largest producers of wood products.

This chapter begins with Augusta, the state capital, proceeds northward to Waterville, and then detours to the west. The route then takes up with Bangor, proceeds directly north, and then loops south along the Canadian border to Houlton.

C E N T R A L   R E G I O N

AUGUSTA

Augusta had been settled for over 200 years when it became Maine's capital in 1831. The earliest pioneers did well trading with the Indians for furs, fish, and timber, but they abandoned the settlement around 1700. Settlers returned, however, in the mid-eighteenth century as timber for construction became highly val-ued, and the town developed on both sides of the Kennebec River. Augusta became an active port, sending timber, furs, and other goods forty-five miles downriver to the sea. One of its chief exports was ice, harvested from the Kennebec each winter and packed in sawdust for points south. In 1832 the capital was moved from Portland to Augusta. Within a decade not only sawmills but cotton mills as well were adding to the prosperity of the thriving city.

Maine State House

While citizens of Portland made several attempts to move the capital back to their city, their cause faded in the face of Charles Bulfinch's impressive structure in Augusta. The architect based the classical design of Maine's capitol on his earlier one for the Massachusetts State House; the building material, however, was indigenous to Maine: granite from Hollowell. Construction began in 1829 and lasted until January 1832. Its completion was a prelude to many alterations, additions, and renovations, beginning with a remodeling of the interior in 1857. Between 1890 and 1891 a three-story wing was added to the rear of the building according to

The Maine State House in Augusta as it has appeared since 1910, when final elaborations were made on Charles Bulfinch's 1829 original.

architect John Calvin Spofford's design, attuned to Bulfinch's original plans. Architect G. Henri Desmond paid less attention to maintaining the integrity of the earlier designs; in 1909–1910 he added two large side wings and replaced the original low dome with an almost 200-foot steel dome covered in copper and topped by *Wisdom,* a gold-covered statue sculptured by W. Clark Noble. Bulfinch's mark is still visible in the front Greek Revival portico and its recessed wall. As the demands of civil government varied, the structure that housed it followed suit; the State House reflects its own history. A self-guided tour of the capitol grounds and State House includes temporary exhibits about Maine and local history, dioramas of native wildlife, portraits of governors, and legislative chambers.

> LOCATION: State and Capitol streets. HOURS: 9–5 Monday–Friday, 10–4 Saturday, 1–4 Sunday. FEE: None. TELEPHONE: 207–289–2301.

The **Maine State Museum** (207–289–2301), about a hundred yards south of the State House, offers an excellent overview of the state's natural, industrial, and social history. Curators have devised dioramas of Maine's natural settings, and there is a gem and mineral exhibit. An extensive exhibit, "Made in Maine," presents the history of the state's products and industries. Historical settings of both factory and home display the various crafts of sewing, weaving, furniture making, and shoe making. Principal industrial tools and methods are explained.

Across from the capitol is **Blaine House** (207–289–2301), the Federal-style residence of Maine's governor. As governors' mansions go, the clapboard, green-shuttered house, sitting behind a picket fence, is modest. Sea captain James Hall built it for himself in 1833; the house takes its name from a later resident, James G. Blaine, a Maine congressman who became Speaker of the House, a U.S. senator, a presidential candidate, and secretary of state under presidents Garfield and Harrison. Blaine died in 1893, and in 1919 his descendants gave the house to the state, to be used as the official residence of Maine's governors and their families.

Fort Western (16 Cony Street, 207-626–2385), a 1754 fortification, also served as a store and, in the nineteenth century, as a tenement for factory workers. The main building, a 100-by-32-foot

OPPOSITE: *The three-story Maine capitol rotunda soars 185 feet above the first floor.*

Fort Western, raised on the east bank of the Kennebec River in the mid-eighteenth century.

rectangle of hewn logs covered in shingles and topped by four huge chimneys, is one of the finest remnants of colonial America. Today it is a **museum** that interprets the military, economic, and social history of the Kennebec River Valley.

In 1827 the U.S. government built an **arsenal** in Augusta to defend the frontier at the time of the boundary dispute with England. The arsenal consisted of fifteen buildings, most of them of granite. Ammunition manufactured here supplied the Mexican War, the Civil War, and the Spanish-American War. Ten of the granite buildings survive and are still in use by the state. Known as the **Kennebec Arsenal Historic District,** they are located at the end of Arsenal Street, on the river.

The **Kennebec County Courthouse** (95 State Street) is one of the earliest Greek Revival structures in Maine (1829), with a full Ionic colonnade. Also of architectural interest is the **Old Post Office** (1886), a fabulous Romanesque edifice, and one of the distinguished Victorian buildings on Water Street in downtown Augusta. A central round tower set on a square base is echoed by a rounded tower at each of the building's corners, heavy rounded arches, and ornate dormers with rounded detail. It houses a bank, postal station, and offices.

ALNA

The town of Alna is known chiefly for the village it encompasses, **Head Tide,** located on the Sheepscot River. The lovely siting is the raison d'être of the village: Mills of all kinds operated on the Sheepscot, giving Head Tide an active economy for 200 years, from pre-Revolutionary times into the twentieth century. One of Head Tide's mills produced thousands of cedar shingles every day.

Along the north and south banks of the Sheepscot, within the **Head Tide Historic District,** are the village's eighteenth- and nineteenth-century houses, a store, church, stable, and school. The 1789 **Alna Meeting House** (Route 218) is one of Maine's superior Colonial buildings. The **Schoolhouse,** also on Route 218, is impossible to miss—its tall cupola pokes above the gently rolling landscape. Built in 1795, it is Maine's second-oldest one-room schoolhouse, fifty years younger than York's.

Clustered on the Sheepscot River, one- and two-century-old buildings define the Head Tide Historic District.

East of Waterville, where the Kennebec merges with the Sebasticook River, lies **Winslow,** primarily a farming community. In 1754,
English colonists built **Fort Halifax** on the Sebasticook to protect
their fragile settlements from the French and Indians. The fort was
also a crucial link during the Revolution and a way station for
Benedict Arnold on his ill-fated march to Quebec. Its blockhouse,
believed to be the oldest in the United States until its demise in
1987 floodwaters, is being reconstructed (1988).

WATERVILLE

Just south of Skowhegan, the aptly named Waterville was born on
the Kennebec's Tionic Falls, which drove the town's lumber mills.
River drivers also took advantage of the water's power, sending
logs over the falls to be milled in town.

The Redington Museum

Housed in an 1814 frame house built by one of Waterville's early
pioneers, this well-appointed museum is administered by the Waterville Historical Society and documents the early years of the
town. Asa Redington, a Revolutionary War veteran of George
Washington's elite Honor Guard, built the house with an eye to the
elegance of the time, as evidenced by the spiral staircase, the
original fireplaces, and the woodwork. Five period rooms of the
late eighteenth and early nineteenth centuries contain antiques and
furnishings original to the Redingtons and other pioneering families, including Chippendale and Hepplewhite pieces; a collection
of clocks; kitchen utensils; period children's toys, among them a
Victorian and a Colonial Revival dollhouse; and family portraits.

The museum's library includes diaries and archives from the
mid-eighteenth century to the twentieth, plus an extensive collection of local newspapers and early photographs. Other exhibits
include displays of early craftsmanship, technological developments in the logging and transportation fields, firearms, Civil War
memorabilia, early business marquees, musical instruments, Indian
artifacts, and period costumes. Adjacent to the museum is the
LaVerdiere Apothecary Museum, housing an extensive collection
of pharmaceutical paraphernalia and furnishings, such as brass
and mahogany cabinets, shelves filled with early patent medicines,

Waterville's authentically furnished and stocked nineteenth-century LaVerdiere Apothecary.

extracts, oils, herbs, and equipment. With an authentic prescription-preparation area and a mirrored fountain backed with stained-glass trim, the museum recalls the soda fountain–drugstore of the nineteenth century.

LOCATION: 64 Silver Street. HOURS: May through September: 2–6 Tuesday–Saturday. FEE: Yes. TELEPHONE: 207–872–9439.

Another particularly picturesque element of the past resides in the **Waterville Opera House** on Castonguay Square. Built at the turn of the century, this well-preserved Colonial Revival structure predates the movie house, harking back to the age of local and traveling theater companies. An early example of Art Deco architecture, the concrete-and-steel **Professional Building** (177 and 179 Main Street), was built in 1923 with stylistic detailing in the reliefs, shield motifs, and low archways.

North of Waterville is some of the most beautiful countryside in Maine—rolling hills, enormous lakes, waterfalls, and streams. Along the waterways grew such mill towns as Hermon, Newburgh Center, Plymouth, Burnham, and Damascus. After 1856, the railroads gave birth to other communities—Fairfield, Shawmut, Anson, and Sidney. **Skowhegan** (an Indian word for "a place to watch fish") was settled in 1771 by two homesteaders, Peter Heywood and Joseph Weston, who brought their families and a few head of cattle from Concord, Massachusetts.

The mid- to late-nineteenth century prosperity of Skowhegan as a regional business center is apparent in its **historic district,** which comprises nearly forty commercial buildings along Water and Russett Streets, as well as Madison Avenue. Virtually all late-nineteenth-century architectural styles are represented here in varying states of renovation. The **Skowhegan History House** (Norridgewock Avenue, 207–474–3140), a dignified, Greek Revival brick residence, is furnished appropriately for its year of construction, 1839. Local documents and artifacts are also on display.

Farther west are fertile agricultural lands, settled for the most part by the English in the 1770s. Highways here roll past fields of corn, potatoes, and pumpkins and past apple orchards. **Farmington,** as its name implies, is a typical farming community on the banks of the Sandy River in the Oxford Hills. The **Little Red Schoolhouse Museum** (Route 2) is complete with desks and books from the last century; built in 1852, it served Farmington's students for over 100 years. It is a visitor center in summer.

Downriver at **Farmington Falls** is the **Old Union Meeting House,** completed in 1827 by a Farmington carpenter, Benjamin Butler. In style the meetinghouse harks back to the eighteenth century, with a steeple in the mode of the London architect Christopher Wren. Used by a variety of denominations before they built their own churches, it now houses the Union Baptist Church. On Holly Road, the **Nordica Homestead Museum** (207–778–2042) pays tribute to the famous opera soprano Lillian Nordica (née Norton). The 1840 Cape Cod–style home, built by her father, was Nordica's home before her mother launched her operatic career. In 1891, Nordica made her debut at the Metropolitan Opera. Her expertise lay in Wagnerian roles, and she in fact studied under Wagner's widow. Nordica spent her last summer here in 1911; she died in 1914. The museum includes concert gowns, programs, stage jewels, music, and other Nordica memorabilia from her career and the family home.

RUMFORD

The largest town in the Oxford Hills, Rumford developed as an industrial and a resort center. The Ellis, Swift, and Concord rivers flow into the Androscoggin, whose powerful falls have driven the town's pulp and paper mills since the late 1800s. The commercial **historic district** reflects the town's fortunes at the turn of the century when Oxford Paper and other companies boosted the local economy. Major downtown buildings, all within sight of the Androscoggin Falls, include the Colonial Revival **Municipal Building,** designed by Harry S. Coombs in 1916; the 1906 Beaux-Arts **Rumford Falls Power Company Building;** the 1910 **Strathglass Building,** also of Beaux-Arts design; and the 1911 Classical Revival **Mechanic Institute.**

The **Strathglass Park Historic District** is an example of an early twentieth-century planned community. Hugh J. Chisolm, a developer for Rumford Falls and the Oxford Paper Company, hired noted architect Cass H. Gilbert to design a residential development for the millworkers. Between 1901 and 1902 fifty-one solid and attractive duplexes, surrounded by gracious lawns, were built on blocks divided by tree-lined avenues. Public services, such as garbage and snow removal, were taken care of by the company. Not until 1948 and 1949 were the lots sold privately.

NEWRY

One of the best-preserved one-room schoolhouses in the country, with its 1895 furnishings intact, is the **Lower Sunday River School** on Sunday River Road in Newry. The town's graceful covered bridge, the **Sunday River Bridge,** was built in 1870. One half of the bridge was assembled on each shore and then settled into place and joined in the center.

The narrow roads and highways heading northwest of Newry toward Baxter State Park seem hardly more than wilderness trails themselves, barely penetrating the heavy forests. But they lead to Maine's lake country. From the mid-1800s, while the sailing set summered at the state's coastal resorts, inland sportsmen stalked moose and fly-fished at Flagstaff and Rangeley lakes. In **Rangeley,** the **Rangeley Lakes Region Historical Society** (Main and Richardson streets) has a large collection of photographs from the resort era. Funds to build the classically designed **Rangeley Public Library** (Lake Street, 207–864–5529) were raised in the early 1900s by summer and permanent residents. The library houses an exceptional collection of material written by—and about—the natural scientist Wilhelm Reich, who fled Nazi Germany and eventually settled in Maine. A student of Sigmund Freud, Reich developed a controversial theory based on a universal biological energy he called orgone. (He named his compound in Maine "Orgonon.") Three miles west of Rangeley is the **Wilhelm Reich Museum** (Dodge Pond Road, 207–864–3443), housed in Reich's observatory. Built of native fieldstone in the Bauhaus style, the building contains his equipment and paintings as well as exhibits on his work. Reich, who died in 1957, enjoyed the region's low humidity and abundant forests, lakes, and mountains, which reminded him of Europe. His study and library are also on view.

THE   EASTERN   INTERIOR

BANGOR

In his journal of 1604, Samuel de Champlain recorded his impressions of the hilly west bank of the Penobscot River. The land there, twenty-three miles inland and thick with oak trees, struck the French explorer as "pleasant and agreeable," as did the Indians who inhabited the area. It would be another century and a half before a Massachusetts pioneer, Jacob Buswell, settled at the pleasant and agreeable spot that would grow into one of Maine's most rollicking towns. Buswell's community, at first known as Kenduskeag Plantation after the tributary stream that runs through town, made its living by exporting fur pelts and lumber. In about 1800 Bangor got its present name—apparently from the title of a favorite hymn of the town's pastor. Bangor now began to come into its own, with businesses and population expanding even as the War of 1812 brought blockades and other British aggressions.

Harvesting pine and spruce trees upstream from Bangor along a great length of the Penobscot, timbermen floated logs to Bangor mills. From them in the 1850s came an enormous supply of lumber, shingles, clapboards, and lath. Much of that wood went out to sea from Bangor in locally made ships—the river town was an active port with a lively overseas trade. Bangor traded with the West Indies, too, exchanging its large winter ice harvest for their molasses, sugar, and rum.

In the mid-nineteenth century, railroads tied Bangor and its timber goods to all points south. The town boomed as many came

OPPOSITE: *Nineteenth-century buildings on Broad Street, in Bangor's Market Square Historic District.*

to make their fortunes—in lumber, milling, shipbuilding, and land speculation. The newcomers created an exciting city, full of cultural diversions. And as with most boom towns, the lumberjacks and sailors found no shortage of saloons and brothels.

The citizens built an extremely good-looking town, which is still in evidence, despite the ravages of a 1911 fire and the urban renewal of the late 1960s. The **West Market Square Historic District** consists of two downtown blocks, defined by State, Main, and Broad streets and the Kenduskeag Stream. The first open marketplace in Bangor, it was also where many set up shop in handsome brick and granite buildings—doctors, booksellers, grocers, shoemakers, druggists, hatters. Much of the area was the 1830s design work of Charles G. Bryant, a prominent hometown architect. His best-known commercial commission is **Bangor House** (174 Main), a grand hotel of its day (built 1833–1834), receiving such guests as Ulysses S. Grant, Daniel Webster, and Theodore Roosevelt. It is now an apartment building.

In the same decade Bryant drew up plans for the **City Common,** east of Broadway, and for **Mount Hope Cemetery.** Landscaped with ponds, trees, and pathways, the cemetery was inspired by Mount Auburn in Cambridge, Massachusetts, the nation's first garden cemetery. Mount Hope is filled with elaborate Victorian monuments, marble urns, granite obelisks, and ironwork. A cannon marks the site of the Grand Army Lot, a burial ground consecrated in 1864 for Civil War veterans.

The city's increasing number of rich entrepreneurs commissioned Bryant and other architects to design houses. Most of the clients preferred to build just south of Main Street in what is now called the **High Street Historic District** (a triangle defined by Union, Columbia, and Hammond streets). Rising above the district is the **Hammond Street Congregational Church,** built in 1853. Built in 1822, the **William Mason House** (62 High Street, private) is probably the oldest brick house in the district. Bryant's **George W. Brown House** (43 High Street, private) and **Pickering House** (39 High Street, private), both built in 1833–1835, are gable-roofed twins with Greek Revival porticoes.

Another of Bangor's historic residential neighborhoods is bounded by Essex, Center, Garland, and State streets. Developed in the 1830s, the **Broadway Historic District** includes several houses designed by architect Charles Bryant, including the Greek

Revival **Smith-Boutelle House** (private) on Broadway near Cumberland. The elaborate doorway, contained within a Doric portico, sports a top panel of anthemion leaves, a popular motif of the Greek Revival style. One resident of the house was Charles Boutelle, Civil War naval officer, publisher of the Bangor *Daily Whig and Courier,* and nine-term congressman. Among Boutelle's guests were three U.S. presidents—Garfield, Harrison, and McKinley. On Penobscot off Broadway is Bryant's **Ken-Cutting House** (private), a graceful Greek Revival double house with wrought-iron railings.

Perhaps the city's most beloved landmark is the 1898 **Bangor Standpipe and Observatory,** which dominates Thomas Hill, the highest elevation in the city, a hilly former Indian hunting ground. Probably the only Shingle-style standpipe in the nation, it handsomely shrouds a huge water tank (now used only in emergencies). The balustrade is lit at night. Also notable in the area is the massive, red brick **Bangor Children's Home.** Built 1868–1869 as an orphanage, it is now a day-care center and private school.

The **Bangor Public Library,** boasting nearly half a million volumes and renowned as a great repository of state and local history, was founded in 1845, but its present building on Hammond Street was built in 1912, after the fire that gutted the area. In fact, the neighborhood is known as the **Great Fire Historic District** for the reconstruction that occurred between 1911 and 1915. Among the library's neighbors are the **Bangor Savings Bank,** the **Bangor High School** (now an apartment building called the Schoolhouse), and the Romanesque **Graham Building.**

One of the earliest examples in the state of the Greek Revival temple style is the 1832 **Zebulon Smith House** (55 Summer Street, private), once one of a line of fashionable residences that announced the wealth of their owners. Smith was a jeweler and silversmith. Another Greek Revival structure is the **Nathaniel Hatch House** at 117 Court Street, with porticoes at both the front and back of the house. The history of the house's owners reflects the boom-time fluctuations of American mid-nineteenth-century society. Nathaniel Hatch, a prosperous banker, built the house in 1832–1833 and sold it soon afterward to Samuel Farrar, who worked with his father in lumber after ill health forced him to give up studying law. In 1857, when his successful business floundered, Farrar sold the house, packed up, and moved to Wisconsin. The house is currently run by the Bangor Housing Authority.

The mahagony-rich entrance hall of Isaac Farrar Mansion in Bangor.

Lumber baron and merchant Isaac Farrar ordered the finest materials for his house, which was the first known U.S. commission of English architect Richard Upjohn. The 1833 **Isaac Farrar Mansion** (166 Union Street, 207–941–2808) contains marble mantles, stained-glass windows, mahogany wainscotting, and much carved woodwork. It has been extensively remodeled. Across from it is the Greek Revival cottage that Upjohn designed in 1836 for lawyer Thomas A. Hill. Now headquarters of the Bangor Historical Society and Museum, the **Hill House** (159 Union Street, 207–942–5766) has a completely restored downstairs floor, the highlight of which is a grand double parlor, furnished to Victorian perfection. In the 1840s the house passed to Samuel Dale, mayor of Bangor, whose guests included Ulysses S. Grant. Among the rotating exhibits are nineteenth-century letters and diaries, photographs, and paintings, as well as household tools and utensils, many of them made in Bangor.

The ornate wallpaper in the Farrar entrance hall is original, dating from 1833.

   In the front hallway of the Hill House is a desk that belonged
to Hannibal Hamlin, a prominent Maine politician before he became Abraham Lincoln's vice president. Born in Paris Hill in 1809,
he died in Bangor in 1891 and is buried in Mount Hope Cemetery.
A farmer and lawyer based in Hampden, just south of Bangor,
Hamlin entered politics as a Jacksonian Democrat. He served first
in the state House of Representatives (1836–1841), was elected to
the U.S. House of Representatives in 1843, and then to the Senate.
His abolitionist views led him to resign from the Democratic Party,
and in 1856 he was elected Maine's first Republican governor. The
following year he was reelected to the U.S. Senate. Although chosen by Lincoln as his running mate in 1860, Hamlin was passed
over in 1864 for Andrew Johnson, who became president upon
Lincoln's assassination. The Maine electorate returned Hamlin to
the U.S. Senate in 1869, where he served until 1881. Before retir-
ing to Bangor, he served as U.S. minister to Spain.

In Bangor, Hamlin lived at 15 Fifth Street, in an 1848 mansard-roofed house that is now the official residence of presidents of
the **Bangor Theological Seminary.** Moved to Bangor from Hampden in 1819, the seminary boasts significant buildings, including
the 1827 **Old Commons Building,** the 1833 **Maine Hall,** and the
1858 **Chapel.**

Bordering the seminary is the **Whitney Park Historic District.**
Clustered around West Broadway between Union and Hammond
streets, it was developed during the Civil War era by a generation
of prosperous newcomers to Bangor. They built large houses in the
popular Victorian styles such as Queen Anne and Shingle. One of
the most exuberant is the Italianate **William Arnold House** (47
West Broadway, private) built by a local merchant in 1857. The
Penobscot Nation Museum (207–827–6545) in Old Town exhibits
a range of Indian artifacts including basketry, clothing, stone tools
and sculpture, and birchbark artwork.

The heritage of Bangor's logging industry is the subject of
exhibits at the **Maine Forest and Logging Museum** (Route 178 in
Bradley, 207–942–4228), scheduled for completion in 1991. The
centerpiece of the complex is a re-creation of Leonard's Mills,
active in 1797. Exhibits explain the sawmill process—from northern wood harvesting, spring log drives, the establishment of logging camps, and forest management to the actual milling (the
waterwheel driven by Blackman Stream). Froes, adzes, broad axes,
pick poles, and other eighteenth-century tools are on display. The
chronology ends with the modern lumber and paper industries.

At **Greenville,** summer residents got around Moosehead Lake on
the *Katahdin,* one of Maine's last and largest steamboats. Built at the
Bath Iron Works in 1914, the powerful vessel carried passengers
and logs between various points on the forty-mile-long lake. Resort
hotels such as the **Mount Kineo House** (207–695–2702) comman-
deered her services for popular excursions. She made her farewell
passenger run in 1938 and her final run in 1976. Now a steamboat-
era exhibit at the **Moosehead Marine Museum,** the *Katahdin* has
been restored and outfitted with displays of her history.

KATAHDIN IRON WORKS

East of Greenville, on **Silver Lake,** are the Katahdin Iron Works,
abandoned in 1890. The blast furnace and kiln remain, survivors

of the once-fiery operation, the only one of its kind in the state. Katahdin was a factory town, built along with the ironworks in 1843—the workers' houses, town hall, train depot, school, stores, auxiliary farms, and boardinghouses are now gone. Taking raw materials from its mineral-rich location, Katahdin produced about twenty tons of pig iron a day in the early 1880s, sending it to markets by rail and river. For a while, the Katahdin furnace blasted nonstop, and the factory produced iron farm tools, parts for machinery, and wheels for railroad cars. After the 1880s, Katahdin could not compete with the newer and more centrally located technology in Pittsburgh, Pennsylvania. Of Katahdin's extensive operation, only one of fourteen kilns and the blast-furnace tower remain and have been renovated, massive and impressive monuments to the passage of boom-time prosperity and society.

LOCATION: Off Route 11, five miles north of Brownsville Junction. HOURS: Memorial Day through Labor Day: 9–5 Daily. FEE: None. TELEPHONE: 207–645–4217.

Chamberlain Lake is just above **Baxter State Park** (207–723–9616), established in 1931. Near the southeast corner of the park is **Mount Katahdin,** northern terminus of the **Appalachian Trail,** blazed by foresters in the 1920s. The 2,100-mile wilderness trail connects Maine's Baxter Peak to Georgia's Mount Springer.

South of Fort Kent, beginning at **Eagle Lake** and stretching southwest to Chamberlain Lake, lie the remains of a remarkable logging-transportation system in the **Tramway Historical District.** The steam-driven Tramway was engineered in 1902 to solve the problem of getting logs from lumbering areas to the waterways for transportation to markets.

In 1841 the waters of Chamberlain Lake had been diverted into the east branch of the Penobscot River. By the beginning of the twentieth century, lumber in the surrounding area had been depleted. The Tramway was developed to carry logs 3,000 feet over land from the timber-rich Eagle Lake area to Chamberlain Lake, which had links to the mills on the Penobscot and the overseas markets. A 6,000-foot steel cable formed a single loop between the two lakes, along which trucks were attached every 10 feet. The trucks ran along 22-inch-gauge rails, with the delivery line on a

OVERLEAF: *Mount Katahdin rises 5,268 feet above autumnal forests.*

raised wooden structure directly above that of the return line. A 9-foot sprocket wheel was driven by steam at the Chamberlain end, drawing the cable and trucks along the route. A log spanned two trucks on its way to Chamberlain Lake, and the trucks returned empty and upside down to Eagle Lake.

Although it was made obsolete by more powerful log haulers and locomotives, the Tramway was never destroyed, and its entire length remains virtually intact. Between 1927 and 1933 a railroad line ran each summer from the Tramway district to Umbazooksus Lake to continue feeding the lumber-mill market, this time to the west branch of the Penobscot River. The railroad engines were subsequently stored in Eagle Lake in a structure that later burned to the ground. The Tramway and the exposed engines of the railway are extraordinary relics of Maine's land, technology, and logging industry.

FORT KENT

Maine's northern border with Canada became a focal point of conflict between the United States and Britain beginning in 1755, when French-Acadians moved into the region known as the Madawaska Territory to escape increasing British domination in Canada. After the American Revolution, the United States and Britain competed for the region's wealth in game, lumber, and minerals. Each country trespassed against the other, creating disputes that continued over fifty years and culminated in the Aroostook War of 1838–1839. This purely diplomatic but potentially bloody confrontation resulted in the establishment of the St. John River as Maine's international border with New Brunswick, Canada.

In the winter of 1838–1839, military troops, sent by the governments of the United States, Great Britain, Maine, and New Brunswick, converged on the lumbering region of the Aroostook Valley. Each was determined to exercise control over the land rich in spruce, cedar, and white pine. Within six weeks officials had settled on an uneasy truce, and the troops withdrew. At the end of 1839, however, a Maine public-land agent hired a local force to establish and monitor the state's claim to the area. The militia, numbering thirty-six men, chose the meeting of the Fish and St. John rivers to locate the **Fort Kent Blockhouse** (Blockhouse Road and West Main Street, 207–834–3866), named for the then-governor of Maine, Edward Kent. New Brunswick and Great Britain

The stocky Fort Kent Blockhouse, a landmark of Maine's border disputes.

countered with an establishment twenty miles away, and the heated confrontation continued. In 1841 the U.S. government sought to end the persistent and potentially dangerous dispute by relieving the civil militia and installing federal troops at Fort Kent. The threat of serious conflict forced negotiations that ended in the Webster-Ashburton Treaty in 1842.

In 1843 the last of the federal troops left Fort Kent. It was sold into private hands in 1858 and was used as a family residence. The state purchased the blockhouse in 1891.

Built of thick, squared cedar logs, the blockhouse, with its prominent second-story overhang, most closely resembles fortifications erected a century before 1839, perhaps as a result of the lack of modern engineering expertise of the local civil militia when it began its task. Inside the rough-hewn structure are pictorial displays of the dispute era, as well as a selection of lumbering equipment.

In 1785 the Acadians landed upriver at St. David in the Madawaska area. They planted a cross on the southern shore of the St. John River to commemorate their safe passage from British persecution in Canada and their establishment in Maine. The **Madawaska Historic Museum** and **Acadian Cross Historic Shrine** (Route 1, 207–728–4518) now mark that point of entry; exhibits include a century-old Acadian schoolhouse and 150-year-old homestead.

VAN BUREN

Each year profitable timber harvests enliven towns up and down the St. John River—Hamlin, Grand Isle, Notre Dame, Lille, Cyr Plantation. One of the larger logging towns is Van Buren, named for President Martin Van Buren, who once visited here. Many of its loggers (as well as most of the river valley's farmers and business-men) are descendants of the original French Acadians. The local economy is based on lumbering, farming, and small businesses.

Van Buren's **Acadian Village** (Route 1, 207–868–2691) con-sists of reconstructed and relocated eighteenth- and nineteenth-century houses and cabins, barns, a railroad station, general store, church, and barber, shoe, and blacksmith shops. The houses are appointed with period furnishings and crafts; the barns, shops, and other buildings are set up with appropriate equipment from plows to blacksmith's anvils to barber chairs. The entire grouping gives visitors a look into early life on Maine's northern frontier.

At the junction of Route 1 and four state highways is **Caribou,** a shipping center for Aroostook potato farmers. Some of them are descendants of Scandinavians who came to northern Maine in the 1870s, settling in the communities they named **New Sweden** and **Stockholm.** Their history is preserved by the **New Sweden Histori-cal Society Museum** (off Route 161, 207–896–5639), whose exhib-its include two Swedish log cabins and a replica of an 1870 commu-nity hall. Immigrant artifacts, documents, and photographs also are housed in the **Stockholm Museum** (Main and Lake streets), which occupies the town's old general store and post office.

Just above Houlton, in **Littleton,** is the youngest and northernmost covered bridge in the state. The 150-foot **Watson Settlement Bridge,** spanning the Meduxnekeag Stream, was built in 1911.

HOULTON

Hub of three railroads—the Bangor and Aroostook, the New Brunswick, and the Aroostook Valley lines—the pioneer community of Houlton grew into a real market town in the 1890s, with impressive commercial buildings constructed along **Market Square.** Built in 1907, the **First National Bank** is of a particularly noble Grecian design. The **Aroostook Historical and Art Museum** (109 Main Street, 207–532–4216) occupies a 1903 Colonial Revival house, the finest residence of its time in Houlton. Surviving from the town's earlier days, and indeed the earliest surviving structure in Aroostook County, is the 1813 **Black Hawk Putnam Tavern** at 22 North Street. Now an office building, the structure served as the town's hotel during its frontier years. The original exterior has been preserved.

One of New Sweden's log cabins contains a spinning wheel and other belongings of the family who built it in 1894.

Notes on Architecture

EARLY COLONIAL

JOHN PERKINS HOUSE, ME

In the eastern colonies, Europeans first built houses using a medieval, vertical asymmetry, which in the eighteenth century evolved toward Classical symmetry. Roofs were gabled and hipped, often with prominent exterior chimneys. Small casement windows became larger and more evenly spaced and balanced on each facade.

GEORGIAN

LADY PEPPERRELL HOUSE, ME

Beginning in Boston as early as 1686, and only much later elsewhere, the design of houses became balanced about a central axis, with only careful, stripped detail. A few large houses incorporated double-story pilasters. Sash windows with rectilinear panes replaced casements. Hipped roofs accentuated the balanced and strict proportions inherited from Italy and Holland via England and Scotland.

FEDERAL

PORTSMOUTH ATHENAEUM, NH

The post-Revolutionary style sometimes called "Federal" was more flexible and delicate than the more formal Georgian. It evolved from archaeological discoveries at Pompeii and Herculaneum in Italy in the 1750s, as well as in contemporary French interior planning principles. A fan-shaped window over the door is its most characteristic detail.

GREEK REVIVAL

FOLLETT HOUSE, VT

The Greek Revival manifested itself in severe, stripped, rectilinear proportions, occasionally a set of columns or pilasters, and even, in a few instances, Greek-temple form. It combined Greek and Roman forms—low pitched pediments, simple moldings, rounded arches, and shallow domes—and was used in official buildings and many private houses.

COUNTRY VERNACULAR

NORTHPORT, ME

The builders of many modest structures in northern New England were concerned only with function, not with stylistic considerations. Many farmhouses and barns do not fit easily into any stylistic designation, although they grew out of building traditions of the colonial period. One distinctive regional building type is the connected house and barn, which developed in the severe climate of Maine and New Hampshire. Simple wooden farmhouses are connected—by means of a rear ell, woodshed, carriage house, and outhouse—to the barn, an arrangement that ultimately proved to be a fire hazard.

GOTHIC REVIVAL

After about 1830, darker colors, asymmetry, broken skylines, verticality, and the pointed arch began to appear. New machinery produced carved and pierced trim along the eaves. Roofs became steep and gabled; "porches" or "piazzas" became more spacious. Oriel and bay windows were common and there was greater use of stained glass.

ITALIANATE

MORSE-LIBBY HOUSE, ME

The Italianate style began to appear in the 1840s, both in a formal, balanced "palazzo" style and in a picturesque "villa" style. Both had round-headed windows and arcaded porches. Commercial structures were often made of cast iron, with a ground floor of large arcaded windows with smaller windows on each successive rising story.

SECOND EMPIRE

PARK-McCULLOUGH HOUSE, VT

After 1860, Parisian fashion inspired American builders to use mansard roofs, dark colors, and varied textures, including shingles, tiles, and ironwork, especially on balconies and skylines. With their ornamental quoins, balustrades, pavilions, pediments, columns, and pilasters, Second Empire buildings recalled many historical styles.

QUEEN ANNE

The Queen Anne style emphasized contrasts of form, texture, and color. Large encircling verandahs, tall chimneys, turrets, towers, and a multitude of textures are typical of the style. The ground floor might be of stone or brick, the upper floors of stucco, shingle, or clapboard. Specially shaped bricks and plaques were used for decoration. Panels of stained glass outlined or filled the windows. Gabled or hipped steep roofs, and pediments, Venetian windows, and front and corner bay windows were typical.

SHINGLE STYLE

The Shingle Style bore the stamp of a new generation of professional architects led by Henry Hobson Richardson (1838–1886). Sheathed in wooden shingles, its forms were smoothed and unified. Verandahs, turrets, and complex roofs were sometimes used, but they were thoroughly integrated into a whole that emphasized uniformity of surface rather than a jumble of forms. The style was a domestic and informal expression of what became known as Richardsonian Romanesque.

RICHARDSONIAN ROMANESQUE

Richardsonian Romanesque made use of the massive forms and ornamental details of the Romanesque: rounded arches, towers, stone and brick facing. The solidity and gravity of the masses were accentuated by deep recesses for windows and entrances and by rough stone masonry, stubby columns, strong horizontals, rounded towers with conical caps, and repetitive, botanical ornament.

RENAISSANCE REVIVAL OR BEAUX ARTS

Later, in the 1880s and 1890s, American architects who had studied at the Ecole des Beaux Arts in Paris brought a new Renaissance Revival to the United States. Sometimes used in urban mansions, but generally reserved for public and academic buildings, it borrowed from three centuries of Renaissance detail—much of it French—and put together picturesque combinations from widely differing periods.

ECLECTIC PERIOD REVIVALS

CASTLE IN THE CLOUDS, NH

During the first decades of the twentieth century, revivals of diverse architectural styles became popular in the United States, particularly for residential buildings. Architects designed Swiss chalets, half-timbered Tudor houses, and Norman chateaus with equal enthusiasm. Many of these houses were modeled on rural structures and constructed in suburban settings. Although widely divergent in appearance, they have similar plans, site orientations, and general scale, brought about by similarities in building sites and by clients' desires for spacious interiors.

I N D E X

Numbers in *italics* indicate illustrations; numbers in **boldface** indicate maps.

Abbe Museum, 246
Abbot-Spalding House, 114
Acadia National Park, *4*, 245
Acadian Cross Historic Shrine, 280
Acadian Village, 280
Acworth, NH, 136, *137*
Adams Old Stone Grist Mill, 81
Allen, Ethan, 13, 18, 19, 23, 52
Allen, Ira, 13, 14, 18, 32, 49, 50-51, 58
Alna, ME, 263, *263*
Alstead, NH, 135
American Boathouse, Camden, ME, 232
American Precision Museum, 76
America's Stonehenge, 107
Amherst, NH, 114
Amoskeag Manufacturing Company, 111, *112-13*
Appalachian Trail, 8-**9, 257,** 275
Arnold, Benedict, 18, 44, 221, 264
Arnold Trail, Popham, ME, 221
Aroostook Historical and Art Museum, 281
Aroostook War, 258, 278
Arthur, Chester A., 54-55; Historic Site, 54-55, **55**
Auburn, ME, 199, 203-04
Augusta, ME, 258-59, 261-63, **262;** State House, 259, *259, 260,* 261

Babb's Covered Bridge, ME, 195
Bailey's Island, ME, *211*
Baltimore Covered Bridge, VT, 79

Bangor, ME, 268, *269,* 270-74, *272, 273*
Bangor House, 270
Bangor Theological Seminary, 274
Baptist Church, Grafton, VT, 79
Baptist Meeting House, Yarmouth, ME, 198
Bar Harbor, ME, 246
Bar Harbor Historical Society Museum, 246
Barker Mill, 203
Barnstead, NH, 123
Barracks Museum, 250
Barre, VT, 68
Barre Museum, 68
Barrett House, 116
Basin Harbor, VT, 44
Basin Harbor Museum, 44
Bates College, 203
Bath, ME, 219-21; Custom House and Post Office, 220
Bath Iron Works, 220
Baxter State Park, *252, 255, 275, 276-77, 278*
Belfast, ME, 236-37
Belfast Museum, 237
Belknap-Sulloway Mill, 158
Bellows Falls, VT, *80,* 81
Benjamin, Asher, 24, 34, 76, 114
Bennington, VT, 23-26, *24, 25*
Bennington Battle Monument, 24-25, *25*
Bennington Museum, 26
Bennington and Rutland Railroad Station, 26
Berlin, NH, 154-55
Bernard, ME, 245
Berwick Academy, 173
Biddeford, ME, 180-81
Big Mill, Bennington, VT, 26
Billings Farm and Museum, 74
Black, Colonel, Mansion, 242, *242, 243,* 244

Blaine House, 261
Blue Hill, ME, 241-42
Boothbay, ME, 225
Boothbay Theatre Museum, 225
Boscawen, NH, 159
Boston and Maine Railroad Station, 158
Bow, NH, 123
Bowdoin College, 207-09, *208;* Museum of Art, 210; Peary-Macmillan Arctic Museum, 209-10
Bradley, ME, 274
Brandon, VT, 39
Brattleboro, VT, *59,* 82-83
Brattleboro Museum and Art Center, 82
Bretton Woods, NH, 149-50, *150, 151, 152-53*
Brewster Free Academy, 156
Brick Meeting House, Grafton, VT, 79
Brick Store, Center Sandwich, NH, 156
Brick Store Museum, Kennebunk, ME, 178
Bristol, ME, 226-28, *227*
Bristol, VT, 42-43
Brookfield, VT, 69
Brooks Memorial Library, 82
Brownington, VT, 58-59, *62*
Brunswick, ME, 204-05, *205, 206,* 207-10, *208*
Bryant, Charles G., 270, 271
Bryant, Gridley J. F., 122, 203
Buck, Pearl S., 32
Bulfinch, Charles, 230, 259
Burlington, VT, 49-52, *51*
Burnham Tavern, 249
Burnt Island Light Station, Boothbay, ME, 225
Busiel-Seeburg Mill, 158

Cabot, John, 226, 236
Calais, ME, 251, *251*
Caledonia County
  Courthouse, 63
Camden, ME, 232, *233,
  234-35*
Canaan, NH, 142-43
Canaan, VT, 62
Canaan Historical
  Museum, 142
Canadian-Pacific Depot,
  63
Canterbury, NH, 159
Canterbury Shaker
  Village, 159
Cape Elizabeth, ME, *160,
  182,* 183
Caribou, ME, 280
Castin, Baron de, 214, 238
Castine, ME, 238-40, *240*
Castle in the Clouds, 156,
  157, 283
Castle Tucker, 224, *224*
Cather, Willa, 134
Center Sandwich, NH,156
Center Shaftsbury Baptist
  Church, Shaftsbury,
  VT, 27
Central Congregational
  Church, Eastport, ME,
  250
Central Vermont Railway
  Depot, Randolph, VT,
  69
Chaffee Art Center, 35
Chamberlain, Gen. Joshua
  L., Civil War Museum,
  205
Chamberlain Lake, ME,
  275
Champlain, Samuel de,
  18, 41, 53, 86, 214, 215,
  236, 244, 251, 268
Chapman-Hall House,228
Charlestown, NH, 135-36
Cheshire Mills, 134
Chester Village, VT, 79
Chestnut Street United
  Methodist Church,
  Portland, ME, 192

Chimney Point Tavern, 41
Chocolate Church, Bath,
  ME, 220
Cincinnati Hall, 106
Civil War, 54, 237
Claremont, NH, 136, 138
Clark Building,
  Kennebunkport, ME,
  180
Clark House, Wolfeboro,
  NH, 157
Clarksville, NH, 154
Colby-Sawyer College, 138
Cole, Thomas, 245
Colebrook, NH, 154
Colonial Pemaquid, 227
Colony, Horatio, House
  Museum, 133
Colony House Museum,
  132-33
Columbia Falls, ME, *248,
  249*
Columbian Mill, 116
Concord, NH, 121-23;
  State House, *120,* 121-
  22
Congregational Church,
  Exeter, NH, 107
Congregational Church,
  Middlebury, VT, 41-42
Congregational Church,
  Newbury, VT, 69
Congregational Church,
  Orford, NH, 146
Congregational Church,
  Peacham, VT, 65
Congregational Church,
  Stoddard, NH, 135
Congregational Church,
  Woodstock, VT, 74
Congregational Church of
  Christ, Berlin, NH, 155
Continental Mill, 202
Contoocook Mills, 117,*117*
Conway House, 232
Conway Scenic Railroad,
  155
Cooley Bridge, VT, 38
Coolidge, Calvin,
  Birthplace, 72-73, *72-73*

Coombs, George M., 202,
  203
Coos County Courthouse,
  154
Cornish, NH, 139, *139,*
  141
Cornish-Windsor Bridge,
  NH, *75,* 138
Counting House, South
  Berwick, ME, 176
Coventry, VT, 58
Covered bridges, 23;
  Maine, 195, 267, 281;
  New Hampshire, 138,
  154, 156; Vermont, 38,
  41, 52, *53, 75,* 79, 82
Craftsbury Common, VT,
  63
Cranberry Isles, ME, 245
Criterion Theatre, Bar
  Harbor, ME, 246

Damariscotta, ME, 228
Dana House, 74
Danby, VT, 32
Dartmouth College, 143,
  143, 144, 145
Davis Island, ME, 224-25
Deer Isle, ME, 241
Derby Line, VT, 59
Derry, NH, 110, *110*
Dorset, VT, *30-31,* 32
Douglas, Stephen A., 39
Dover, NH, 123-24
Dow, Neal, Memorial, 191
Drewsville, NH, 135
Dummerston, VT, 82
Durgin Covered Bridge,
  NH, 156
Durham, NH, 124-25
Dyces Head Lighthouse,
  239
Dyer Library, 181

Eagle Island, ME, 211
Eagle Lake, ME, 275
Eagle Tavern, 34
East Poultney, VT, 33-34
Eastern Cemetery,
  Portland, ME, 192

Eastport, ME, 250
Eddy, Mary Baker, 123
Effingham, NH, 156
Ellsworth, ME, 242, *242,*
243, 244
Ellsworth Congregational
Church, 242
Emerson, Ralph Waldo,
134
Emerson-Wilcox House,
172, 173
Enfield, NH, *140,* 141-42
Episcopal Church, Barre,
VT, 68
Equinox Hotel, 28
Essex County Courthouse,
63
Eureka Schoolhouse,
Springfield, VT, 79
Exeter, NH, 104-07, *108-
09*

Fair Haven, VT, 34
Fairbanks Museum and
Planetarium, 63
Fairfield, VT, 54-55, *55*
Farmington, ME, 266
Farmington Falls, ME, 266
Farnsworth Homestead,
231, *231*
Farrar, Isaac, Mansion,
272, *272, 273*
Ferrisburg, VT, 43-44
Fillmore, Lavius, 24, 42
Fire Museum, Wolfeboro,
NH, 157
First Church, Nashua,
NH, 114, *115*
First Church in Belfast,
ME, 236
First Church of Christ,
Scientist, Concord, NH,
123
First Congregational
Church, Kittery, ME,
169
First Congregational
Church, Lebanon, NH,
141
First Congregational
Church, Woodstock,
VT, 74

First Congregational
Society Unitarian
Church, Hampton Falls,
NH, 104
First Parish Church,
Brunswick, ME, 205
First Parish House,
Portland, ME, 192
First Parish Meeting
House, Biddeford, ME,
181
First Unitarian-
Congregationalist
Society, Nashua, NH,
114
First Universalist Church,
Auburn, ME, 203
Fisher, Jonathan,
Memorial, 242
Fisher Covered Railroad
Bridge, VT, 52, *53*
Fishermen's Museum,
Bristol, ME, 227
Fitzwilliam, NH, 134
Follett House, 50, *282*
Forestdale Iron Furnace, 39
Fort at No. 4, NH, 135-36
Fort Constitution, NH,
104, *105*
Fort Edgecomb, ME, 224-
25
Fort George, ME, 238, 239
Fort Gorges, ME, 194
Fort Halifax, ME, 264
Fort Kent, ME, 278-80,
279
Fort Knox, ME, 237
Fort McClary, ME, 166-67,
167
Fort Popham, ME, 221-22,
221
Fort Western, ME, 261-62,
262
Fort William Henry, ME,
227
Foster, Reverend Dan,
House, 78
Francestown, NH, 116
Franconia, NH, 146, *147,*
148, *148-49*
Franconia Notch State
Park, 148, *148-49*

Franklin, NH, 158
Franklin County Museum,
54
Freeport, ME, 198
French and Indian wars,
88, 124-25, 128, 135-36,
163, 244
Frost, Robert, 24, 28, *110,*
146; Farm, Derry, NH,
110, 110; Place,
Franconia, NH, 146, *147*
Fryeburg, ME, 197

Gale Memorial Library,
158
Gates House, 250
Gilman Garrison House,
106
Gilmanton Ironworks,
NH, 123
Goodrich Memorial
Library, 59
Gorges, Ferdinando, 10,
86, 92, 162, 171
Gorham Bridge, VT, 38
Grace Episcopal Church,
Manchester, NH, 112
Grafton, VT, *78,* 79
Grafton Historical Society
Museum, 79
Grand Isle, VT, 52
Grand Trunk Railroad
Station, Lewiston, ME,
202
Grand Trunk Railroad
Station, Yarmouth, ME,
198
Great Stone Dwelling,
Enfield, NH, *140,* 142
Greeley, Horace, 34, 114
Green Mountain Boys, 13,
18, 23, 25, 43
Greenfield, NH, 114
Greenmount Cemetery,
Burlington, VT, 52
Greenville, ME, 274
Guildhall, VT, 62

Hamilton House, *174-75,*
176, *176*
Hamlin, Hannibal, 164,
273-74

Hammond Bridge, VT, 38
Hammond Street
  Congregational Church,
  Bangor, ME, 270
Hampton, NH, 104
Hampton Falls, NH, 104
Hancock, John,
  Warehouse, York, ME,
  173
Hanover, NH, 143, *143,*
  144, 145
Harding, George M., 194,
  236
Harpswell, ME, 211
Harpswell Meeting House,
  211
Harrington Meeting
  House, Bristol, ME,
  227-28
Harris Mill, 134
Harrisville, NH, 134
Haskell Free Library and
  Opera House, 59
Hatch, Nathaniel, House,
  271
Haverhill, NH, 146
Hawthorne, Nathaniel,
  148
Head Tide, ME, 263, *263*
Henniker, NH, 121
Hildene, 28, *29*
Hill House, 272-73
Hillsboro, NH, 117, *117,*
  118-19
Hillside Cemetery,
  Eastport, ME, 250
Hobb House, 177
Hollis, NH, 114
Holt House, 242
Homer, Winslow, 182
Hope Cemetery, Barre,
  VT, 68
Houlton, ME, 281
Howells, William Dean,
  169
Hubbardton, VT, 18-19,
  38
Hunniwell, Richard,
  House, 181
Hussey Plow Company,
  177
Hyde Log Cabin, 53

Intervale, NH, *129*
Irasburg, VT, 58
Island Pond, VT, 62
Isle la Motte, VT, 53
Isles of Shoals, ME, 169-
  71, *170*
Islesford, ME, 245

Jackson, NH, 155
Jackson, Richard, House,
  94-95, *94*
Jaffrey, NH, 134
Janquish Island, ME, *211*
Jefferds Tavern, 172
Jericho, VT, 52
Jewett, Sarah Orne,
  House, 173
Jones, John Paul, 103,
  166; House, 99

Katahdin (steamboat), 274
Katahdin Iron Works,
  274-75
Keene, NH, 132-34, *133*
Kennebec County
  Courthouse, 262
Kennebunk, ME, 177-78,
  179
Kennebunkport, ME, 178,
  180
Kipling, Rudyard, 82
Kittery, ME, 166-67, *167,*
  168, 169
Kittery Historical and
  Naval Museum, 166
Knight House, 203-04
Kora Temple, Lewiston,
  ME, 202

Laconia, NH, 158
Ladd-Gilman House, 106
Lancaster, NH, 151, 154
Langdon, John, 99, 104;
  House, *84, 98,* 99
Larrabee's Point, VT, 40-41
LaVerdiere Apothecary
  Museum, 264-65, *265*
Lebanon, NH, 141
Lee-Tucker House, 224,
  224
Leonard, Nathaniel,
  House, 76

Lewiston, ME, 199, 202-03
Libby Museum, 157
Lincoln, Robert Todd, 28
Lincoln County Museum
  and Old Jail, 223
Lisbon, NH, 146
Little Red Schoolhouse
  Museum, Farmington,
  ME, 266
Littleton, ME, 281
Littleton, NH, 151
Longfellow, Henry
  Wadsworth, 185, 186,
  205
Lord, Captain, Mansion,
  Kennebunkport, ME,
  180
Lord's, Squire, Great
  House, Effingham, NH,
  156
Loudon, NH, 123
Lower Shaker Village,
  140, 141-42
Lower Sunday River
  School, Newry, ME, 267
Lyme, NH, 146

Machias, ME, 249-50
Machiasport, ME, 250
McKim, Mead & White,
  51, 83, 208, 210
McLellan-Sweat House,
  188
Macmillan, Donald B.,
  209, 210
MacPheadris-Warner
  House, 96
Madawaska Historic
  Museum, 280
Madison, NH, 156
Madison Corner, NH, 155
Maine, **8-9,** 162-64. *See also*
  Maine, coast of; Maine,
  interior of; Maine,
  southern
Maine, coast of, 214-15,
  216-17, 219, 228, 236,
  238-39, 250; Bar
  Harbor, 246; Bath, 219-
  21; Belfast, 236-37;
  Blue Hill, 241-42;
  Boothbay, 225; Bristol,

226-28, *227;* Calais, 251, *251;* Camden, 232, *233, 234-35;* Castine, 238-40, *240;* Columbia Falls, *248,* 249; Damariscotta, 228; Deer Isle, 241; Eastport, 250; Ellsworth, 242, *242, 243,* 244; Fort Edgecomb, 224-25; Fort Knox, 237; Machias, 249-50; Monhegan Island, 226, *226;* Mount Desert Island, *4,* 244-46; Popham, 221-22, *221;* Rockland, 230-31, *231;* Rockport, 232; Searsport, 237; Sedgwick-Brooklin, 240-41; Thomaston, 229-30, *229, 230;* Waldoboro, 229; Wiscasset, *212,* 222-24, *222, 224*
Maine, interior of, *252,* 254, *255,* **256-57,** 258, 264, 265-66, 267-68, 274, 275, *276-77,* 278, 280-281, *281;* Alna, 263, *263;* Augusta, 258-59, *259, 260,* 261-62, *262;* Bangor, 268, *269,* 270-74, *272, 273;* Fort Kent, 278-80, *279;* Houlton, 281; Newry, 267; Rumford, 266-67; Silver Lake, 274-75; Van Buren, 280; Waterville, 264-65, *265*
Maine, southern, **165,** 197, *211;* Auburn, 199, 203-04; Biddeford, 180-81; Brunswick, 204-05, *205, 206,* 207-10, *208;* Cape Elizabeth, *160, 182,* 183; Freeport, 198; Fryeburg, 197; Harpswell, 211; Isles of Shoals, 169-71, *170;* Kennebunk, 177-78, *179;* Kennebunkport,

178, 180; Kittery, 166-67, *167, 168,* 169; Lewiston, 199, 202-03; Naples, 197; New Gloucester, 198-99, *199, 200-01;* North Berwick, 177; Porter, 197; Portland, *163,* 183, *184,* 185-86, 188-95, *189, 190;* Saco, 181; Sanford, 177; Scarborough, 181-82; South Berwick, 173, *174-75,* 176, *176;* South Windham, 195; Standish, 195-96, *196;* Yarmouth, 198; York, 171-73, *172*
Maine Forest and Logging Museum, Bradley, ME, 274
Maine Maritime Museum, Bath, ME, 219-20
Maine State Museum, Augusta, ME, 261
Manchester, NH, 111-12, *112-13*
Manchester, VT, 28, *29*
Maple Grove Maple Museum, 63
Mariner's Church, Portland, ME, 192
Marrett House, 195-96, *196*
Marston, Elisha, House, 156
Mason, John, 86, 87, 92, 162
Masonic Temple, Belfast, ME, 236
Matteson, Peter, Tavern, 28
Meeting House, Canterbury, NH, 159
Memorial Library, Dorset, VT, 32
Merrill, Rev. Daniel, House, 241
Merrimack, NH, 112-13
Methodist Church, Newbury, VT, 68
Middlebury, VT, *40,* 41- 42

Middlebury College, *40,* 41
Middletown Springs, VT, 32-33, *33*
Milford, NH, 114
Moat Mountain, Intervale, NH, *129*
Moffatt-Ladd House, 97, *97*
Monadnock Mills, 136
Monhegan Island, ME, 226, *226*
Montpelier, VT, 65, 68; State House, 65, *66-67*
Montpelier, Thomaston, ME, *229,* 230, *230*
Moose Island, ME, 250
Moosehead Marine Museum, 274
Morrill, Justin, Homestead, *70,* 71
Morrisville, VT, 52
Morse-Libby House, 189-91, *189, 190, 283*
Moses, Anna Mary Robertson (Grandma), 22, 26
Moultonborough, NH, 156
Mount Desert Island, ME, *4,* 244-46
Mount Desert Island Historical Society Museum, 245
Mount Hope Cemetery, Bangor, ME, 270
Mount Independence, VT, 39, *39*
Mount Katahdin, ME, *252,* 254, *255,* 275, *276-77*
Mount Kineo House, 274
Mount Washington, NH, *151*
Mount Washington Cog Railway, 150, *150*
Mount Washington Hotel, 150, *152-53*
Munro-Hawkins House, 28
Museum of Yarmouth History, ME, 198

Museum Shipyard, Bath,
ME, 219-20

Nahanda Village Site,
226-27
Naples, ME, 197
Nashua, NH, 113-14, *115*
Naskeag Point, ME, 241
New Castle, NH, 103-04,
105
New England Maple
Museum, 38
New Gloucester, ME, 198-
99, *199, 200-01*
New Hampshire, **8-9,** 86-
88, 90-91. *See also* New
Hampshire,
southeastern; New
Hampshire, western
and northern
New Hampshire,
southeastern, **89,** 114,
125, *125;* Concord, *120,*
121-23; Derry, 110, *110;*
Dover, 123-24;
Durham, 124-25;
Exeter, 104-07, *108-09;*
Francestown, 116;
Henniker, 121;
Hillsboro, 117, *117,*
118-19; Manchester,
111-12, *112-13;*
Merrimack, 112-13;
Nashua, 113-14, *115;*
New Castle, 103-04,
105; New Ipswich, 116;
North Salem, 107;
Portsmouth, *84, 87,* 92-
97, *92-93, 94, 95, 97, 98,*
99-101, *101, 102,* 103;
Rochester, 123
New Hampshire, western
and northern, *126,* 128-
29, *129,* **130-31,** 132,
134, 138, 141, 154, 155,
156, *157,* 158, *158,* 159;
Acworth, 136, *137;*
Alstead, 135; Berlin,
154-55; Bretton Woods,
149-50, *150, 151, 152-*
53; Canaan, 142-43;

Canterbury, 159;
Center Sandwich, 156;
Charlestown, 135-36;
Claremont, 136, 138;
Cornish, 139, *139,* 141;
Effingham, 156;
Enfield, *140,* 141-42;
Franconia, 146, *147,*
148, *148-49;* Hanover,
143, *143, 144,* 145;
Jaffrey, 134; Keene,
132-34, *133;* Laconia,
158; Lancaster, 151,
154; Lebanon, 141;
Littleton, 151;
Stoddard, 135; Walpole,
134-35; Wolfeboro, 156-
57
New Hampshire Historical
Society Museum and
Library, 122
New Ipswich, NH, 116
New London, NH, 138
New Sweden, ME, 280,
281
New Sweden Historical
Society Museum, 280
Newbury, VT, 68-69
Newcastle, ME, 228
Newfield, ME, 197
Newington, NH, 125, *125*
Newport, NH, 138
Newport, VT, 59
Newry, ME, 267
Nickels-Sortwell House,
223
Nordica Homestead
Museum, 266
North Bennington, VT,
26-27, *27*
North Berwick, ME, 177
North Congregational
Church, St. Johnsbury,
VT, 63
North Conway, NH, 155
North Dorchester, NH,
146
North Salem, NH, 107
North Yarmouth
Academy, 198
Northeast Harbor, ME, 245

Northport, ME, *282*
Norumbega, 232, *233*

Oak Street School,
Lewiston, ME, 202
Old Coal Kiln, Lisbon,
NH, 146
Old Colony Maple Sugar
Factory, 59
Old Constitution House,
74-75
Old First Church,
Bennington, VT, 24, *24*
Old German Church,
Waldoboro, ME, 229
Old Jail, Ellsworth, ME,
244
Old Ledge School,
Yarmouth, ME, 198
Old Man of the Mountain,
Franconia, NH, 148,
148-49
Old Meeting House,
Canaan, NH, 142
Old Meeting House,
Jaffrey, NH, 134
Old Meeting House,
Newington, NH, 125
Old North Church,
Canaan, NH, 142
Old Parsonage,
Newington, NH, 125,
125
Old Red Church,
Standish, ME, 196
Old Red Mill, Jericho, VT,
52
Old Round Church,
Richmond, VT, 44, *45*
Old Schoolhouse, York,
ME, 173
Old South Congregational
Church, Windsor, VT,
76
Old Stone House
Museum, Brownington,
VT, 58-59, *62*
Old Stone Shop,
Wallingford, VT, 32
Old Tavern Inn, Grafton,
VT, *78,* 79

Old Union Meeting
  House, Farmington,
  ME, 266
Old York Gaol, York, ME,
  172
Olmstead, Frederick Law,
  46
Orford, NH, 146
Orthodox Church of the
  Holy Resurrection,
  Berlin, NH, 155
Orwell, VT, 39, *39*
Ossipee, NH, 156
Ottaquechee D.A.R.
  House, 74
Owl's Head, ME, *238-39*
Oxbow Cemetery,
  Newbury, VT, 69

Park-McCullough House,
  26-27, *27, 283*
Parris, Alexander, 76, 186,
  188
Peacham, VT, 65
Peary, Robert E., 209, 211
Pejepscot Historical
  Museum, 207
Pemaquid Lighthouse,
  227, *227*
Penobscot Bay, *234-35*
Penobscot Marine
  Museum, 237
Penobscot Nation
  Museum, 274
Pepperrell, Lady, House,
  168, 169, *282*
Pepperrell, William,
  House, *168*, 169
Perkins, Elizabeth, House,
  173
Perkins, John, House,
  239-40, *240, 282*
Perkins Tide Mill, 180
Pettengill House and
  Farm, 198
Phillips Exeter Academy,
  107, *108-09*
Pierce, Franklin, 117-19,
  123; Homestead,
  Hillsboro, NH, 117-19,
  118-19; Manse,
  Concord, NH, 123

Piermont, NH, 146
Pinkerton Academy, 110
Pittsburg, NH, 154
Pittsfield, NH, 123
Pittsford, VT, 38
Pleasant Point, 250
Plymouth Notch, VT, 72-
  73, *72-73*
Popham, George, 162, 221
Popham, John, 10
Popham, ME, 221-22, *221*
Porter, ME, 197
Portland, ME, *163,* 183,
  184, 185-86, 188-95,
  189, 190; Customhouse,
  193
Portland Fire Museum,
  193
Portland Head Light,
  Cape Elizabeth, ME,
  160, 182, 183
Portland Museum of Art,
  193, *194*
Portland Observatory, 192
Portsmouth, NH, *84, 87,*
  92-97, *92-93, 94, 95, 97,*
  98, 99-101, *101, 102,*
  103
Portsmouth Athenaeum,
  100, *101, 282*
Poultney, VT, 33-34
Poultney Historical Society
  Museum, 34
Proctor, VT, 35-37, *35, 36,*
  37

Randolph, VT, 69
Randolph Historical
  Museum, 69
Rangeley, ME, 267-68
Red Brick Schoolhouse,
  Wiscasset, ME, 223
Redington Museum, 264-
  65, *265*
Reich, Wilhelm, 267-68;
  Museum, 268
Revere, Paul, 104, 214
Revolutionary War, 13,
  18-19, 33, 39, 41, 44,
  104, 105, 106, 136, 214,
  238-39, 241, 249;
  Bennington, VT, 24-25;

Hubbardton, VT, 18-
  19, 38; Portland, ME,
  164, 183
Richards, Dexter, and
  Sons Mill, 138
Richmond, VT, 44, *45*
Rochester, NH, 123
Rock of Ages Company,
  68
Rockingham, VT, 82, *83*
Rockingham Free Public
  Library, Bellows Falls,
  VT, 81
Rockland, ME, 230-31,
  231
Rockport, ME, 232
Rokeby Museum, 44
Ruggles, Thomas, House,
  248, 249
Rumford, ME, 266-67
Rundlet-May House, 100
Rutland, VT, 34-35

Saco, ME, 181
St. Albans, VT, 54
St. Anne's Catholic
  Church, Berlin, NH,
  155
St. Anne's Shrine, 53
St. Croix, ME, 251
St. John the Evangelist
  Church, St. Johnsbury,
  VT, 63
St. John's Church,
  Portsmouth, NH, 100-
  101
St. Johnsbury, VT, 63-64,
  64
St. Johnsbury Athenaeum,
  64, *64*
St. Luke's Episcopal
  Church, Charlestown,
  NH, 135
St. Mary's Church,
  Claremont, NH, 138
St. Mary's Church,
  Lewiston, ME, 202
St. Patrick's, Newcastle,
  ME, 228
St. Paul's Episcopal
  Church, Brunswick,
  ME, 205

St. Paul's Episcopal
Church, Lancaster, NH,
154
St. Paul's Episcopal
Church, Windsor, VT,
76
St. Peter's Episcopal
Church, Drewsville,
NH, 135
St. Thomas' Episcopal
Church, Dover, NH,
124
Saint-Gaudens, Augustus,
139, 141; National
Historic Site, 139, *139*,
141
Sanford, ME, 177
Sayward-Wheeler House,
171
Scarborough, ME, 181-82
Scarborough Historical
Society Museum, 182
Schoolhouse, Alna, ME,
263
Schoolhouse, Wolfeboro,
NH, 157
Scott Covered Bridge, VT,
82
Searsport, ME, 237
Sedgwick-Brooklin, ME,
240-41
Sellers, Salome, House, 241
Seven Ponds, ME, 15
Sewall House, 220
Shaftsbury, VT, 27-28
Shaftsbury Center, VT,
27-28
Shaftsbury Historical
Society Museum, 27-28
Shaker Village, New
Gloucester, ME, 199,
199, 200-01
Sheafe Warehouse,
Portsmouth, NH, 103
Shelburne, VT, *12*
Shelburne Farms, 46-47,
46-47
Shelburne Museum, 47,
48, 49
Sheldon Museum, 42
Sherman Zwicker
(schooner), 220

Shoreham Covered
Railroad Bridge, VT, 41
Silver Lake, ME, 274
Skolfield-Whittier House,
206, 207
Skowhegan, ME, 265-66
Skowhegan History
House, 266
Smith, John, 86, 162, 169,
225, 226, 232, 236
Smith, Gov. John B.,
House, 117
Smith, Joseph,
Monument, 71
Smith, Parson, House, 195
Society of Friends Meeting
House, Dover, NH, 124
Somesville, ME, 245
South Baptist Church,
Laconia, NH, 158
South Berwick, ME, 173,
174-75, 176, *176*
South Bristol, ME, 228
South Church,
Portsmouth, NH, 101
South Congregational
Church, Newport, NH,
138
South Congregational
Church, St. Johnsbury,
VT, 63
South Lyndeborough,
NH, 132
South Royalton, VT, 71
South Shaftsbury, VT, 27-
28
South Windham, ME, 195
South Woodstock, VT, *56*
Southwest Harbor, ME,
245
Springfield, VT, 78-79
Standish, ME, 195-96, *196*
Stanwood Wildlife
Sanctuary, 244
Stark, John, 19, 25, 88, 90,
111, 136
Stark, NH, 154
Stark Park, 111
Stevens, John Calvin, 192,
195
Stockholm, ME, 280
Stockholm Museum, 280

Stoddard, NH, 135
Stone Brothers and Curtis
Mill, 134
Stowe, Harriet Beecher,
204-05; Brunswick, ME,
home of, *205*
Stowe, VT, 52
Strafford, NH, 123
Strafford, VT, 69, *70*, 71
Strawbery Banke, 101,
102, 103
Strong, John, Mansion, 42
Sullivan, John, 88, 104,
125
Suncook, NH, 132
Sunday River Bridge, ME,
267

Tate House, 185
Taylor-Barry House, 178,
179
Thayer's Hotel, Littleton,
NH, 151
Thomaston, ME, 229-30,
229, 230
Thompson Ice House, 228
Tinmouth, VT, 32
Tisdale, Seth, House, 244
Townshend, VT, 82
Tramway Historical
District, ME, 275, 278
Tremont, ME, 245
Troy, VT, 58
Two Lights, Cape
Elizabeth, ME, 183

Union Church,
Claremont, NH, 136,
138
Union Church, Stark, NH,
154
Union Railroad Station,
Brattleboro, VT, 82
Unitarian Church,
Burlington, VT, 50
United Baptist Church,
East Poultney, VT, 33-
34
United Church of
Acworth, NH, 136, *137*
United Church of
Craftsbury, VT, 63

United Church of Dorset
and East Rupert,
Dorset, VT, 32
United Church of
Randolph, VT, 69
Universalist Church,
Alstead, NH, 135
University of Vermont,
50-52, *51*
Upjohn, Richard, 108,
112, 135, 205, 210, 272

Van Buren, ME, 280
Vergennes, VT, 43
Vermont, **8-9**, 18-19, 22-
23. *See also* Vermont,
eastern; Vermont,
western
Vermont, eastern, *56*, 58-
59, *59*, **60-61**, *62*, 62-63,
65, 69, 76, *77*, 78, 82,
83; Barre, 68; Bellows
Falls, *80*, 81;
Brattleboro, *59*, 82-83;
Chester Village, 79;
Craftsbury Common,
63; Grafton, *78*, 79;
Montpelier, 65, *66-67*,
68; Newbury, 68-69;
Plymouth Notch, *72-73*,
72-73; Randolph, 69; St.
Johnsbury, 63-64, *64;*
South Royalton, 71;
Springfield, 78-79;
Strafford, 69, *70*, 71;
Windsor, 74-76, *75;*
Woodstock, 74
Vermont, Republic of, 13,
19, 129
Vermont, western, *16, 19*,
20-21, 32, 41, 52-53, *53;*
Basin Harbor, 44;
Bennington, 23-26, *24,
25;* Brandon, 39;
Bristol, 42-43;
Burlington, 49-52, *51;*
Danby, 32; Dorset, *30-
31*, 32; East Poultney,

33-34; Fair Haven, 34;
Fairfield, 54-55, *55;*
Ferrisburg, 43-44;
Hubbardton, 38; Isle la
Motte, 53; Larrabee's
Point, 40-41;
Manchester, 28, *29;*
Middlebury, 41-42, *40;*
Middletown Springs,
32-33, *33;* Mount
Independence, 39, *39;*
North Bennington, 26-
27, *27;* Pittsford, 38;
Poultney, 33-34;
Proctor, 35-37, *35, 36,
37;* Richmond, 44, *45;*
Rutland, 34-35; St.
Albans, 54; Shaftsbury,
27-28; Shaftsbury
Center, 27-28; South
Shaftsbury, 27-28;
Stowe, 52; Vergennes,
43
Vermont Marble Exhibit,
35, *35*
Vermont Museum,
Montpelier, VT, 65
Victoria Mansion, 189-91,
189, 190

Wadsworth-Longfellow
House, 185-86
Waldo County
Courthouse, 236
Waldoboro, ME, 229
Wallingford, VT, 32
Walpole, NH, 134-35
Walpole Meeting House,
South Bristol, ME, 228
Waponahki Museum, 250
War of 1812, 14, 18, 43,
214, 225, 239, 250
Ward Library, 62
Warner, Seth, 18, 23, 25,
32, 38
Washington, NH, *126*
Waterville, ME, 264-65,
265

Watson Settlement
Bridge, ME, 281
Weathersfield Bow, VT,
76
Weathersfield Center, VT,
76, *77*, 78
Webster, Daniel, 90, 145,
148, 158; Birthplace,
158, *158*
Wentworth, Benning, 13,
18, 34, 88, 95, 101
Wentworth-Coolidge
Mansion, 95-96, *95*
Wentworth-Gardner
House, 100
White Columns, 180
Wilder-Holton House, 154
Williston-West United
Church of Christ,
Portland, ME, 192
Willowbrook, 197
Wilson Castle, 36, *36, 37*
Wilson Museum, 239-40,
240
Wilton, NH, 114
Windsor, VT, 74-76, *75;*
U.S. Post Office, 76
Windsor County
Courthouse, 74
Windsor-Cornish Covered
Bridge, VT, *75*, 138
Winslow, ME, 264
Winter Street Church,
Bath, ME, 220
Wiscasset, ME, *212*, 222-
24, *222, 224*
Wolfeboro, NH, 156-57
Woodman Institute, 124
Woodstock, VT, 74
Wyman Tavern, 132, *133*

Yarmouth, ME, 198
York, ME, 171-73, *172*
York Institute Museum,
181
Young, Ammi B., 35, 50,
65, 76, 141, 142, 145,
220, 236

230: Brian Vanden Brink, Rockport, ME
231: Brian Vanden Brink, Rockport, ME
234-235: Fred M. Dole/ f/STOP Pictures
238-239: The Museum of Fine Arts, Boston, MA. Bequest of Martha C. Karolik for the Karolik Collection of American Paintings, 1815-1865
240: Helga Photo Studio
248 (lower right): Brian Vanden Brink, Rockport, ME
251: Clyde H. Smith/ f/STOP Pictures
252: Clyde H. Smith/The Stock Shop

255: Yale University Art Gallery, New Haven, CT, Stanley B. Resor, B.A. 1901, Fund
259: Helga Photo Studio
262: Lynn F. Gustin, courtesy of Fort Western, Augusta ME
276-277: Clyde H. Smith/ f/STOP Pictures
279: Voscar The Maine Photographer, Presque Isle, ME
282 (top left): Helga Photo Studio
282 (lower left): Douglas Armsden, Kittery Point, ME
282 (top center): Peter E. Randall, Portsmouth, NH

282 (right): Brian Vanden Brink, Rockport, ME
283 (top left): Brian Vanden Brink, Rockport, ME
283 (lower left): Douglas Armsden, Kittery Point, ME
Back Cover: Clyde H. Smith/f/STOP Pictures

The editors gratefully acknowledge the assistance of Honi Brett, Ann J. Campbell, Rita Campon, Ann ffolliott, Amy Hughes, Carol A. McKeown, Klaske Piebenga, Martha Schulman, and Patricia Woodruff.

Composed in Basilia Haas and ITC New Baskerville by Graphic Arts Composition, Inc., Philadelphia, Pennsylvania. Printed and bound by Toppan Printing Company, Ltd., Tokyo, Japan.